ARABS
IN THE
NEW WORLD

ARABS IN THE NEW WORLD

Studies on Arab-American Communities

Edited by
Sameer Y. Abraham and Nabeel Abraham

Wayne State University
Center for Urban Studies

This book was supported in part by the U.S. Department of Education, Ethnic Heritage Studies Program, Grant number G008100726 under Title IX of the Elementary and Secondary Education Act of 1965. The opinions expressed herein do not necessarily reflect the position or policy of the U.S. Department of Education or the Ethnic Heritage Studies Program, and no official endorsement by the U.S. Department of Education should be inferred. The opinions expressed herein are solely those of the individual authors.

Library of Congress Cataloging in Publication Data

Main entry under title:

Arabs in the New World.

   Bibliography: p.
   Includes index.
   Contents: A historical overview of Arabs in America / Alixa Naff — Emigration from Syria / Najib E. Saliba — Arab Christians in the United States / Philip M. Kayal — [etc.]
   1. Arab Americans — Addresses, essays, lectures. 2. Arab Americans — Michigan — Detroit — Social conditions — Case studies. 3. Detroit (Mich.) — Social conditions — Case studies. 4. Arab Americans — Bibliography. I. Abraham, Sameer Y. II. Abraham, Nabeel.
E184.A65A73   1983   305.8'927'077434   83-1401
ISBN 0-943560-00-4

The cover photograph, taken in 1878, is of one of the earliest Arab families to settle in the United States—Professor Yusif Arbili (seated second from right) and his family. The Arabic caption reads, "Here [at last] I am with the children exulting in freedom." The empty chair to his left appears to be a symbolic gesture of respect, representing the reserved place of a beloved relative left behind in Damascus to whom this photograph was probably sent.

Printed in the United States of America

To the early Arab immigrants whose sojourns to the New World were undertaken in the hope of a better life for themselves and those they left behind.

Contents

Introduction / 1

Part One: Historical Overview and National Profile

Arabs in America: A Historical Overview / 8
    Alixa Naff
Emigration from Syria / 30
    Najib E. Saliba
Arab Christians in the United States / 44
    Philip M. Kayal
Arab Muslims and Islamic Institutions in America: Adaptation
 and Reform / 64
    Yvonne Haddad

Part Two: Case Studies of Arab-American Communities in Detroit

Detroit's Arab-American Community: A Survey of Diversity
 and Commonality / 84
    Sameer Y. Abraham
The Yemeni Immigrant Community of Detroit: Background,
 Emigration, and Community Life / 109
    Nabeel Abraham
Detroit's Iraqi-Chaldeans: A Conflicting Conception of Identity / 135
    Mary C. Sengstock
The Lebanese Maronites: Patterns of Continuity and Change / 147
    May Ahdab-Yehia
The Southend: An Arab Muslim Working-Class Community / 163
    Sameer Y. Abraham, Nabeel Abraham, and Barbara Aswad

Part Three: Select Bibliography on Arab-Americans

A Select Bibliography on Arab-American Immigration
 and Settlement / 186
    Mohammed Sawaie

Appendix: National Arab-American Organizations, Publications,
 and Elected Officials / 201

Index / 203

Acknowledgements

This book was made possible in part through a grant from the U.S. Department of Education's Ethnic Heritage Studies Program. While the larger project we have been involved in has included the research and development of materials about the Arab world and Arab-Americans, we have always considered the publication of this volume the vital core of our work. A large debt is owed to Mr. Lawrence E. Koziarz, the Director of the Ethnic Heritage Studies Program and Mrs. Carmen D. Rodriguez, the Program Officer, for providing us with the support and encouragement for our many endeavors. Through their kind cooperation we have been able to add to our growing knowledge of another of America's ethnic groups.

While the federal government provided the funds, Wayne State University's Center for Urban Studies provided the organization and personnel which were essential in bringing our ideas to fruition. In particular, Dr. Sue M. Smock, the Director, and Mary Clayton, the Administrative Assistant, brought to bear their substantial administrative capabilities to insure that the many bureaucratic details of life would not pose a hindrance. Two other staff members, Bea Sandweiss and Marie Smith, undertook the laborious task of typing some of the manuscripts. Were it not for the helpful assistance of these individuals, it is unlikely that we would have been able to realize our many objectives and deadlines.

Another debt is owed to the staff of the Michigan Metropolitan Information Center which is also housed at the Center for Urban Studies. Bill Simmons, Sandra Abela, and Kathy Ward contributed more than they might suspect by providing us with the U.S. Census data which were used in preparing the article on the "Southend" community. Their earnest responses to our many requests are gratefully acknowledged.

Julia Fitzgerald and Dr. Michael A. Daher brought to bear their respective editorial skills in assisting us in reviewing the articles and preparing them for publication. At times, they forced us to rethink substantive issues while at other times we were questioned about subtle nuances. In both cases, they undertook their roles with conscientious and meticulous care.

Much of the cartographic work was performed by Karen L. Wysocki. Her greater talent was revealed in the ability to translate seemingly meaningless information into meaningful maps without making apparent our general ignorance of the cartographic process.

Finally, a belated debt is owed to a colleague and friend, Dr. Lorraine Majka, who has patiently awaited the completion of this volume. Her past support and assistance were considerable and continue to be irreplaceable.

Introduction

In the fall of 1981, the newly established American-Arab Anti-Discrimination Committee (ADC) held its first national convention in Detroit, Michigan. The convention theme, "Arab Americans Come of Age," reflected the overwhelming sentiment of the many second- and third-generation Arab-Americans who participated in that convention. For them, the time was long overdue for a concerted effort by Arab-Americans to make their presence felt in the United States. In the century since their parents and grandparents began immigrating to the New World, Arab-Americans, with only a few exceptions, have gone largely unnoticed in American society. Their lack of visibility has been so pronounced that one writer has characterized them as part of a "hidden minority."[1] The reasons behind their lack of ethnic visibility lay partly in their small numbers relative to most ethnic groups in America and partly in the fact that they were generally well integrated, acculturated, and even assimilated into mainstream society. If Arab-Americans as a group had an ethnic presence at all, it was on the local level, in the vaguely defined "Little Syrias" which formed part of the larger ethnic quilt that characterized much of urban-industrial America.

Today, there are an estimated two to three million Arab-Americans in the United States. Included in this estimate are early immigrants as well as many second-, third-, and even some fourth-generation Americans who identify with their Arab cultural heritage. Like other immigrants, Arabs tended to settle in the major urban centers near points of commerce and industry. The largest population concentrations appear to be widespread, with some convergence in the northcentral and northeastern states. Figure 1 illustrates the key states in which Arab immigrants and their offspring have settled over the years.

Many present-day Arab-Americans trace their ancestry in this country to the great immigration waves of the late 19th and early 20th centuries. This was the period of the so-called "new immigration," when millions of eastern and southern European immigrants landed on America's shores. Whereas the European immigrations have long since dwindled to a trickle, however, those of the Arabs and other Middle Easterners have steadily increased, in some instances dramatically so. The nature and extent of the "new Arab immigration" can be seen in the Southend, a primary,

---

[1] See Joan H. Rollins, [editor,] *Hidden Minorities: The Persistence of Ethnicity in American Life* (Washington, D.C.: University Press of America, 1981).

1

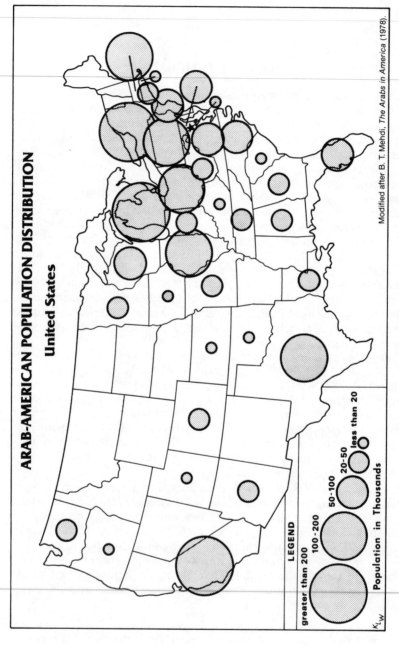

ARAB-AMERICAN POPULATION DISTRIBUTION
United States

LEGEND

greater than 200 100 - 200 50-100 20-50 less than 20

Population in Thousands

Modified after B. T. Mehdi, *The Arabs in America* (1978).

Figure 1

working-class community of Arab Muslims located in Dearborn, Michigan. Unlike the early Arab immigrants who over time have acculturated and assimilated, these mostly post–1967 immigrants are largely unacculturated and unassimilated into mainstream American society. Clearly estranged from Detroit's predominantly white middle-class suburbs, the Southend Arabs re-create in their relatively isolated neighborhood some of the social institutions and practices brought over from the old world— the mosque, the coffeehouse, and Arab nationalism, among others. If the more assimilated second- and third-generation Arab-Americans have felt unnoticed as an ethnic group, then the new immigrants living in clearly visible and often well-known ethnic neighborhoods must surely feel neglected by the rest of society, especially by those public and private institutions entrusted with the task of resolving the social, economic, educational, and cultural problems encountered by the new immigrants.

Generally speaking, the acculturation and assimilation patterns of established Arab-Americans closely resemble those of other ethnic groups. Many, for example, have pursued the "American dream" and some have realized it, if only in part. The new immigrants who continue to make their way to the United States also share similar hopes and dreams. As is the case with all ethnic groups which are constantly being infused with new arrivals, sharp differences between the "old" and "new" immigrants frequently develop. The old immigrants often do not realize the extent to which they have accepted American norms, values, and attitudes even while tenaciously clinging to fond memories of their native lands. The new arrivals, for their part, find their assimilated Arab-American counterparts more American than Arab and out of touch with the changing realities of the Arab world. Where the two groups find common cause, however, is with regard to political events in the Middle East and America's foreign policy in the area which is viewed as biased against the Arabs and strongly in favor of Israel. Arab-Americans of different generations, regional backgrounds, religions, and social classes have been moved into action as a direct result of the Arab-Israeli wars and the injustices they feel have been committed against the Palestinian people. These events have served as a basis for greater self-awareness, political activity, and group cohesiveness. Perhaps the most concrete manifestation of these developments is the emergence of several national Arab-American organizations which are dedicated to serving Arab-American interests and working toward a more balanced American foreign policy.[2]

Just as events in the Middle East stimulated Arab-American organizational activity, Arab-American academics were also stirred into action at another level. In fact, research and writing on Arab-Americans appears to have closely followed the establishment of major Arab-American organizations. With few notable exceptions, most academic interest in

---

[2]See the Appendix for a list of national Arab-American organizations, publications, and elected officials.

Arab-Americans appears in the post-World War II period. One exception is the early and often quoted work of Philip K. Hitti, the noted Arab historian, which has remained the primer on Arab-Americans and is frequently referred to by students in the field. The period between Hitti's *The Syrian Americans* (1924) and the next major published work, *The Arab Moslems in the United States* (1966) by Abdo Elkholy spans almost two generations. While a few social scientists, both Arab and non-Arab, took interest in the community, publishing a number of articles during the interim period, it was not until the June 1967 Arab-Israeli War that an active interest in Arab-Americans emerged and studies were launched in a major way.

The publication of *The Arab Americans: Studies in Assimilation* (1969), edited by Elaine Hagopian and Ann Paden, represented a major turning point in Arab-American studies. The editors included a selection of papers delivered at the first annual convention (1968) of the newly established Association of Arab-American University Graduates (AAUG). In inaugurating the AAUG's monograph series, the Hagopian and Paden book provided a renewed stimulus to Arab-American researchers and scholars across the country to begin the process of self-examination and redefinition. The AAUG's first book was followed by publication of a second volume edited by Barbara C. Aswad, *Arabic Speaking Communities in American Cities* (1974), which was jointly published with the Center for Migration Studies in New York.

The following years witnessed a substantial increase in the number of students engaged in research on Arab-Americans.[3] Since that time, four new books have appeared on the subject: *The Syrian-Lebanese in America: A Study in Religion and Assimilation* (1975) by Philip M. Kayal and Joseph M. Kayal; *An Olive Branch on the Family Tree: The Arabs in Canada* (1980) by Baha Abu Laban; *The Arab World and Arab-Americans: Understanding a Neglected Minority* (1981) edited by Sameer Y. Abraham and Nabeel Abraham; and *The Chaldean Americans: Changing Conceptions of Ethnic Identity* (1982) by Mary C. Sengstock. Two other volumes are nearing completion, one by Alixa Naff which focuses on pre-World War II immigration and settlement and another by Nabeel Abraham on immigrant politics and political factionalism in Detroit's Yemeni community.

The volumes in print or nearing publication do not by any means reveal the full extent of the increasing research and scholarship focused on this group. Numerous papers have been delivered at academic conferences and special conferences, as well as published in various journals and magazines. Social science students both here and abroad have taken an active interest in the study of Arab-Americans, making it the topic for a growing number of theses and dissertations. The Immigration and History Research Center of the University of Minnesota has organized the "First Philip K. Hitti International Symposium on Near Eastern Studies," scheduled for

---

[3]For a list of titles, see the select bibliography by Mohammed Sawaie in this volume.

1983. The conference theme focuses on "Arabic Speaking Immigration to North America to World War II." Similar conferences devoted to other facets of community life are planned for the future, according to the conference sponsors. This year's annual American Sociological Association convention, which is to be convened in Detroit, has also included a special session on Arab-Americans entitled "Emerging Minorities:Patterns of Growth, Conflict and Change among Detroit's Arab-Americans." Both conferences reflect the increasing academic interest in and acceptance of Arab-American studies.

Like many of the above publications and activities, the original impetus for this book centered on the need to increase our knowledge about Arab-Americans, a need all the more apparent in Detroit where the growing number of Arab immigrants has resulted in an explosion of inquiries from journalists, educators, students, politicians, businessmen, and so on. In an earlier volume, we attempted to answer this need in part by preparing a book for public school teachers who had expressed an interest in learning more about the cultural background, history, and problems currently confronting the increasing number of Arab and Arab-American students enrolled in schools throughout the Detroit metropolitan area. Unlike that earlier work, this companion volume has a different focus and responds to a broader set of concerns.

This book was conceived with a number of objectives in mind. First, from a general perspective, our intent was to make available the most current research on Arab-Americans in this country. Our second objective was to present the reader with ethnographic depth in the subject through a number of community case studies. Finally, we were intent upon compiling a volume which would be of value to both the general reader and the academic community. Admittedly these goals were not always easy to fulfill.

Two of the articles (A. Naff and N. Saliba) have been previously published elsewhere, and are included in this volume because they merit wider circulation. The articles by Y. Haddad and S. Abraham are based on previously published works which were rewritten and expanded for this volume. The remaining five articles and the select bibliography by M. Sawaie were prepared explicitly for inclusion in this work. The article by N. Abraham is derived from a previous ethnographic study, while those by M. Sengstock, P. Kayal, and M. Ahdab-Yehia rest on earlier sociological investigations. Finally, the article by S. Abraham, N. Abraham, and B. Aswad presents an indepth profile of an important Arab Muslim community by drawing on previous studies and the authors' firsthand knowledge of the community.

In keeping with our stated objectives, the book was divided into three sections. Part One is designed to provide the reader with a historical overview of Arab-Americans, their reasons for emigration from Greater Syria (the country which is home to a good number of the early immigrants), and a profile of the two religious groups, Muslims and Christians, which comprise the population. Depth of perspective is realized in Part Two where the focus turns from the national community to an examination of several communities located in the Detroit metropolitan area. The choice of Detroit is not fortuitous. Detroit is considered to be home to one of the oldest and largest (if not the largest) Arab-American communities in North America. Because of its size and social heterogeneity, the community has been the focus of a growing number of studies. Moreover, in some quarters Detroit is considered a "leader" community in that it sets the pace for many political and social activities, provides personnel for national organizations, and represents a major source of strength for Arab-American communities throughout the country. Given the history and diversity of Detroit's Arab-American population, it is reasonable to view the various communities here as representative of Arab-Americans elsewhere. For all these reasons, then, Detroit appeared as the logical choice upon which to focus our case studies.

Part Three of the book is devoted to a select bibliography on Arab immigration and settlement in the United States. This section should provide students and colleagues with access to additional sources of information in the hope of stimulating future research and interest in Arab-Americans.

S. Y. A. and N. A.

Part One

Historical Overview
and National Profile

ABSTRACT

The Arab-American community in the United States, two million strong, is the result of a century of immigration. Roughly 90 percent of this community is Christian and 10 percent Muslim, a direct reversal of the Muslim-Christian ratio in the Middle East. Most of the early immigrants were Syrian-Lebanese Christians of peasant stock with economic motives for emigrating. Driven by a competitive spirit and an ethic of hard work, the new immigrants excelled in the peddling trade, around which they established their family life. Since 1948 the majority of Arab immigrants have been Muslim; often they are highly educated and migrate for political reasons. Although nearly a century of assimilation has weakened the effectiveness of Arab institutions such as churches, mosques, the press, and cultural organizations, extensive American participation in Middle Eastern politics combined with the influx of a new, highly articulate immigrant population have led to a regenerated and more unified Arab-American community.

Arabs in America:
A Historical Overview

by Alixa Naff

Arabs had been in America for more than three quarters of a century before the general American public became aware of their existence.[1] In fact, it was not until the series of Middle East crises immediately following World War II that attention was focused on Arab-Americans and their homeland. This is not surprising, since American Arabs, one of the smaller groups in America's mosaic of ethnic peoples, had assimilated relatively rapidly and smoothly.

There are today roughly two million[2] Arabs in the United States—90 percent of them Christian and 10 percent Muslim, and over half of them well-assimilated third- and fourth-generation descendants of immigrants who arrived between 1875 and 1940.

Most of the original Arab immigrants were Christians from the Syrian province of the Ottoman Empire that included the semiautonomous administrative district of Mt. Lebanon, the coastal mountain range between the Syrian port cities of Beirut and Tripoli. They were likely to call themselves Syrians (the independent parliamentary Republic of Lebanon was not established until 1946) and tended to identify themselves in terms of

---

[1] This article is a revised version of an earlier work which appeared in the *Harvard Encyclopedia of American Ethnic Groups* (1980:128–136). It is reprinted here with permission of the author and publisher.

This article relies on primary data collected from in-depth interviews conducted by the author with first- and second-generation Arab-Americans in numerous communities in the United States. Other data sources included primary books, journals, memoirs, and documents from the author's private collection on Arab-Americans, which is to be housed in the Smithsonian Institute in Washington, D.C. In addition, the author is completing work on a forthcoming book entitled, *Becoming American: The Arab Experience, 1875–1940.*

[2] It is difficult to ascertain the exact number of Arab-Americans, given the lack of sound and reliable statistical data. Informed observers and experts generally agree that after more than a century of migration and growth, the total Arab-American population ranges from a low of 2 million to a high of 3 million. —The Editors

9

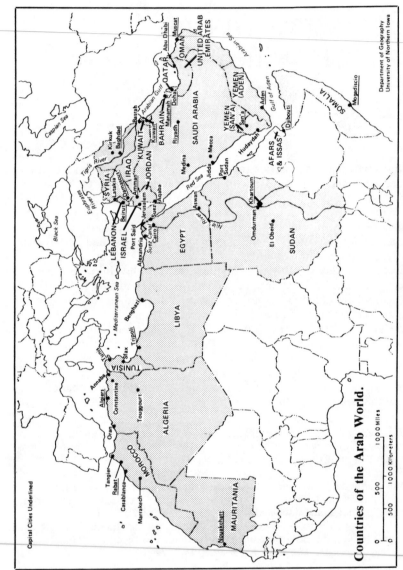

Countries of the Arab World.

Figure 1

their region, village of origin, or religious preference. They were not called Arabs, a term that has become familiar only in recent years. Most of the more recent Arab immigrants are Muslims from independent and often rival Arab states; in contrast to the earlier immigrants, they are frequently ardent Arab nationalists. Perhaps as many as 175,000 have come to the United States since 1948.

Christian and Muslim Arabs share a common heritage, but they are far from unified. Deeply rooted religious and sectarian beliefs as well as politics divide them in the United States as they do in their homelands, but at the same time an overarching Arab-American identity has begun to take shape. The Arab-American movement is little more than a decade old. Before the mid-1960s, and even now in some households, pre-World War II immigrants and their descendants were more comfortable with the designation Syrian or Lebanese-American. Interest in their Arab heritage has been awakened by the presence of Arab nationalists, indignation over U.S. foreign policy in the Middle East, objections to the unfavorable Arab image in the U.S. press, and the general contemporary interest in ethnicity.

Nomenclature is one problem; statistics is another. Official statistics are clearly distorted. In immigration records until 1899 and in census records until 1920, all Arabs were recorded, together with Turks, Armenians, and others, under "Turkey in Asia." After 1920 the increase in their numbers warranted the separate classification "Syria," but religious differences were not noted. Official records have been slow to keep up with political changes; until relatively recently, for example, non-Syrian Arabs might be counted as "other Asian" and North African Arabs as "other African." Since 1948 the Palestinians, who account for much of the post-World War II Arab immigration, have been designated simply as refugees, or as from Palestine or Israel, or as nationals of the country of their last residence.

HISTORICAL BACKGROUND

Propelled by the fervor of a new religion, Arabs rode out of their homeland in the 7th century and in about one hundred years conquered territory from Central Asia through North Africa to Spain. These Arabs were Muslim; their religion, Islam, meaning submission to one God, was revealed to the Arab prophet Muhammad in the Arabian peninsula. His revelations provided the believers with the Quran, a text that became one of the bases for the immutable holy law that governs every activity in the lives of its adherents. In Islam as in Judaism (and in Christianity before the Reformation), religion, politics, and society were inseparably linked. Many of its basic tenets also resemble those of Judaism and Christianity, to which it is loosely tied. But the unity of religion and society as it was envisioned by the Prophet was short-lived. Thirty years after Muhammad's death, schism resulted from a problem of succession. The Muslims first split into two sects—Sunni and Shia; other heterodoxies developed subsequently.

Relations between the ruling Muslim majority and religious minorities among the indigenous populations of the lands they conquered were based upon the belief that Muhammad was the last in a long line of messengers of God that included both Moses and Jesus. As followers of these honored, if lesser, prophets, Christians and Jews enjoyed a wide measure of toleration under the jurisdiction of their own religious hierarchies, although their communities were more heavily taxed as the price they paid for protection by the Muslim army.

One of the great civilizations, Islam in the Middle Ages exerted an intellectual ascendancy unmatched in Europe until the Renaissance. Its decline in subsequent centuries followed cycles of conquest, internal disintegration, and regeneration. The last Islamic empire was ruled by Ottoman Turks for four hundred years, before its fall in 1918.

The modern Arab world encompasses the countries of Algeria, Bahrain, Egypt, Iraq, Jordan, Kuwait, Lebanon, Libya, Morocco, Oman, Palestine, the People's Democratic Republic of Yemen, Qatar, Saudi Arabia, Syria, Sudan, Tunisia, the United Arab Emirates, and the Yemen Arab Republic. Although most Arab-Americans are descendants of Syrian immigrants, all these countries are represented in the Arab-American population, including several thousand who are refugees from Palestine, part of which is now the state of Israel.

To speak of the Arab world, however, implies a cultural unity that ignores a number of cleavages created by differences in geography and history. Mountains and deserts have contributed to the perpetuation of particularisms and parochialisms, particularly in Mt. Lebanon where oppressed heterodoxies had historically sought refuge during periods of religious conflict. The Arab lands lie at the crossroads of major trade routes between East and West and their great commercial cities have been conquered by imperial armies since biblical times. The discovery in the Middle East in the 20th century of the world's largest reserves of oil added another dimension both to Arab politics and to the strategic importance of Arab lands.

Christian sects abound in the Arab world. Conquering Muslims found several rival sects around the Mediterranean; still other sects, differing in both doctrine and rite, came later. Most of these are in Syria and Lebanon; there is a sizable Coptic Christian minority in Egypt. Relations are further complicated by the affiliation of Maronites, Melkites, and Syrian (Jacobite) and Chaldean Catholics with the Roman Catholic church and by the antipathy of the scattered Eastern Orthodox community and the small Protestant group towards Rome.

When the Arabs today discuss the golden age of Arab culture, Muslims tend to emphasize its Islamic content, Christians its Arab. Both date the eclipse of Arab power to the period of Ottoman Turkish rule, but Muslims are apt to attribute it to Western Christian influences inimical to Islam, while Christians may explain it in terms of the poverty and stagnation that centuries of Muslim Ottoman domination produced.

The tradition of accommodation between Muslims and Christians was severely disrupted in the 19th century. European powers competed for influence in the tottering Ottoman Empire by exploiting the loyalties and interests of the various Christian sects. In Syria the French supported the Maronites and the Melkites; the Russians supported the Eastern Orthodox; and England vacillated between the Christians and the semi-Islamic Druze as its interests dictated. France encouraged a Maronite dream of political dominance in Lebanon and alienated Muslims, Druze, and the Orthodox Christians who tended, then as now, to support the Muslims in politics. In Egypt, England's support of the Copts antagonized the Muslim majority. European interference generated hostility between Muslim and Christian and exacerbated factionalism among the rival Christian sects. The higher social and economic status led the Western-supported Christians to treat the already embittered Muslims with arrogance.

American influence at the turn of the century was primarily educational. American Protestants opened numerous schools in Mt. Lebanon and Syria, where they taught at least the rudiments of Arabic (and in a few cases, English) to a significant number of boys and girls and provided food and medical assistance in periods of strife. Of most lasting importance, they established the Syrian Protestant College (later renamed the American University in Beirut) whose numerous graduates went on to make valuable contributions to modern Arab life and thought.

EARLY IMMIGRATION

The first Arabs to discover the economic opportunities in the United States were probably the Christian tradesmen who, encouraged by the Ottoman sultan, came to exhibit Syrian wares at the Philadelphia International Exposition in 1876. Their enthusiastic reports, the activities of steamship agents recruiting labor from all over the world for American industry, and the efforts of native brokers and moneylenders combined to begin a chain emigration from the Mt. Lebanon area, the source of most pre-World War II Syrian migration. The overwhelming majority of these mountain-village emigrants were Christians in pursuit of economic interests.

In the late 19th century, Mt. Lebanon was an autonomous administrative district of the Ottoman Empire under the protection and influence of Western Christian powers and governed by a Christian Ottoman official. This district, according to historian Philip Hitti, was acknowledged to be "the best governed, most prosperous, peaceful and contented country in the Near East." Some residents migrated to escape military service which after 1908 became mandatory for Christians as well as Muslims under the new Turkish revolutionary government. Fear that they would be unable to maintain their Islamic traditions in a Western Christian society discouraged a mass migration of Muslims to the United States. Fragmentary data suggest that only a few thousand young Muslim men joined the Christian emigrants between 1900 and 1914, most of them after 1908.

The pioneers reported their success in letters home and demonstrated it in the amount of money they sent or in their ostentatious behavior if they went back to visit. The evidence attracted so many emigrants that before the turn of the century an entrepreneurial network of independent services developed to assist villagers along the stages of their journey. The operation of the network throughout most of the early period encouraged still more migration.

Adventurous bachelors were soon followed by married men and families. Some were small tradesmen, artisans, and skilled laborers, but most were off the land—owners of small, scattered holdings, tenant farmers, or laborers. Only a handful were intellectuals or professionals. With few exceptions, they came hoping to make a quick profit and return home to enjoy the status and privileges that money would bring; they were not leaving to escape religious or political persecution or economic oppression. Most of them were poor but not destitute. Emigration was generally a family venture and was financed by family resources. It was considered an investment whose return would be both wealth and prestige when the emigrant returned to his native village. Later, relatives already in the United States often paid for the trip.

Despite their unreliability, official immigration records are useful in revealing trends and characteristics of the Syrian migration. Immigration increased dramatically each year, from a few hundred in 1887 to over 4,000 in 1898; it rose to over 9,000 in 1913, but dropped sharply as a result of World War I. Immigration rose again briefly, partly in anticipation of the restrictive Immigration Act of 1924; the threat of restriction hastened the migration or reentry of Syrians with their families and relatives, of emigres dissatisfied with British and French League of Nations mandate governments that had been established after the war instead of promised Arab independence, and of Palestinians migrating as a result of bitter struggles with the British authority over the influx of Jews from Europe who had been promised a Jewish homeland in Palestinian territory. Restrictions, the Depression, and World War II severely curbed immigration between 1925 and 1948. Arab immigration after 1945 included a few from Iraq, Egypt, and Morocco. Immigration records show that 107,593 Syrians and 8,425 Palestinians arrived in the United States before World War II. Census figures to 1940 reveal 206,128 Americans of Syrian and Palestinian origin and descent. But the figures are only a rough approximation resulting from inaccurate record-keeping, illegal entries, and other sources of error.

Few Syrians returned to their villages permanently. Family commitments, economic failures, and temporary dissatisfactions produced a continual two-way traffic, though villagers sometimes remained several years before reemigrating with their families. Figures for 1908–1910 show a 25 percent return rate, mostly of single males, suggesting individual restlessness rather than discontent with life in the United States.

quarrels alike often spilled into the streets.

Unlike the post-1948 Arabs, the Syrians had relatively smooth relations with other Americans. Hostility toward them was neither specific nor sustained and Syrians were only dimly aware of it. They were more sectarian than nationalistic and their population small and dispersed, and this also made them inconspicuous. Driven by economic ambition, they also began rather early to imitate their neighbors and to seek their approval. They became citizens, bought homes, and followed the middle-class course out of old neighborhoods into better ones and ultimately into the suburbs. The process was slower among the few Arab industrial laborers and other wage earners.

RELIGIOUS INSTITUTIONS

A sense of permanence in the Syrian community was signaled first by the establishment of communal institutions—places of worship, newspapers, and associations. Leadership in founding these institutions was assumed by the more enterprising and prosperous men and women in both Christian and Muslim communities.

The first Syrian migration had not included clergy. Their passage was arranged by lay leaders who had already organized the churches and mosques; thus the clergy's dependence on and answerability to these leaders was conditioned even before they arrived. Often overzealous and poorly educated, the immigrant clergy helped transplant sectarian and religious factionalism to the New World.

Founding Eastern-rite churches whose masses would be conducted in Arabic or Syriac was the first concern of the Christian Syrians. The first churches—one Melkite, one Maronite, and one Orthodox—were built in New York between 1890 and 1895. By the early 1920s approximately 75 churches of one or another of the three sects were scattered through 28 states. But more than half of them were in the East, leaving vast areas unserved by a Syrian Eastern-rite church; many communities went more than a generation without one. Some regularly attended other churches; some awaited the sporadic visits of itinerant priests for important ceremonies; some succumbed to the temptation of belonging to churches they considered American—both Roman Catholic and Protestant—draining away adherents of each sect in sufficient numbers to alarm its leaders. They responded by Americanizing several aspects of the service and in the process inadvertently promoted assimilation by diluting the distinction between themselves and the "American" churches.

Defending their traditions against acculturation pressures was much more difficult for the Muslims than for the Christians. Although Muslims have no priesthood and can pray in any ritually uncontaminated space, the mosque and its prayer leader (imam) are central to Muslim religious practice and a symbol of community unity. A Muslim working and living in a non-Muslim society has to make essential religious compromises: it is not usually possible to observe the Sabbath on Friday,

During the depressed 1930s over 60 percent of the approximately 1,500 arrivals left for home or elsewhere.

From 1899 to 1915, women composed about 47 percent of the Arab total; they, too, came to acquire wealth, join spouses, or increase their chances of marriage as villages emptied of single men. Despite their arrival, family, sect, and village traditions still compelled many men to seek wives in the homeland. In the twenties, when a sense of permanence set in, the women immigrants outnumbered the men. Throughout the period of immigration, up to 75 percent of the Syrian immigrants were between the ages of 15 and 45. The 44 percent illiteracy rate before 1910 reflected their humble origins; by the twenties it had dropped to 21 percent, an indication both of better reporting and the development of education at home.

FAMILY VALUES AND ECONOMIC LIFE

Arab traits and values hinge on the central position held by the extended family in Arab society. The enhancement of family honor and status is an inviolable trust for its members; in return for protection, identity, and status, the family demands conformity and the subordination of individual will and interests. The honor or dishonor of an individual reflects on the entire family.

Noble ancestry, a claim few families can credibly make, has been supplanted in the United States by wealth as the basis for status and honor. Although money alone does not confer distinction on a family, it increases the ability of family members to manifest values—magnanimity, munificence, generosity, and hospitality—which even the poorest families cherish. Since in the structure of Arab society family honor is intricately entwined with loyalty to religion, sect, village, and even quarter, individual loyalty must extend to those as well. This system of values breeds family and group ties with strong clannish and factional tendencies. The determination to elevate and defend family honor and status produces a competitive spirit and an ethic of hard work, thrift, perseverance, shrewdness, and conservatism. The fear of shame restrains crime and indigence. Given the economic opportunities and the system of values in the United States, Syrians readily became success-oriented free-enterprisers. No two more dissimilar molds could have produced more similar products.

The Syrian immigrant occupation was peddling; no other immigrant group, with the exception of the German Jews, so completely identified with it. Although the form of peddling as conducted in the United States was a departure from Levantine traditional forms, selling and bartering the products of their labor from village to village and door to door was common to petty farmers, artisans, and tradesmen in the homeland.

Before 1914 at least 90 percent of the immigrants, including women and children, took up the trade in the United States, if only for a short time. Peddling yielded good profits and required little training, capital,

During the depressed 1930s over 60 percent of the approximately 1,500 arrivals left for home or elsewhere.

From 1899 to 1915, women composed about 47 percent of the Arab total; they, too, came to acquire wealth, join spouses, or increase their chances of marriage as villages emptied of single men. Despite their arrival, family, sect, and village traditions still compelled many men to seek wives in the homeland. In the twenties, when a sense of permanence set in, the women immigrants outnumbered the men. Throughout the period of immigration, up to 75 percent of the Syrian immigrants were between the ages of 15 and 45. The 44 percent illiteracy rate before 1910 reflected their humble origins; by the twenties it had dropped to 21 percent, an indication both of better reporting and the development of education at home.

FAMILY VALUES AND ECONOMIC LIFE

Arab traits and values hinge on the central position held by the extended family in Arab society. The enhancement of family honor and status is an inviolable trust for its members; in return for protection, identity, and status, the family demands conformity and the subordination of individual will and interests. The honor or dishonor of an individual reflects on the entire family.

Noble ancestry, a claim few families can credibly make, has been supplanted in the United States by wealth as the basis for status and honor. Although money alone does not confer distinction on a family, it increases the ability of family members to manifest values—magnanimity, munificence, generosity, and hospitality—which even the poorest families cherish. Since in the structure of Arab society family honor is intricately entwined with loyalty to religion, sect, village, and even quarter, individual loyalty must extend to those as well. This system of values breeds family and group ties with strong clannish and factional tendencies. The determination to elevate and defend family honor and status produces a competitive spirit and an ethic of hard work, thrift, perseverance, shrewdness, and conservatism. The fear of shame restrains crime and indigence. Given the economic opportunities and the system of values in the United States, Syrians readily became success-oriented free-enterprisers. No two more dissimilar molds could have produced more similar products.

The Syrian immigrant occupation was peddling; no other immigrant group, with the exception of the German Jews, so completely identified with it. Although the form of peddling as conducted in the United States was a departure from Levantine traditional forms, selling and bartering the products of their labor from village to village and door to door was common to petty farmers, artisans, and tradesmen in the homeland.

Before 1914 at least 90 percent of the immigrants, including women and children, took up the trade in the United States, if only for a short time. Peddling yielded good profits and required little training, capital, or English. The immigrants were not deluded about its hardships, but they preferred its independence to the drudgery of the factory and the isolation of the farm. Peddling drew young men and women from villages in groups of up to sixty or more, allowing the network of transit services to be formed and stimulating a Syrian industry of manufacturers, importers, and wholesalers to supply their needs. Those who did not peddle, or who tried and found its hardships intolerable, turned to work in mills and factories. A very few farmed or homesteaded in the West.

The transit network began in the homeland, but had its base in the new country in a peddling settlement clustered around a supplier, usually an enterprising veteran peddler. The port community of New York was the mother of peddling communities and their major supplier, but by 1900 Syrian peddlers had penetrated the remotest parts of the nation, from where suppliers, sometimes two or more in a town, recruited fellow villagers or attracted others. This proliferation of peddling settlements distributed Syrians throughout the United States; it also spared new arrivals the anxiety of finding work, since they could immediately be absorbed somewhere in the constantly expanding system.

Peddling was initially a trade in rosaries, jewelry, and notions that would fit into a small case. It soon expanded into suitcases filled with a wide range of dry goods from bed linens to lace—almost anything that an isolated farmer's wife or housebound city dweller might want to buy. Horses, wagons, and later automobiles allowed some peddlers to sell imported rugs and linens supplied by international traders in New York's Syrian community. By frugality, resourcefulness, long hours of work, and charging all that the market would bear, peddlers commonly calculated earnings into the thousands annually. Relatively few failed.

Syrian peddlers developed a network of routes from New York to California and from Maine to Texas. The more enterprising and determined, including a few women, remained on the road for weeks or months at a time, covering several states. Others concentrated on a single area. Most women, children, and old people remained within range of the settlement to which they returned in the evening. In addition to peddling, many women crocheted, embroidered, and sewed goods at home for their menfolk to sell, or worked in kimono or garment factories, sometimes also owned by Syrians. They generally continued this economic partnership through the various stages along the family's route to prosperity.

Suppliers were important figures in the early period. As businessman, leader, and often founder of a settlement, a supplier served many functions. He attracted and sometimes recruited peddlers, supplied them (frequently on credit), organized their routes, banked their savings, mediated between them and local authorities, rented them the crowded and poorly furnished quarters suited to their itinerancy, frugality, and temporary status, and involved himself in their social life and communal welfare. Supplier and peddler formed an interdependent relationship firmly based on canons of tradition that validated the supplier's leadership and limited his excesses. No special title attached to him nor was abject obedience demanded. If the peddler disagreed with him, the supplier's prestige and income were both at risk, and he frequently made concessions. The supplier's territory was the peddler's economic base and a refuge made up of relatives and friends. Since the peddler joined the group voluntarily, he could also leave when his personal and material objectives were better served elsewhere. He might join other villagers in more lucrative areas or establish his own supply store or other business.

Peddling hastened acculturation and in the process contributed to its own obsolescence. Peddlers accumulated capital, learned English quickly, and through constant contact with native-born Americans acquired new values, including the notion of settling permanently in the United States. When Syrians settled down, the majority opened family businesses in cities or smaller towns. Dry goods and grocery stores were the most common, but businesses ran the gamut. Numerous Syrian publications reflect the pride Syrians still take in "being in business."

Meanwhile, Muslim Arabs were also arriving, though in far smaller numbers. Higher industrial wages in the United States after 1910 attracted them to such industrial cities as Chicago, Toledo, and Dearborn, Michigan, although industrial labor usually proved to be a transitory occupation for the Muslims as well as for the Christians. When adjustment and capital were sufficient they generally turned to other pursuits.

SETTLEMENTS

From 1910 through 1930, according to census records, over 88 percent of the Syrians lived in or near urban centers, almost half of them on the East Coast. Of the remainder, about 2 percent farmed and the rest were businessmen in small towns or rural areas. New York, the first and the leading business, cultural, and intellectual center for Syrians until well after 1948, sheltered about 2,600 in Manhattan and Brooklyn in 1904; 7,631 in 1930. Only Boston's 3,150 Syrians came close to this number in the early years, but Detroit's colony increased from 417 in 1910 to 5,520 in 1930. Today Greater Detroit is home to the largest Arab-American community in the United States, reputed to number 200,000 members and still rapidly growing.

Syrian-American settlements were modeled on community life in the homeland and reflected the traditional, relatively homogeneous grouping by religion, sect, or village. Its leaders were more apt to be drawn from the most experienced and enterprising than from the high-born. The community served in the first place to ease the adjustment for newcomers; migrants subsequently moved in and out of it as their interests required. In both the cities and the remoter settlements, Syrian village life and values were maintained to some extent. The large communities were often noisy and congested; coffeehouses, stores, and restaurants supplied from New York provided traditional fare. Celebrations and quarrels alike often spilled into the streets.

Unlike the post-1948 Arabs, the Syrians had relatively smooth relations with other Americans. Hostility toward them was neither specific nor sustained and Syrians were only dimly aware of it. They were more sectarian than nationalistic and their population small and dispersed, and this also made them inconspicuous. Driven by economic ambition, they also began rather early to imitate their neighbors and to seek their approval. They became citizens, bought homes, and followed the middle-class course out of old neighborhoods into better ones and ultimately into the suburbs. The process was slower among the few Arab industrial laborers and other wage earners.

RELIGIOUS INSTITUTIONS

A sense of permanence in the Syrian community was signaled first by the establishment of communal institutions—places of worship, newspapers, and associations. Leadership in founding these institutions was assumed by the more enterprising and prosperous men and women in both Christian and Muslim communities.

The first Syrian migration had not included clergy. Their passage was arranged by lay leaders who had already organized the churches and mosques; thus the clergy's dependence on and answerability to these leaders was conditioned even before they arrived. Often overzealous and poorly educated, the immigrant clergy helped transplant sectarian and religious factionalism to the New World.

Founding Eastern-rite churches whose masses would be conducted in Arabic or Syriac was the first concern of the Christian Syrians. The first churches—one Melkite, one Maronite, and one Orthodox—were built in New York between 1890 and 1895. By the early 1920s approximately 75 churches of one or another of the three sects were scattered through 28 states. But more than half of them were in the East, leaving vast areas unserved by a Syrian Eastern-rite church; many communities went more than a generation without one. Some regularly attended other churches; some awaited the sporadic visits of itinerant priests for important ceremonies; some succumbed to the temptation of belonging to churches they considered American—both Roman Catholic and Protestant—draining away adherents of each sect in sufficient numbers to alarm its leaders. They responded by Americanizing several aspects of the service and in the process inadvertently promoted assimilation by diluting the distinction between themselves and the "American" churches.

Defending their traditions against acculturation pressures was much more difficult for the Muslims than for the Christians. Although Muslims have no priesthood and can pray in any ritually uncontaminated space, the mosque and its prayer leader (imam) are central to Muslim religious practice and a symbol of community unity. A Muslim working and living in a non-Muslim society has to make essential religious compromises: it is not usually possible to observe the Sabbath on Friday, pray five times a day, and fast during the sunlight hours of the holy month of Ramadan. Clues to the effect of American society on a Muslim group are provided by a small community established near Ross, North Dakota, around 1900. Before a mosque was built in the 1920s, prayer and ritual were conducted in private houses and led by the best informed among the group. Without a mosque for almost thirty years and without any cultural reinforcement from newcomers, the Muslims rapidly lost the use of Arabic, assumed Christian names, and married non-Muslims. The community dwindled as children moved away, and the mosque was abandoned by 1948. Elsewhere the sparse and scattered Muslim communities rarely even built mosques; only three are known to have been constructed in the twenties.

THE PRESS, CULTURE, AND ETHNIC ORGANIZATIONS

The first Arabic newspaper was published in New York in 1892; by 1907 there were seven daily or weekly competitors; by 1920 that number doubled, and numerous other periodicals were in circulation as well. The impetus was provided by a few Syrian immigrant intellectuals influenced by a literary revival led by Syrians in Egypt. Competition was keen, the quality mixed, and the papers often short-lived. The most durable and influential was *al-Hoda* (The Enlightener), which began in 1898 and was the organ of the Maronites, followed by the Orthodox *Mirat al-Gharb* (Mirror of the West) in 1899 and the Druze *al-Bayan* (The News) in 1910. Established from the start on a sectarian basis, the Arabic press did nothing to discourage community fragmentation. Its editors published news and opinion on events in the homeland and in the United States, social news, literature and literary criticism, and encouraged good citizenship. Textbooks for learning English, American customs, and procedures for naturalization were also published.

The decline in both the number and quality of Arabic publications between the wars reflected the ignorance of Arabic language among the descendants of Syrian immigrants. Attempts to teach Arabic to children at home and in private schools competed unsuccessfully with the Americanization process. The number of Arabic readers was also diminished by restrictive immigration laws and political stability in the homeland. Too few immigrants came, and the Syrian Americans turned their attention to domestic news. Arabic newspapers also lost their intellectual quality. They had to compete in style and technology with the American press and simplify their language for readers whose lack of facility in Arabic required an easy, clear journalistic style.

By the mid-1920s the editors who had earlier contributed to the acceleration of Americanization began pressing for a revival of the community's ethnic consciousness, but with little success. The all-English journal *Syrian World,* founded by *al-Hoda* in 1926 for that purpose, lasted about six years. English predominated in the ethnic press, whose content and transience both indicated a diminished awareness of the

Arab heritage.

The Syrian literati influenced by European and American free verse, who were active in New York before 1914, had little influence on Syrians in the United States, notwithstanding the revolutionary effect they had on literature in the Arab world. Syrian-Americans had little appreciation for Arabic literature. Its content was so alien to their experience that hardly a single name from this prolific literary group is known to them. Gibran Khalil Gibran (1883–1931) is the only exception, and even his works were introduced to most Syrians by the non-Arab Americans who popularized them. Concerned primarily with the impact of their innovations on general Arab literature, this literary elite failed in the United States to preserve or transmit any work of lasting ethnic social or cultural significance. The works of a few talented American authors of Syrian descent such as William Blatty (1928–) and Vance Bourjaily (1922–) reflect little or no influence either of their Arab predecessors or of their ethnic origins.

Early ethnic organizations formed around the religious sects. They built places of worship, buried the dead, and helped the needy. In time, others were formed to maintain sectarian solidarity, promote American patriotic ideals and citizenship, further understanding between Syrians and other Americans, and make philanthropic contributions to benefit their respective ancestral villages. With the exception of an influential Maronite group founded just before World War I to support a French-backed Maronite-dominated Lebanon, organizations to influence homeland politics were not a consideration until after 1948. Whatever their other aims, the paramount objective of all these societies was perpetuation of the group, mainly through in-group marriage. To arrest the growing drift of youth away from it, parents and priests sponsored local, and later regional, family, village, and sectarian organizations.

Syrians had such a propensity for organizing that at any given time the number of organizations was out of all proportion to the number of Syrians in the population. Their fondness for organization reflected their factional tendencies and slowed the erosion of group solidarity and traditional values in the United States. Their contributions made possible the building of numerous churches, orphanages, hospitals, and schools in the homeland. They did not establish comparable charitable or educational institutions in the United States that transcend subgroups, although individual Arabs have contributed generously to American philanthropic causes.

Although the early Syrian organizations were not political in purpose, they were not immune to political vicissitudes in the homeland. When in 1920 Greater Lebanon was created by the pro-Maronite French mandatory government from Mt. Lebanon and land belonging to Syria proper, many non-Maronite immigrants from the incorporated Syrian areas refused to use the term Lebanese. The controversy over whether organizations should be called Syrian-American, Lebanese-American, or both, subsided only when Lebanon and Syria achieved full independence after

World War II.

Unification of the Syrian community was attempted in 1932 when a regional federation of local organizations was formed in Boston. By that time leadership had passed to the American-born, English-speaking generation who were less sectarian in their interests and who hoped to transcend the divisions perpetuated by their elders. Although hampered by the depression and by internal conflicts, the Eastern Federation was successful enough to inspire other regional federations. They sponsored social activities, provided scholarships, and sought to improve relations between Syrian-Americans and others. Aside from some interest in Arabic food, music, and dance, little Arab ethnic heritage was apparent in these organizations. The degree to which Americanization had overtaken their institutions explains in part why Syrian-Americans were so slow to comprehend the significance of the Arab political and social issues that so preoccupied the post-1948 arrivals. Even when they did, it was primarily as Americans and only secondarily as Arabs.

GROUP MAINTENANCE

The breakdown of the patriarchal, extended family into nuclear units and the reduction in the father's authority were the first effects of immigration on Arab family life. Long hours, even days, away from home, peddling or minding the store, and the participation of wives in the family business weakened the paternal authority. The father lost ground as a disciplinarian, although he retained the respect due him as head of the family. American influence, education, and economic opportunities might impel sons to establish their own households when they married, but sentimental attachments and concern for the welfare of the family still tied the various units together.

The energy that women devoted to the economic goals of the family gradually freed them from some Old World customs. Muslim women usually abandoned the veil when they emigrated. Covering the head, a custom common to both Christian and Muslim women, was also soon abandoned except by the most traditional-minded. Working wives and mothers did not relinquish their domestic roles, but they adjusted to necessity by having fewer children, cooking fewer time-consuming Arabic meals, and gradually adopting the custom of prearranged social visits.

Their labors helped build and support churches and kept the youth within the group. Their independence ended some time-honored traditions: by World War II the segregation of sexes at social gatherings in homes and churches had vanished except in mosques and among the most traditional Mulsims. Only after the war did later marriages and unarranged ones become the rule; daughters were allowed to remain single if they wished, and the preference for male children lost much of its force.

Any hope for keeping marriage within the ethnic, religious, sectarian, or regional group was thwarted in the earliest years by a shortage of

Syrian women, attendance at non-Syrian churches, and desire for acceptance in the larger American society. Interethnic, though not interreligious, marriages were sufficiently common to elicit admonitions
against them in the Arabic press before 1914. An increase in the number
of immigrant Syrian women, churches, and associations slowed the trend
but did not entirely reverse it. Both convention and religion allowed men
greater latitude than women in the choice of spouses. Until World War II
unmarried women usually remained under the surveillance of the family,
and their choices were carefully controlled and arranged to serve its interests. Women were expected to adhere to the faith of their husbands; if
they married outside the sect, they and their children would be lost to it.
Marriage was consequently a frequent source of conflict between the immigrant and the next generation. The children yearned for the aspects of
American middle-class life that they had been exposed to through school,
movies, radio, and military service. Marriage was for many an escape
from parental authority; a non-Arab marriage presented itself as a solution to the dilemma of living in two cultures. Only occasionally did interethnic marriage result in permanent rupture in family relationships,
however, and by the 1950s it was in any case so commonplace, especially
among returning servicemen, that it ceased to be a major source of contention.

Marriage for the few Muslim Arabs posed more serious problems. In
the early years women were few, and departure from custom, which had
the force of holy law behind it, was attended with greater concern. The
traditional-minded initially sought spouses in the homeland, but eventually the rate of interethnic (which for Muslims also meant interfaith)
marriages among them increased as well. Beginning in the mid-sixties it
soared among the professional and educated classes of both religious
groups.

The attempts of the immigrant generation to maintain Arab culture
ran afoul of their eagerness to succeed in the United States; the requirements of success relegated tradition to second place. Immigration
restrictions after 1924 encouraged assimilation and prepared the way for
the gap that developed between the descendants of the early immigrants
and the culture-conscious Arabs of more recent times. The participation
of the early immigrants in American life was somewhat cursory; coupled
with their prosperity, however, it was nevertheless sufficient to allow
their children to enter the larger American society with relatively little
psychological stress.

The family, the keystone of Arab identity and social organization, had
already been modified in the first generation to a degree determined by
the family's economic status, the number of Syrians in the community,
and the family's own inclinations regarding its cultural heritage. Hardly
a family was unaffected at least to some extent by the assimilation process. The second generation maintained those elements of their parents'
culture that were not incompatible with an American household. They
raised their children according to local practices; they still relished ethnic

food, but usually only on special occasions; if they did not attend church regularly, they at least observed religious holidays. They maintained family bonds but also developed relations with non-Syrian Americans of their own class.

The third and fourth generations are considerably more remote from the culture of the first. A recent awakening to their ethnicity has caused them to turn to their parents for cultural pegs on which to hang their identity; but parental knowledge is often superficial, based only on being Syrians of one religious sect or another. Grandparents add little more than nostalgic reminiscences of an outdated past. If political and economic events had not reactivated Arab immigration and an interest in Arab culture, Syrian-Americans might have Americanized themselves out of existence.

THE POSTWAR IMMIGRATION

For more than a century the West altered both social relations and political boundaries within the Arab world. By 1920 France ruled Morocco, Algeria, Tunisia, and Syria, including Mt. Lebanon. England governed Egypt, Sudan, Palestine, Transjordan, Iraq, and the eastern and southern shores of the Arabian peninsula, and exerted considerable influence in Libya. Only Saudi Arabia and Yemen remained independent. Greater Syria, which was supposed to be the basis for an independent, unified Arab nation promised by the West in return for Arab military aid to the Allies in World War I, was artificially divided in 1920 into a truncated Syria, a Maronite-dominated Greater Lebanon (incorporating the Syrian port cities of Sidon, Tyre, Beirut, and Tripoli), Transjordan, and a promised homeland in Palestine for the Jews. Lingering separatist feelings hardened and new ones developed. Arab nationalist ideology was born out of resentment and frustration over broken promises and thwarted aspirations. Arab nationalists set about building up Arab self-esteem and encouraging unity to counter foreign rule. The Arab nations gradually won their independence after World War II, but Arab unity foundered on separatist nationalist ideologies and sentiments that were reinforced by religious differences.

Between the wars, Western influence had led the upper and middle classes to send their sons, and some daughters, to be educated in Europe. After independence, governments committed to modernization subsidized education abroad, particularly in the United States. The rate of modernization lagged well behind the rate of education, however, as competing revolutionary ideologies, military coups, and wars with Israel sapped economies and career opportunities. As a result, despite the emigration restrictions imposed by several Arab governments and the dedication to the development of their countries of the individuals involved, hundreds of Muslim and Christian students sent to the United States for training simply remained there. Many professionals also emigrated, entering the United States under the terms of the professional-preference clause in the

Immigration and Nationality Act of 1965. This Arab "brain drain" reached its highest point between 1968 and 1971, but from 1965 through 1976 "professional, technical, and kindred workers" averaged about fifteen percent of Arab immigrants—Egypt alone lost nearly seven thousand. A high percentage of immigrants from Jordan, Lebanon, and Syria are undoubtedly Palestinians; other Palestinians were admitted as refugees or under Israeli passports.

This immigration wave began in 1948, but it accelerated greatly after the Arab defeat in the Arab-Israeli war of 1967. From 1948 through 1979 arrivals totaled approximately 216,000; about 142,000 came during and after 1967. More than 44,000 came from Egypt; Jordan, Lebanon, Iraq, and Syria together provided about 126,000, most of them Palestinians; about 9,200 were listed as Palestinians; the rest came from North African countries, aside from a few thousand from the Arabian Peninsula. Some, like the stateless Palestinians, were pushed by political events; some by economic uncertainties. But most of them came to improve their prospects. In this group Muslims exceeded Christians by about 60 percent. About 45 percent were women, and over 50 percent were between 20 and 49 years old. From 1965 to 1976 skilled workers averaged 15 percent and unskilled workers 10 percent of Arab immigration; wives, children, and others reporting "no occupation" averaged over 50 percent. Recent arrivals under these classifications include Palestinians and Lebanese displaced by civil war in Lebanon.

Settlement and adjustment have been considerably easier for these Arabs. They have the advantages of education, language, special skills, and the communities and precedents already established by the Syrians. Most of them intended to return home eventually, and were simply awaiting a change in the circumstances that had precipitated their migration. Few actually go back. Some, like the unskilled Yemeni farmers and factory laborers, travel back and forth several times before finally deciding to settle.

The immigrants preferred to live among their own kind, but where they actually settled was necessarily determined by employment opportunities. With the exception of the 0.6 percent (mostly Yemeni) listed in the 1970 U.S. Census as farm laborers and the 1.0 percent as farmers and farm managers, they are predominantly city dwellers. If they came to join relatives, they generally found them in mixed neighborhoods, for by the postwar period few urban Arab communities remained. Some, like the Egyptians Copts and the Yemenis have formed new communities. They have already experienced considerable upward mobility. The professionals, best equipped to deal with the problems of settlement and adjustment, have already become almost indistinguishable from other Americans of their class.

The few communities of Arab industrial workers are more unified. In south Dearborn, Michigan, a predominantly Muslim community dating from about 1916 has received a steady stream of Palestinians, Yemenis, and refugees from Lebanon since the mid-1960s. The residents have organized to house, guide, instruct, and generally serve the needs of the newcomers.

The recent immigrants are considerably less sectarian, a trend that parallels declining sectarian allegiance among the American-born. Wherever they settle, postwar immigrants find American-born Arabs. Before the Arab-Israeli war of 1967, the two groups had difficulty understanding each other's concerns and tended to associate mainly with those Arabs who did not seriously challenge their views on Arab issues. After 1967 what they perceived as general American hostility toward Arabs drew the two groups closer together.

Arabs of the recent immigration are nationalistic and are eager to maintain their traditions. Their efforts harmonize with those of the newly ethnicized American-born Arabs. One result has been a sharp increase in the number of mosques in the United States. Since its use is essential to the Muslim faith, Arabic is also being revived. Mostly immigrant imams are trying to revive religious discipline and knowledge both of Arabic and modern Islamic thought. Many Christian Arab churches have also begun to offer classes in Arabic language, history, and culture. Social events feature modern Arab food, songs, and dances; discussions at the parish level consider ways of encouraging a sense of community.

Outside the religious institutions a growing number of Syrian-Americans are also showing an interest in their ethnicity, learning about their culture, and taking at least some colloquial Arabic at college or doing research on Arabs and Arab-Americans in graduate school. One group, in concert with the recent arrivals, is trying to improve the quality of the teaching of Arab history and culture in high school. The long-term effects of all this activity remain to be seen, for in the meantime the children of the immigrants again experience the temptations of assimilation.

The Arab-American press reached its nadir in the forties. After 1950 several new newspapers in Arabic appeared, along with several journals in English. They stress the politics and economics of the Arab world, although they do not entirely neglect social and cultural items. Editorials interpret events in terms of the publisher's attitude toward American involvement in Arab-Israeli affairs. Competition for a limited audience still results in constant turnover. None of these papers has attained the journalistic and literary quality or enjoys the national success of the earlier Arab publications.

The formation of associations by the new immigrants coincided with important changes in those established earlier by the Syrian community. The Eastern Federation of American Syrian-Lebanese Clubs, under a younger, more educated leadership, attempted to influence American foreign policy toward the emerging Arab nations and inform American public opinion. In 1950 regional federations coalesced into a more politicized National Association of Federations. Editorials in its monthly publication, however, revealed conformity to American political attitudes and fear of condemnation from other Americans. In the decade of McCarthyism, its Syrian readership was particularly sensitive to

Syria's sharp swing to the political left. The national organization had all but dissolved by the sixties, its leadership claiming in its waning days that integration into American life had rendered ethnic organizations obsolete. As it turned out, its attempts to become a national ethnic interest group had simply been premature. The Syrian community was too disunited to pursue a common goal.

In the fifties the loyalties of the new Arabs in America were confounded by the intensity of competing Arab ideologies in the Arab world, by U.S. refusal to sell arms to the pro-Western revolutionary government in Egypt, by President Gamal Abdul Nasser's consequent arms deal with the Soviet bloc, withdrawal of U.S. funds for the Aswan Dam, nationalization of the Suez Canal, and the Suez War of 1956. Yet in their diffuse and confused way these organizations initiated the consciousness-raising process in the United States that would accelerate after the 1967 Arab-Israeli war. The unexpected Israeli victory, followed by hostility toward the Arabs in the American press, brought the two Arab-American communities together. The Association of Arab-American University Graduates held its first convention in 1968. It proposed to unify the Arab-American community, influence American Middle East policy, and correct misinformation about Arabs in general and the image of Arab-Americans in particular through a public information program and publications by its members. Dominated by post-1948 immigrants, it takes a militant stand on solutions to the Arab-Israeli conflict. The National Association of Arab Americans, founded in 1972 in Washington, D.C., and dominated by American-born Arab businessmen and professionals, has among its aims the involvement of Arab-Americans in the American political process. It is registered as a lobby on behalf of Arab-Americans to influence U.S. Middle East policy. More recently a third more broadly based national organization was formed in response to what it perceives to be persistent and pervasive defamation of the Arab image in the United States, and to an American Middle East foreign policy which, in favoring Israel, contributes to "Arab cultural denigration." Established in 1980, the American-Arab Anti-Discrimination Committee "combats stereotyping of Arabs in the media and discrimination against Arab-Americans in employment, education, and political life." These national organizations are much more viable than their predecessors.

Before 1948 Arab-Americans did not feel the need to gain influence as a group in American life, although individuals attained positions of prominence in party politics, labor unions, entertainment, education, and the press. Emphasis on individual achievement required neither unions nor political parties, and the general satisfaction of Syrian-Americans with their way of life obviated their participation.

A sizable percentage of Arab-Americans today are professional and semiprofessional people in practically all fields. Their rate of achievement is high; Arabs have a long roster of public personalities in law, consumerism, finance, medicine, politics, government, journalism, the sciences, education, show business, and literature.

POLITICS

Syrians became naturalized, voted at least as faithfully as the rest of the population, and joined Rotary and Kiwanis clubs, if only because these were the "American" things to do. If city machines thought them too few to court, small-town ward bosses did not. One or two Syrians in the United States aspired to public office as early as 1910. Later, Syrians won election as mayors, city councilmen, and state legislators, and were appointed to public office. In 1958 the first Syrian won a seat in Congress. In 1980, James Abourezk of South Dakota became the first Arab-American to be elected to the U.S. Senate. Other Arab-Americans from Connecticut, Maine, Ohio, Texas, and West Virginia have been elected to the House of Representatives. However, Arabs are more likely to win elective office in small towns where their families have been prominent and where their ethnic origins play little or no part in their political success. They are too individualistic and scattered to be relied on as a political bloc.

On domestic matters Arabs vote their private interests. Although five of the six Arabs in Congress are Democrats, the majority of Arab-Americans are conservative and generally Republican, in part because most Syrians began moving up the economic ladder in the twenties when the Republican party was ascendant. Arab Democrats generally adhere to the party's social and economic platform, conservative in the South, more liberal in the North; they are rarely radicals.

Likewise, in national elections the Arab vote does not seem to have been significantly affected by U.S. policy in the Middle East, which in any case was neutral or nonexistent before President Harry S. Truman's recognition of the state of Israel in 1948. Despite ethnic awakening and the outspoken criticism by Arab-American leaders of America's Middle East policy since 1948, the situation has not perceptibly altered.

Recent Arab immigrants have succeeded in arousing ethnic loyalty among the Americanized generations and have also taught them what their parents had not—that the label Arab includes both Muslims and Christians. They have precipitated a movement toward Arab cohesion; it is frequently superficial and still meets with resistance from many quarters, but that any cohesion at all could be generated among the descendants of the early immigrants is itself remarkable. The elements of Arab culture that survived, fostered in churches, mosques, and the family, have proved to be tenacious.

The relations between Arabs and other Americans have generally been amicable, marred only by occasional anger and disillusionment in recent years. The problem for the second generation was to avoid assimilating to the point of becoming invisible. The task for Arab-Americans today is to breach factional divisions and form a cohesive Arab-American community.

REFERENCES

Aswad, Barbara C., ed.
   1974   *Arabic Speaking Communities in American Cities.* New York: Center for Migration Studies and the Association of Arab-American University Graduates, Inc.

Benyon, E. D.
   1944   The Near East in Flint, Michigan: Assyrians and Druse and Their Antecedents. *Geographic Review* 24:234–274.

Bisharat, Mary
   1975   Yemeni Farmworkers in California. *MERIP Reports* (January):22–26.

Elkholy, Abdo
   1966   *Arab Moslems in the United States: Religion and Assimilation.* New Haven: College and University Press.

Hagopian, Elaine C., and Ann Paden, eds.
   1969   *The Arab-Americans: Studies in Assimilation.* Wilmette, Ill.: The Medina University Press International.

Hitti, Philip
   1924   *Syrians in America.* New York: George H. Doran Co.

Houghton, Louise Seymour
   1911   The Syrians in the United States. *Survey* 26(1–4):480–495; 647–665; 786–802; 957–968.

Jaafari, L.
   1973   The Brain Drain to the United States: The Migration of Jordanians and Palestinian Professionals and Students. *Journal of Palestine Studies* (Autumn):119–131.

Kayal, Philip M., and Joseph M. Kayal
   1975   *Syrian Lebanese in America: A Study in Religion and Assimilation.* Boston: Twayne.

Othman, Ibrahim
   1974   *Arabs in the United States: A Study of an Arab-American Community.* Amman, Jordan: Shashaa and the University of Jordan.

Sengstock, Mary C.
   1970   Telkaif, Baghdad, Detroit: Chaldeans Blend Three Cultures. *Michigan History* 54:293–310.

Tannous, Afif
1943 Acculturation of an Arab-Syrian Community in the Deep South. *American Sociological Review* 8(3):264–271.

Wasfi, Atif A.
1971 *An Islamic-Lebanese Community in the U.S.A.: A Study in Cultural Anthropology.* Beirut: Beirut Arab University.

ABSTRACT

The vast majority of Arabs who immigrated to the United States at the turn of the century originated in the Ottoman province of Syria. A variety of economic, political, and social factors led to their emigration. With the exception of the district of Mount Lebanon, the general economic and political conditions in Syria, even before World War I, were chaotic and depressed. The collapse of the once prosperous silk industry and Ottoman alliance with Germany affected the economic and political stability of Mount Lebanon as well. These disruptive conditions, combined with reports of economic opportunity in the West and a certain amount of political persecution, led to a steadily increasing flow of emigrants. Consequently, Syria suffered a serious manpower shortage during the early years of the 20th century. A significant number of emigrants, however, did invest newly acquired capital in their home country.

Emigration from Syria

by Najib E. Saliba

The background and causes of emigration from Syria in the last four decades of Ottoman rule are examined in this article.[1] This period witnessed the first wave of emigration, an outflow which was interrupted by World War I and, as far as emigration to the United States was concerned, was afterwards limited by more stringent U.S. immigration laws.[2]

SYRIA ON THE EVE OF WORLD WAR I

During most of the period under study, Syria was administratively divided into three provinces (vilayets) and three autonomous districts called *mutasarrifiyyas* (usually subdivisions of vilayets).[3] The province of Aleppo included northern Syria and parts of southern Turkey, the province of Syria included central Syria (mainly the cities of Hama, Hims, and Damascus) and Transjordan; the province of Beirut, which was created in 1888, included the coastal districts of Latakia, Tripoli, Beirut, southern Lebanon, and northern Palestine (the districts of Akka and Nablus). The autonomous districts included the district of Jerusalem, that of Dayr al-Zawr in eastern Syria, and the district of Mount Lebanon.

Of all these administrative divisions, that of Mount Lebanon played a pioneering role in emigration. The district of Mount Lebanon was set up as a consequence of a tragedy and was abolished in the midst of another tragedy, World War I. It was established in the wake of European, mostly French, intervention in a sectarian civil war in Syria in 1860, during which

---

[1] This article originally appeared in *Arab Studies Quarterly* Vol. 3, No. 1. It is reprinted here with permission of the author and publisher. The term Syria includes, in addition to present-day Syria, the Republic of Lebanon, Palestine, and the Kingdom of Jordan.

[2] In 1917 the U.S. Congress introduced literacy restrictions, thus closing the United States to illiterate immigrants. Moreover, the more stringent immigration laws introduced in 1924 almost totally closed the United States to Asiatic immigrants.

[3] For a brief account of Ottoman administration in Syria see the author's doctoral dissertation (1971). See also al-Hakim (1966:5).

several thousand Christians perished. Under European pressure on behalf of the Christians, the Ottoman sultan issued a decree setting up Mount Lebanon, an area of about two thousand square miles, as an autonomous district with its governor responsible directly to the Sublime Porte in Istanbul. The governor was to be an Ottoman Catholic Christian but not from Mount Lebanon and was to be appointed by the sultan and approved by the six European powers which guaranteed Mount Lebanon's autonomy (Salibi 1965:110). Assisting the governor was an administrative council composed of four Maronite Christians, two Greek Orthodox, one Greek Catholic, three Druze, one Sunni Muslim, and one Shia Muslim.

From its inception in 1861 to its fall in mid-1915, Mount Lebanon was better governed, administered, and policed and its people better educated than the rest of Syria. Many observers noted that its people enjoyed unprecedented tranquillity, security, and prosperity (al-Hakim 1964:14). They also enjoyed exemption from military conscription and high taxation, two notorious aspects of late Ottoman rule. Because of these favorable conditions the residents of Mount Lebanon were envied by their less fortunate neighbors. As the saying went, "Happy was he who had a goat's resting place in Lebanon."

The situation was not totally satisfactory because Mount Lebanon was cut off from its fertile hinterland, the Biqa plain, as well as the plains of Sidon and Tyre. Its territory was largely mountainous and little suitable for agriculture. With a high birth rate, little farming, and virtually no industry, emigration served as a safety valve to what might otherwise have been an explosive situation.

The relative peace and tranquillity which prevailed in Mount Lebanon for over half a century totally disappeared with the onset of World War I. As soon as the Ottoman Empire entered the war on the side of Germany, the Allied fleets blockaded the coasts of Syria and prohibited the importation of all foodstuffs. Local production was not sufficient to feed the population. In addition, Ottoman military authorities confiscated wheat and other grains in order to assure adequate food supplies for the army. Famine spread throughout Syria and hit particularly hard in Mount Lebanon.[4] Survivors of that calamity still relate horrible stories of the years of war, stories of people who starved to death in the streets while others frantically went through garbage looking for something to eat. People of moderate means sold or mortgaged their land, homes, and other belongings for small quantities of food. Ironically, food supplies, according to some accounts, were not always absent from the market. Monopoly and high prices, however, placed them beyond the reach of the common man. The absence of private and public relief agencies contributed to the severity of the situation. Although Ottoman authorities

---

[4]There are many moving accounts about the famine which afflicted Mount Lebanon during World War I. See al-Hakim (1964:245–251); Khatir (1967:200–207); Aridah (1916:459–462); al-Aswad (1930). The 1916 issue of *al-Funun* was dedicated to the famine in Syria.

undertook some relief measures, those measures were totally inadequate. Some Ottoman officials, allied with wealthy local opportunists, benefited at the expense of the poor. While thousands starved to death during the four years of war,[5] suspected leaders and politically conscious notables suffered from imprisonment, house arrest, exile, and hanging.[6] Jamal Pasha, the Turkish military governor of Syria, drew no distinction between Muslim and Christian.

If Mount Lebanon enjoyed adequate living conditions before the war, the same was not true of the rest of Syria. Although conditions varied slightly from one province to another, public security on the whole was wanting. The people were exposed to the arbitrariness of government officials, the police, and tax collectors. There was hardly any security for life and property.[7] Villages at the edge of the desert were constantly exposed to bedouin raids and pillage; urban areas, in turn, suffered from sectarian and other sources of tension. The government was weak and its intervention could not always be counted upon. High public officials were sometimes unwilling or unable to preserve public order. Insufficiency or inaccessibility of security forces tied the governor's hands. The commander of army troops in a given province did not always work harmoniously with the governor, the highest public official in the province. Furthermore, peaceful relations between the empire on the one hand and its dissatisfied minorities and the imperial powers on the other were a rarity from 1850 onward. War circumstances invariably led to the withdrawal of almost all security forces from the provinces to the scenes of hostility, leaving the Syrian provinces underpoliced and exposed to lawlessness and domestic strife. At those times public security was obviously at its worst.

The general economic situation also left much to be desired. Ottoman authorities followed a *laissez-faire* economic policy. Without official concern and encouragement, agriculture—the cornerstone of the economy—and industry were in a state of decline (Saliba 1971:307–309). Agriculture, for example, had long suffered from neglect, peasant ignorance, pests, inadequate rainfall, bedouin depredation, foreign competition, and dependence on centuries-old methods of farming, threshing, and winnowing. Whole villages at the edge of the desert were abandoned by the peasants for lack of security and the fields turned into desert. The annual yield of wheat, barley, and maize had progressively fallen. Particularly affected was the cultivation of cotton. Left unprotected from the competition of Egyptian and U.S. cotton, Syrian production of that

---

[5]Estimates vary. Khatir (1967:200) put the number of Lebanese victims at 100,000; Ali put the number of victims in all Syria at 120,000 (1925:135).

[6]About forty people were hanged in Beirut and Damascus in 1916 because of political activities. See al-Hakim (1964:234–238); see also Ali (1925:141–145).

[7]See Chapter 6 of the author's dissertation (1971) on government and public security in Syria.

commodity had practically ceased by World War I (Himadeh 1936:79; Issawi 1966:208; 1977).

The situation in industry was hardly better. For years observers of the Syrian economy had noted the decline of the previously vigorous textile industry. Although estimates of the number of workers and looms left in operation varied, there was general agreement that the trend was downward. The problems which hurt the cotton and silk industry the most included high domestic taxation and the lack of protective tariffs in the face of heavy competition by cheap machine-made goods imported from abroad (Himadeh 1936:80; Issawi 1977:99, 221, 281–282). In addition, a shift in native tastes to European-made clothing led to a shrinking market. The opening of the Suez Canal in 1869 not only hurt Syria's transit trade with Iraq and Iran, it also dealt a serious blow to its silk industry in the international market for it greatly facilitated the transportation of Chinese and particularly Japanese silk to European markets at competitive prices. Syrian silk could not hold its ground. Subsequent attempts to open the American market to compensate for the loss of the French one proved fruitless. In 1889, Syrian production of silk was reported to have been twenty-five percent below that of previous years. Silkworm disease and the cutting down of mulberry trees during World War I accelerated the decline. In the early 1920s, Syria's production of raw silk (cocoons) was little more than one-sixth of what it had been in 1910, down from 6,100,000 kilograms to 1,300,000 (Saliba 1971:313; Hitti 1922:120; Bisharah 1922:355, 358; Himadeh 1936:123, 137). The problems of the textile industry, however, were not unique. The same situation was generally true in other industries such as the production of olive oil and alcoholic beverages, tanning, dyeing, wood engraving, and jewelry making.

An already bad economic situation was made worse by the empire's entry into the war and the establishment of the draft. Males between 18 and 45 years of age were drafted. In a land not accustomed to military service, conscription was very unpopular. Of the 240,000 conscripts about 40,000 were killed and approximately 150,000 deserted (Ali 1925:145; al-Hakim 1964:223). Many others fled their homes and lands to escape the draft. Undoubtedly, this reflected negatively on the security situation, the economy, and, particularly, agriculture.

THE EARLY YEARS OF EMIGRATION: 1878–1920

The number of emigrants from Syria was small, and largely to Egypt, prior to 1878 (Ali 1925:93; Safa 1960:10, 120). Emigration picked up steadily in the 1880s and the 1890s and increased sharply in the first fourteen years of this century. There is a virtual concensus among sources that the Christians of Mount Lebanon were the first to emigrate. Although conflicting estimates make it virtually impossible to state with certainty the number of Lebanese who emigrated before 1900, it is estimated that about 5000 emigrants had settled in the United States by 1899 and about

1000 in Canada by 1901 (Hagopian and Paden 1969:21; al-Id 1959:529, 613). Others went to Australia and the countries of South America. Of a population estimated at 442,000 in 1913, Mount Lebanon had lost more than 100,000 to emigration by 1914 (Rondot 1947:28–29; Hitti 1965:207; Ruppin 1966:270), more than one-fourth of its population. It did not take other Syrians long to catch up with the Lebanese. Very soon, emigrants were leaving from Damascus, Jerusalem, Ramallah, and the many other towns and villages (al-Hakim 1964:42–43; Hitti 1922:22–23, 121; Issawi 1966:272). By the 1920s, the Syrian community in Egypt numbered over 50,000 of whom more than 15,000 were Orthodox Christians.[8] Probably about 4000 Syrian emigrants had settled in Australia by 1903, over 3000 in Canada by 1921, and some 80,000 to 100,000 in Brazil by 1922 (al-Khuri 1903:600–602; Hagopian and Paden 1969:21, n.7; Daun 1922:228–231).[9] Others settled in Argentina and Mexico.

A large number went to the United States before 1920. It is virtually impossible to accurately determine their number and place of origin in Syria. Part of the difficulty stems from the fact that early Syrian emigrants were entered as Arabs, Turks, Asiatic Turks, and sometimes as Armenians and Greeks in U.S. immigration records (Hitti 1922:16–17). It was only after 1899 that the Immigration Service began to classify such immigrants as Syrians. Even then, the 1910 U.S. census listed no immigrants of Syrian origin in the United States. Following an inquiry, however, another official report put the number of Syrian emigrants who entered the United States between 1899 and 1910 at 56,909 (Hitti 1922:16–18, 22). Table 1 shows the number of Syrians who entered the United States annually from 1899 to June 30, 1919, a total of 89,971.

The sharp decline in the number of immigrants beginning in 1915 and continuing through 1919 reflects the war years' conditions as well as U.S. literacy restrictions. The above figures, however, require explanation. The total number included only those who had declared their intention to stay in the United States permanently. It did not include those who might have subsequently returned or those who might have decided to stay after they had entered. Moreover, it ignored the deceased and did not include those who had entered the United States before 1899. Taking these factors into account, a conservative estimate of Syrian-born immigrants in the United States in 1920 might well have exceeded 100,000.

Although we do not know exactly how many emigrants left, we are

---

[8] Issawi (1966:269); *al-Kalimah* (1914:108–111). Reid put the number of Syrian Christians in Egypt in 1907 at 34,000, according to the Egyptian census of that year (1975:27). He estimated their total number for the year 1920 as "barely" exceeding 30,000 (1975:51). Since the great bulk of Syrian emigrants came to Egypt following the British occupation of 1882 (see Ali 1926:153–154; Reid 1975:22), it is conceivable that Syrian Christians continued to settle in Egypt after 1907.

[9] Safa put the number of emigrants who entered Brazil between 1904 and 1913 under the designation of "Turk" or "Syrian" but mostly of "Lebanese origin" at 46,003 (1960:190).

Table 1. Syrian Emigration to the United States, 1899-1919

Year	Emigrants	Year	Emigrants
1899	3,708	1910	6,317
1900	2,920	1911	5,444
1901	4,064	1912	5,525
1902	4,982	1913	9,210
1903	5,551	1914	9,023
1904	3,653	1915	1,767
1905	4,822	1916	676
1906	5,824	1917	976
1907	5,880	1918	210
1908	5,520	1919	231
1909	3,668		
Total			89,971

Source: *Annual Report Commissioner General Immigration,* 1919:168 (cited by Hitti 1924:62-65).

much better informed as to why they left. The vast majority left for economic reasons. Whether to Egypt, Australia, North or South America, the main motive was economic betterment (*al-Manar* 1899:490; *al-Mahabbah* 1903:382; *al-Kalimah* 1909:348; Ali 1925:153–154; Hitti 1924:56; Reid 1975:20–21; Safa 1960:176; Himadeh 1936:16–17). Perhaps foreign missions spread the idea that better economic prospects existed overseas. In the case of Mount Lebanon (unlike the rest of Syria) overpopulation was also an important factor. As already stated, the Lebanese had no access to the fertile plains of the Biqa, Sidon, and Tyre. The rest of Syria was unattractive to them because of its economic backwardness and its lack of political and economic security; thus they turned their attention to emigration (Hitti 1965:206; al-Hakim 1964:43; 1966:240). The opening of the Chicago fair in 1893 and that of St. Louis in 1906 did much to attract Syrian emigrants. There are abundant references to the importance of those fairs in attracting and spreading immigrants all over the country (Hitti 1922:22–24; Nahhas [1923?]:16; Miller 1969:5; *al-Kalimah* 1909:27–28). Among the Syrian goods displayed were icons, strings of beads, and crosses, items for which Palestine was noted. There is hardly any doubt that the general economic backwardness of Syria, the lack of economic enterprise, economic insecurity, ruinous taxation, and, above all, the awareness of a better life elsewhere drove the Syrians to emigrate.

Political insecurity and an almost total absence of freedom of expression drove many intellectuals to leave. Because of the native and foreign schools which were established in Syria, that country experienced an intellectual awakening in the second half of the nineteenth century.[10] The city of Beirut was the hub of this intellectual activity. Besides its native schools, there was the Syrian Protestant Mission (later known as the

[10]On the general state of education, see: Birru 1960:14–17; al-Hakim 1964:98–101; Salibi 1965:139–140; Saliba 1971:317–332.

American University of Beirut) and Saint Joseph's University. In addition, Beirut was the center of several printing presses, newspapers, and magazines. In 1881, the American printing press alone published 57,500 books, more than two-thirds of which were sold that same year. As a result, a renaissance occurred in the Arabic language. The reading public increased and writers began to discuss serious topics such as better government, social equality, due process of law, improved economy, and improved communications. Stimulating this intellectual movement was the relative freedom of thought and expression which existed in Syria until 1880. However, with the expulsion of Midhat Pasha, a great Ottoman liberal and reformer as governor of the province, censorship was applied to the press and to other forms of intellectual expression. Sultan Abd al-Hamid and his agents gradually squeezed life out of the press and subjected writers and journalists to imprisonment, fines, and expulsion. Thousands of books were burned or buried in the ground in an attempt to keep inspectors away.

Faced with tightening Hamidian censorship and economic emaciation at home, Christian and Muslim intellectuals alike fled Syria and took refuge in Egypt, Europe, and the Americas (al-Hakim 1964:33, 1966:60; Hitti 1922:121; al-Bustani 1908:27–28, 42–45). Perhaps the largest community of these intellectuals settled in Egypt after 1882. Under British control, the Egyptian press was relatively free to publish, especially on topics unrelated to Egyptian-British relations. Consequently, authors, editors, and journalists flocked to Cairo and Alexandria, 28 to Cairo, 19 to Alexandria. This colony of political refugees left its mark on the Egyptian press by establishing well-known and long-lasting Egyptian papers and magazines (Salibi 1965:147–148; Saliba 1971:332–342; Himadeh 1936:16; Issawi 1966:272; Cioeta 1979:167–186).

Religious persecution in Syria, particularly the 1860 massacres, has often been cited as a major factor in emigration. The literature dealing with this topic is controversial and not entirely consistent; popular belief and some accounts tend to overemphasize its importance. Said B. Himadeh found that emigration developed gradually from 1860 to 1900 at an average of 3000 emigrants annually (Himadeh 1936:16; Issawi 1966:269; Reid 1975:20). The American missionary Henry H. Jessup told of a "thousand refugees," presumably Christians, who emigrated to Alexandria aboard a Russian steamer in the wake of the Damascus massacre of 1860 (Jessup 1910:204). Muhammad Kurd Ali, on the other hand, referred to "some" who emigrated to Egypt, Istanbul, and elsewhere in the Mediterranean area (1925:93). An examination of much of the literature dealing with emigration, including accounts written by emigrants, indicates that on the whole, religious persecution was a supplementary rather than a primary factor in emigration. While available evidence supports growing emigration from Syria after 1880, there is no convincing proof of a significant and sustained outflow of people in the previous two decades. Hence, the assertion that religious persecution drove Christians to emigrate needs considerable modification and further study. Accounts written by many emigrants do not generally substantiate the persecution thesis, for seldom did an emigrant indicate that he had left his homeland because of religious persecution.

Also seldom did an emigrant indicate he had left his homeland permanently. On the contrary, many entertained a desire to return after having made some money. A. Ruppin, a German scholar, reported that one-third to one-half of the emigrants returned and invested their savings in land and in new homes (Ruppin 1966:271–272). It is highly unlikely that so many would have returned if religious persecution had been their primary reason for leaving. The fact that sustained and progressive emigration came after 1880, two decades after the 1860 massacres, coupled with the fact that the early emigrants came largely from the autonomous district of Mount Lebanon which had a Christian majority and enjoyed political stability indicates that religious persecution had little to do with emigration. Surely, some emigrants complained of religious fanaticism and bigotry. These complaints, however, followed others such as Ottoman misrule, political oppression, lack of freedom, inequality, and lack of economic opportunity (Nahhas [1923?]:12–14; Abu Madi 1952:9; Arbili 1913:152–153). In only one account, the case of the Orthodox Christian Arbili family, the first Syrian family to emigrate to the United States, is religious persecution named as a primary reason (al-Kalimah 1905:27–28; al-Kalimah 1913:488–497, 490, 495). The Arbilis, an upper-class family, witnessed and miraculously survived the sectarian massacres of Damascus in 1860. Having moved to Beirut, a relatively secure place, Yusuf Arbili decided, eighteen years after the massacres, to leave the Ottoman Empire altogether "for the progress of my children." Having been discouraged by the Russian consul in Beirut from emigrating to Russia, he then turned his attention to the United States.

Religion was an important factor in determining the destination of the emigrants. Most emigrants to Egypt were Muslims and almost all the early emigrants to the West were Christians.[11] Despite the fact that the Christian was usually Maronite, Orthodox, or Melkite, denominations not very common in the Western world, he was still Christian, subscribed to the same basic beliefs, and worshiped and prayed to the same God, and thus could blend into the new society. The Muslim emigrant faced psychological, religious, and cultural obstacles in the West. What would become of him, his children, and his religion in the land of the "infidel"? For these reasons the Syrian Muslim, at first, shunned emigration to the West, leaving that option almost totally to the Christian.

Other factors also influenced Syrian migration. Stories of economic success abroad created a psychological disposition favorable to emigra-

---

[11]Hitti estimated the number of Maronite Christians in the United States around 1922 at 100,000; Orthodox, 90,000; Muslims 8,000; Druze, 1,000. See Hitti 1922:16; Hagopian and Paden 1969:4; Ruppin 1966:272; Elkholy 1966:17, 22.

tion (Hitti 1922:122; al-Hakim 1966:240). The early emigrants themselves, either through correspondence or after an occasional return home, encouraged their relatives and former neighbors to emigrate (Abu Rizq 1903:381–385, 382; al-Hakim 1964: 42–43; Hitti 1922:122; Daun 1922:228–229).

Emigration became popular. Some even borrowed the money for their tickets abroad (Hitti 1922:122; Daun 1922:228), which cost approximately 230 to 250 francs to South America and 190 francs to New York (Issawi 1966:271–272). Transportation was regular, monthly and sometimes weekly, and emigrants were not encumbered in those days by lengthy forms to fill out, visa applications, and passports or medical examinations. They only needed to go to the port where they could buy their tickets. Agents there often determined their destination for them. Emigrants to the United States took their physical examination before landing at New York City or Boston. The sick were not permitted to disembark and had to return home. In one case, a Lebanese mother and her two children came to join the father who had already settled in Worcester, Massachusetts; the children were not allowed to land because of illness. In another case, a Lebanese was denied entry in 1908 because of trachoma; after returning home, he came back to the United States in 1913. As Ottoman international problems multiplied, bringing with them military conscription and a ban on emigration, smuggling thrived with the connivance of high Ottoman officials (al-Hakim 1966:241; Hitti 1922:121; al-Bustani 1908:115–116; Himadeh 1936:14).

Evidence indicates that some 68 percent of the early emigrants were men and the majority of the men (probably 60 percent) were young, unmarried, and on the average in their mid-twenties (Hitti 1922:125; Hagopian and Paden 1969:8; Abu Jamrah 1924:161–171, 166). A small minority were married and perhaps twelve percent of these brought their families with them. The emigration of the young, the unattached, was most serious. Many villages lost their young blood and became shelters for senior citizens. A village in Mount Lebanon called "Bayt Shabab," or the home of youth, later was referred to as "Bayt al-Ajazah," or the home of the aged!

With the possible exception of the educated minority and the intellectuals, the early emigrants predominantly were poor peasants. A very few had some education while the majority were illiterate (Hagopian and Paden 1969:5; Abu Jamrah 1924:165; Issawi 1966:271; Himadeh 1936:16–17).[12] As emigrants, they became so absorbed in economic matters that they neglected the world of the mind and failed to avail themselves of the educational opportunities in their adopted country (Hitti 1922: 436–438; Abu Rizq 1903:382).

---

[12]This is to be contrasted sharply with the emigrants of the 1950s and the following years. See A. Hossein and J. Cummings (1977).

THE IMPACT OF EMIGRATION ON SYRIA

The impact of emigration from Syria appeared to be uneven, with both negative and positive consequences. Initially, it depleted Syria's manpower, causing a shortage of labor and reinforcing economic stagnation. The loss of the labor force had serious effects on the weaving industry in Mount Lebanon and on agriculture as well. Terraces which the Lebanese peasant had laboriously constructed over the years to preserve his soil lay untended. In the long run, emigration may well have been the cause for the retardation of Syria's economic, political, and social development. Not all the consequences of emigration were negative, however. The emigrants contributed to the relief effort in Syria during World War I and their remittances figured significantly in the economy before the war. In the case of Mount Lebanon, remittances from abroad made up some 41 percent of its budget (Ruppin 1966:271) by the beginning of the war. Many of those red-roofed houses, so characteristic of the present-day landscape, were paid for with money earned overseas. In addition, the emigrants lobbied extensively for the independence of the modern republics of Syria and Lebanon from France during and after World War II. As that independence was achieved and foreign armies withdrew, both governments initiated serious efforts to tie the emigrants closer to their native land. Soon plans were underway to encourage the emigrants not only to pay annual visits to the "old country" but to invest part of their capital in it as well. Moreover, in the effort to consolidate emigrant Lebanon with resident Lebanon, the Lebanese government has made Lebanese citizenship readily available to the emigrants (who actually never lose their Lebanese citizenship) and to their offspring. They can hold property, public office, and even vote in elections.

REFERENCES

Abu Jamrah, Said
    1924   Nimah Yafith. *al-Muqtataf* 65.

Abu Madi, Murad
    1952   *al-Sanabil.* New York.

Abu Rizq, Wadi
    1903   al-Suri fi Ustralya. *al-Mahabbah.* No.321. Beirut.

al-Aswad, Ibrahim
    1930   *Tanwir al-Adhhan fi Tarikh Lubnan.* Beirut.

al-Bustani, Sulayman
    1908   *al-Dawlah al-Uthmaniyyah qabl al-Dustur wa badah.* Cairo.

al-Hakim, Yusuf
    1964   *Beirut wa-Lubnan fi Ahd al-Uthman.* Beirut.

    1966   *Suriyyah wa-al-Ahd al-Uthmani.* Beirut.

Ali, Muhammad Kurd
    1925   *Khitat al-Sham.* Damascus.

al-Id, Yusuf
    1959   *Jawlat fi al-Alam al-Jadid.* Buenos Aires.

al-Kalimah
    1905   *al-Kalimah* (Antiochian Orthodox Church, New York). No.1:
            27–28.

    1909   *al-Kalimah.* No.18:348.

    1913   Fi Muhajarat al-Duktur Yusuf Arbili. *al-Kalimah.*

    1914   *al-Kalimah.* No. 2:108–111.

al-Khuri, Yusuf Abbud
    1903   al-Suriyyun fi Ustralya. *al-Mahabbah.* No.237.

al-Mahabbah
    1903   *al-Mahabbah.* No.321:382.

al-Manar
    1899   *al-Manar* (Beirut), p. 490.

Arbili, Ibrahim
  1913 Fi Tarikh al-Ailah al-Arbiniyyah wa-Muhajaratiha ila al-Wilayat al-Muttahidah. *al-Kalimah* (Antiochian Orthodox Church, New York).

Aridah, Nasib, ed.
  1916 *al-Funun,* Part 5 (October). New York.

Birru, Tawfiq Ali
  1960 *al-Arab wa-al-Turk fi al-Ahd al-Dusturi al-Uthmani, 1908–1914.* Cairo.

Bisharah, Edmond
  1922 al-Sina'at fi Suriyyah wa-Lubnan. *al-Muqtataf.* No. 60.

Cioeta, D. J.
  1979 Ottoman Censorship in Lebanon and Syria, 1876–1908. *International Journal of Middle East Studies* 10(2):167–186.

Daun, Tawfiq
  1922 al-Suriyyun fi al-Barazil. *al-Muqtataf* 61.

Elkholy, Abdo A.
  1966 *The Arab Moslems in the United States.* New Haven, Conn.: College and University Press.

Hagopian, Elaine, and Ann Paden, eds.
  1969 *The Arab-Americans: Studies in Assimilation.* Wilmette, Ill.: The Medina University Press.

Himadeh, Said B.
  1936 *Economic Organization of Syria.* Beirut.

Hitti, Philip K.
  1922 al-Suriyyun fi al-Wilayat al-Muttahidah. *al-Muqtataf.* Nos. 60–61.

  1924 *The Syrians in America.* New York: George H. Doran Co.

  1965 *A Short History of Lebanon.* St. Martin's Press.

Hossein, A., and J. Cummings
  1977 The Middle East and the United States: A Problem of Brain Drain. *International Journal of Middle East Studies* 8(1):65–90.

Issawi, Charles, ed.
  1966   *The Economic History of the Middle East, 1800–1914.* Chicago: University of Chicago Press.

  1977   British Trade and the Rise of Beirut. *International Journal of Middle East Studies* 8(1):91–101.

Jessup, Henry H.
  1910   *Fifty-Three Years in Syria.* New York: Fleming H. Revell Co.

Khatir, Lahd
  1967   *Ahd al-Mutasarrifin fi Lubnan: 1861–1918.* Beirut.

Miller, Lucius H.
  1969   *Our Syrian Population.* San Francisco.

Nahhas, Nicholas A.
  [1923?] *The Mirror of Antioch in North America* (in Arabic). Np.

Reid, Donald
  1975   *Odyssey of Farah Antun.* Chicago: Bibliotheca Islamica.

Rondot, Pierre
  1947   *Les Institutions Politiques du Liban.* Paris.

Ruppin, A.
  1966   Syrien als Wirtschaftsgebiet. In *The Economic History of the Middle East: 1800–1914.* Charles Issawi, ed. pp. 269–273. Chicago: University of Chicago Press.

Safa, Elie
  1960   *L'Emigration Libanaise.* Beirut.

Saliba, Najib E.
  1971   Wilayat Suriyya (The Province of Syria). Ph.D. dissertation, University of Michigan, Ann Arbor.

Salibi, K. S.
  1965   *The Modern History of Lebanon.* London: Weidenfeld and Nicolson.

ABSTRACT

Arab Christians who have emigrated to the United States from Syria and Lebanon reflect distinctive patterns of acculturation and assimilation in their host society. Three recognizable patterns appear in the experience of Maronite, Melkite, and Orthodox Christians. Maronite Christians emigrated having already established close cultural and political links with the West. Their Western allegiance, together with the primacy of village and familial ties over national identity, led to willing and rapid assimilation of Maronites into American and, in particular, American Catholic culture. By contrast, the Melkites came to America with a liturgical tradition more closely allied to Byzantine rites. Only after arriving in the United States did Melkites latinize their rite in the interest of assimilation and social mobility. Of all the Arab Christians, the Syrian Orthodox have been the most resistant to cultural integration. They have maintained a distinctive ethnic identity by preserving an Eastern liturgical tradition and acknowledging a heritage rooted in Arab civilization. Recent political conflicts in the Middle East have made Maronites and Melkites more inclined to follow the Orthodox example.

Arab Christians
in the United States

by Philip M. Kayal

Most Westerners are unaware and often startled to learn that there are over nine million Christians living in the Arab world with perhaps another three million Arab Christians scattered throughout North and South America. Americans, in particular, have become conditioned to view all Arabs as long-robed, desert-dwelling, wandering bedouins of the Islamic faith. Only when the Arab Christians are seen as "converts" (rather than members of indigenous, authentic, and locally significant communities) or "strange Protestants" are they able to escape these stereotypes. While both Arab Muslims and Christians suffer under the burden of proving their humanity and civility to Westerners, the Christians have the added problem of defending their Eastern Christian patrimony and its Arab cultural heritage. In addition, being a Christian minority in the Middle East has aroused suspicions that they are under Western control and influence. They themselves are torn between loyalty to their country and traditions, and the plea for Arab unity, which they often fear would lead to subjugation and loss of their own distinct identities (Malik 1964). This problem of remaining faithful to their Eastern Christian and Arab heritage is again being played out in the American context and is centered around the relationship of religion and ethnicity in American life.

To appreciate the situation and experience of Arab-American Christians requires some understanding of the differences between Eastern and Western Christianity and the interplay between their theological and organizational systems. Likewise, we need to be aware of how the Latin-rite French crusaders and the Ottomans influenced the identities, consciousness, and development of the Arab Christian sects or "rites" which migrated here. In the American context, we would have to note the effects of American foreign policy on the life and organization of the Arab-American Christian community.

EASTERN CHRISTIANITY

Unlike in the West, Eastern Christianity developed in small, provincial enclaves which allowed for a great deal of diversity within a broader cultural unity. Rather than develop a centrist political-religious organization like that of the Roman Catholic church, the Eastern Christian communities emerged pluralistically and relatively independently of one another. They used native languages and cultures in creating their liturgies, rites, and organizational style. They emphasized the "life of the community" and depended on collegiality and participation for development and guidance. Membership in a community of faithful believers became the source of identity and loyalty (Kayal 1979). Whereas uniformity dominated the West, the East was characterized by "catholicity" or universality and diversity. While Christianity was essentially "catholic" until the great schism of 1054, not all Christians were Roman. In the East, for example, the clergy were encouraged to marry. Eastern spirituality encouraged a fluid theology and sacramentology as well as a Platonic mysticism. The East drew most of its inspiration from Greek philosophy rather than the "Latin fathers," and the faithful were encouraged to fully participate in the life of the church.

The symbiotic relationship between environment and faith resulted in the formation of distinct traditions which are known as "rites." A "rite" is an entire way of life that is spiritually and liturgically unique. Eventually, Christian rites were organized under the direction of bishops and patriarchs who acted collegially in the development and enunciation of doctrine and practice. In the West, the dominant rite was known as "Latin" or Roman. Its counterpart in the East was the tradition of Constantinople and is known as the Byzantine rite. Because of political rivalries and tensions, these two socioreligious systems broke relations with one another. The Roman rite then claimed the title Catholic and the Byzantine church began to call itself Orthodox. Since the West was interested in both political and religious control of the East, they sent French missionaries among these Byzantines to "convert" them to Catholicism. Around 1724 many of the Byzantine Christians in Syria reaffiliated themselves with the Roman church and became known as Melkites. The Melkites and Orthodox Syrians are offshoots of each other and share exactly the same tradition but not the same hierarchy. The Christians of Syrian extraction who migrated to America came largely from these two groups of believers. Unfortunately, the Orthodox saw the Melkites as "uniates," that is, traitors who succumbed to Latin bribes of economic success and respectability. The Melkites were thus drawn into the Western cultural tradition by their affiliation with the Roman church.

Another important group of Easterners to emigrate to America were the Maronites of Lebanon. They claim to have remained faithful to Rome throughout their history. They are Antiochian in origin (rather than Byzantine) and dominate the modern-day country of Lebanon both economically and religiously. They represent a liturgical and administrative system totally different from that of the Melkites and Orthodox. They fell under the influence of the French who promised them autonomy and prosperity if they stayed faithful to the West and Catholicism. They are very Western in theology and culture despite their Arab and Eastern Christian heritage and this has interfered with their relationships with other Arab Christians and Muslims. The Maronites never understood that the French were using them to gain a foothold in the Middle East and that the Maronite religious tradition was authentic and viable on its own terms, and did not need to become more and more like that of the West.

The influence of the French on the life of the Christian Arabs cannot be underestimated. The French crusaders and their modern counterparts, for example, taught the Christian Arabs that they were backward and illegitimate Christians because "real" Christians were Westerners, prosperous, and educated. They successfully implanted the idea that Arab meant Muslim and that Christian Arabs would never be accepted as real Arabs even though their history, thought, and way of life was and still is essentially Arab. When the Turkish Muslim oppression intensified, the Christian Arabs used this as undeniable evidence of inherent Islamic hostility. They did not understand that their Arab Muslim neighbors were also suffering under the Turks and that the Ottoman oppression was directed at a growing Arab nationalism. Consequently, the Arab Christians (especially the Maronites) bargained with the French and English for "protection" and for help to defeat the Turks. The Maronites were particularly interested in securing an independent homeland for themselves in Lebanon. These Eastern Christians were using the Western imperialists to gain more economic and political power for themselves, which in turn antagonized their Muslim compatriots, whose own emerging nationalism transcended sectarian and national interests.

The Ottomans also capitalized on the divisions present among the Christians by encouraging each religious group or rite to think of itself as a separate nation or "millet" under the leadership of its own patriarch. The ruling Turkish powers, who had to integrate a heterogeneous population, capitalized on the Christian diversity by playing sects against one another and by structuring each rite both politically and socially into a separate "nation." The millet became a church organized as a separate nationality within which "the laws of personal statute were based on religious sanctions" (Cahnman 1944:526). This occurred because religion and nationality were interchangeable to the Turkish mind. Thus, when the Christians refer to their "nation," that is, their church, they do not realize that it is a purely artificial creation introduced by the Ottomans because the latter had no other way of classifying or treating their non-Muslim subjects.

As a result of this peculiar form of national identity and religious organization, familial and religious systems invariably overlapped and interfered with the development of other, broader identities. Sometimes whole villages belonged to and derived identity from the same religious group. Social life rarely existed beyond the extended family, which was

more or less religiously homogeneous. The village represented the outer
limit for secondary social discourse, but a sense of belonging was reserved
to the family, which was made up of coreligionists (Tannous 1942). This
explains why Hitti (1924:25–26) could write that the Syrian Christian immigrant is a man "without a country par excellence," for his patriotism
takes the form of love of religion and family. The church replaces the
state and all cooperation between individuals is governed by this traditional grouping. For the early Syrian-Lebanese immigrants to America,
membership in clubs and organizations was almost always based on some
geographical or religious distinction (Hitti 1924:30). They were united
and divided by social and religious issues, rather than by broad political
questions.

SYRIAN CHRISTIANS IN AMERICA

Prior to World War II, it is very difficult to speak of a "Syrian" or
Arab ethnic group assimilating or adjusting to American society. They
were not only religiously divided but separated as well by regional
origins, as in the case of the political distinction between Syrians and
Lebanese. They arrived here with Turkish passports yet thought of themselves as *Roum-Orthodox, Ruom-Catholique,* or "Maronites." They were
called "Arabs" by those who wanted to insult them. They felt that they
were anything other than Arab. Eventually, as Syria became an independent state and nationality became an acceptable American identity,
they called themselves Syrians only to find that the "Lebanese" among
them resented that appellation once Lebanon also became a free and
separate entity.

Ironically, they referred to themselves in private as *owlad Arab* (i.e.,
"children of Arabs"), but they did not want the public to see them as
"hostile" outsiders or as Muslims, so they resisted this identification.
More significantly, the early immigrants brought with them a view of history which is now dated and inappropriate to Middle Eastern political
realities. To speak of oneself in terms of a religious identification is no
longer functional or feasible either within today's Arab-American community or in the Arab world. When we speak, therefore, of the present
Syrian-Lebanese community as an Arab-American Christian community,
it must be understood developmentally and historically.

The Syrians began arriving in this country in ever-increasing numbers
after 1850 when the Turkish oppression intensified and Syrians wished to
avoid conscription into the army and unreasonable taxation. Being traders,
they scattered themselves throughout the known world. They came to
America in search of a better life. Typhoid, disease, pestilence, and war-
fare with the Druze population on Mt. Lebanon had made life intolerable for them. With the arrival of philanthropic American missionaries
(mainly Presbyterians), the Syrians became overwhelmed by the generosity
of these foreigners who, they concluded, must have come from a country
with streets "paved with gold." By 1924, there were about 125,000

Syrians scattered in the major cities of North America. Brooklyn, New York became their most vibrant center, producing offshoots in Rochester, Utica, Paterson, Boston, Detroit, Miami, and Los Angeles (Kayal 1982:222).

Because of confusion about their own identity and because they were few in number, the Syrians remained a politically irrelevant and disorganized social entity, only occasionally drawing together to fight discrimination. There was a time at the turn of the century when they were denied citizenship because they were defined as nonwhite (Jabara 1979). After winning their case, however, they again became politically and religiously divided and inactive. Mary Treudley (1953:261) was quick to observe the lack of sociopolitical organization among the Syrians when she noted that even the designation "Syrian" was nothing more than a term which labeled the category to be dealt with but did not indicate the source or the sense of belongingness.

Studying Arab-American or Syrian-Lebanese Christians, then, means focusing on an emerging ethnic group which has had difficulty in creating an institutionally viable community outside of the religious sphere. The Syrian-Lebanese community has been further weakened by its emphasis on material success and wealth and by its desire to assimilate or Americanize without acculturating completely. These goals altered their religious institutions and community life more than any other factor. The Catholic Syrians had to accommodate themselves to an American Catholicism which was not only Latin but Irish as well. The Orthodox had to literally explain themselves to Catholics and Protestants alike since Americans had little knowledge of Eastern Christianity. In their early years, the Orthodox Syrians were enmeshed in jurisdictional problems with their fellow Greeks and Russians and had to contend with Presbyterian and Episcopalian attempts to convert them. As Arabs, they expected their faith to preserve their ethnic identity. But they were also in America and had to adjust to their new environment so as not to lose their American-born second generation. Catholic Syrians faced a similar problem. Unlike the Catholic Syrians, however, the Orthodox were not forced to Americanize since they were free from the pressures to conform which the Catholic Syrians experienced as members of the American Catholic church.

In American society, it is generally agreed that assimilation means entrance into one of the three major American religious categories: Protestant, Catholic, or Jew. Unprecedented problems awaited assimilation-oriented Syrians who shared a common culture but not a common religion. They had to emerge as an integrated ethnic group with common interests and goals while at the same time being expected to forfeit their traditional identities for American ones. The Catholic Syrians were being pulled away from their Oriental roots, a process which alienated them from the Orthodox and made their own disappearance as an identifiable group more likely. The Orthodox, on the other hand, also had to Americanize and learn to mix with other Orthodox nationalities like the Greeks, while still keeping their ethnic heritage alive. Both Orthodox and Catholic Syrians eventually learned to separate religion and nationality and to join together over common secular interests. The second- and third-generation Syrian-Lebanese were confronted with the task of making it work.

One of the major integration conflicts that the Catholic Syrians faced was with the American Latin-rite Catholic church, which was culturally and institutionally dominated by the English-speaking Irish (Will Herberg 1960:160). Being the most assimilationist of all Catholic ethnic groups, the Irish wanted to build a single, unified American Catholic church devoid of any ethnicity but their own. They believed everyone could share the Mass since they thought it to be the same throughout the world. The Syrians would have to be socially and religiously marginal to this development since they were Easterners. The conflict between the Irish and Syrians, therefore, was never just an ethnic one. It was "rather a confrontation between two religious disciplines, two ecclesiologies and two religio-cultural traditions which never fully understood one another" (Kayal 1973:414). Since their ethnic and religious identities were so intertwined, any change in one would have to affect the other.

The Melkites especially were determined to hold onto their traditions, since they saw the Church as "catholic" or universal. The Maronites, forever wanting to be recognized as Catholic and Western, accepted the Irish pressure to "Latinize." The Melkites knew that too much latinization would alienate them from their Orthodox "cousins" whose rite they shared. Yet Rome never responded adequately to the legitimate request of the Melkite and Maronite groups here for autonomy. Indeed, it was not until the mid-1960s that both these rites received semiautonomy from the Latins to establish their own dioceses. Until then it was felt that it would be in the best interest of the American Catholic church that the Melkites and Maronites turn their rites into latinized "American" traditions like those in other Catholic "national" parishes. Commenting on this trend of the Syrian Catholics to allow themselves to be "latinized" for acceptance rather than force American Catholicism to become legitimately pluralistic in terms of rite, language, and liturgy, Fr. Alan Maloof, the first American-born Melkite priest ordained in the United States wrote:

> They wanted to be more "American" in all aspects of the word. Americanization remoulded home, family, work and recreation. Some unfortunately, overzealous in their good intentions, confused the word "Americanization" with "Latinization." The general idea seemed to be, "We are in America now—therefore, our churches and customs should be the same as those of other American Catholics (Latin); so that we may all be alike; we should not confuse people. (Maloof 1951:261)

By modifying their rites and the symbols of their "corporate identity" so as to make them more American, the Syrians unwittingly destroyed the basis for their own community life. Ultimately, they would become like every other Catholic ethnic group. Their Melkite and Maronite churches became "Syrian churches" instead of uniquely different forms of Roman Catholicism. They became temporary ethnic establishments until such a time came when they were no longer necessary and would disappear.

From another perspective it might be argued that this cultural accommodation permitted them to give up their old sectarian identities for more modern, ethnic ones. From the religious perspective they were destroying their unique traditions which were supposed to be their *raison d'etre*. But they really were more interested in ethnic and cultural continuity, and latinization was a small price to pay for being allowed to become another Catholic ethnic group like the Poles and Italians with their own churches and culture. Indeed, the ethnic group could only emerge when the Syrian-Lebanese would allow themselves the privilege of treating their culture as seriously as their religion. What they ended up offering their communicants was a distorted Eastern theology, spiritually, and an abbreviated form of Arab culture supported by the churches. This became an acceptable way of being both American and Syrian at the same time, since ethnicity got tagged onto one of the most valid forms of American pluralism—religion. These "Syrianisms," notes Treudley (1953:262), "had a simple meaning: food habits, crafts, music, and dancing, the rites of hospitality, authoritarian family patterns, the closeness and warmth of family ties, a religious ritual with many common features, whether the church was Maronite, Melkite or Eastern Orthodox."

Unfortunately, the Syrian Catholics were not successful in maintaining either a distinct ethnic heritage or a separate religious tradition. They became so similar to the Latins or Americans that it no longer made sense to argue that they were different and had a unique heritage to preserve. Indeed, they lost over half of their faithful to the Latin or American rite. While the official estimates of the Melkite and Maronite exarchates place their numbers at fifty thousand and one hundred thousand respectively, there are less than twenty thousand Melkites registered in the nearly thirty official Melkite "parishes" of the United States. A greater number estimated at thirty thousand are nominally Melkite, but in practice, Latin. The Maronites, on the other hand, who have over forty parishes, claim to have one hundred thousand "active" followers and estimate their loss to other rites to be fifty thousand (Kayal 1975).

Both the Maronites and Melkites came to America from relatively powerless and subdued socioreligious traditions. They themselves did not appreciate their own heritages and when confronted with the power of the Latin church, simply surrendered their autonomy to it. Frequently this was due to the material and social appeal of Latin Christianity rather than to its religious and salvific significance. The Middle Eastern Arab Christians were constantly being proselytized by Catholics and Protestants alike. The Muslims on the other hand refused to permit any Muslim to become a Christian, so these Western missionaries could only work among the Orthodox and Catholic Syrians.

The Melkites, being Orthodox in origin, were disliked and mistrusted by their mother church since they appeared to be opportunists trying to become Westerners. Yet they were distrusted by the West as well because they were Orthodox or Byzantine in inspiration, style, and faith. The Maronites, on the other hand, were more than willing to be "submerged" into Roman Catholicism because they saw Rome and France as their protectors. Indeed, they were known as the "Irish of the East" because of the tenacity of their faith (Maloof 1958).

In the minds of the Latins, however, the Eastern Catholics were backward. This was the Latin attitude towards all Easterners, whether in the Middle East or in America. The Eastern rites were looked down upon socially, being associated with peasant culture, whereas the Latin rite stood for European and Chrisitan civilization, progress, prestige, education, commerce—in short, for being Western (Atwater 1935:18). "In the Syrian immigrant's mind, to be modern, affluent, and American meant to be Latin" (Kayal 1974:125). The Maronites, who were largely Lebanese and French oriented, had less of a conflict with the Latins. For them, and other Easterners, the Latin rite stood for European and Christian civilization and the ideals of progress. It became prestigious to be educated and involved in commerce (Atwater 1935:18).

The Syrian-Lebanese integration into American Catholicism was facilitated by the acute shortage of their own educated priests, and by the lack of unified diocesan organization. Their dispersion throughout the country and their inability to build their own parochial and language schools encouraged integration. More important was their predominantly middle-class status which eventually made them indistinguishable from their American counterparts. Economic success brought them middle-class status within a generation and weakened the basis for a distinctive and separate ethnic identity. The unwillingness of the American Catholic church to be genuinely pluralistic in terms of rite forced them to latinize, and their own ethnic culture became so much like that of the American middle class in overall values and orientation that they hardly could constitute themselves as a distinct ethnic group. Among themselves they maintained certain customs which could be enjoyed and appreciated by any interested American, that is, food, music, dances, and even their rites.

Only the Syrian Orthodox were spared the particular pressure to latinize, since they did not have to confront the assimilationist American Catholic church. Americanization was necessary and inevitable in the case of the second and third generations. Like their Catholic counterparts, the Orthodox also quickly assimilated into the entrepreneurial American middle class. Over time, they learned to structure and organize their religious services along American lines. Choirs were organized, greater decorum prevailed, and the general mores of American church behavior gained acceptance. Unfortunately, the Orthodox were a "minority within a minority" and were coveted by Protestants as well as by other Orthodox jurisdictions. Today they number about seventy-five thousand affiliated members and claim a loss of about forty thousand to other faiths. Eventually the Orthodox secured their independence from the

Russian patriarchate and now are considered the most progressive wing of the Eastern Orthodox church in America. They were the first Orthodox group to introduce English into their liturgy. From an ethnic perspective, this signalled their openness to converts from non-Arab backgrounds. The Orthodox Syrians even went so far as to establish a parish in New Jersey which was composed of Greeks, Russians, and Syrian-Americans. Their philosophy claimed that the richness of the faith, rather than commitment to ethnicity, would attract members. Apparently they were correct in their assumption, as the parish is flourishing much like any typical Catholic parish composed of different ethnic groups.

Until recently, no Arab Christian parish thought it could or even should survive without an Arab constituency to support it. They were committed to maintaining or supporting the modified Arab culture which they had developed in this country. This was especially true of the latinized Maronites, who were the most successful in intertwining an ethnic culture with a religious tradition (Kayal 1974:126). Adhering to the philosophy that "our Lebanese community is supported by our culture and religion...both of them reflecting our soul and spirit" (Maloof 1958:283), the Maronite church has become the primary bearer and preserver of a westernized "Arab culture" as interpreted by the Lebanese, rather than a reflection of a "universal" Eastern Catholic tradition open to everyone. The ethnic culture that evolved, however, was acceptable to the Melkites and Orthodox precisely because it was so apolitical, superficial, and inoffensive.

THE CHRISTIAN ARAB-AMERICAN DILEMMA

Making sense of the assimilation experience of Christian Arab-Americans of Syrian-Lebanese origin is complicated because the ethnic group was divided into two major religious bodies (Catholic and Orthodox), several Catholic rites (Melkite, Maronite, and to a lesser degree Syriac and Armenian), and two emerging nationalities (Syrian and Lebanese). Since Americans preferred immigrants who were identifiable in nationality or ethnic terms, the early immigrants had to constitute themselves as an ethnic group based on some modified cultural traditions which they could pass on to their children and which were similar to those of other ethnic groups. This meant relearning social expectations, in that the Christian Arabs would now have to mix with other "Arabs" across traditional religious and national (home country and even native village) identities. By the second generation, they were able to use their ethnic-cultural heritage to solve the perplexing problem of intermarriage which had more or less devastated their ranks. Unlike other ethnic groups, their small numbers, coupled with their divisiveness, made it almost impossible for the Syrian-Lebanese Christians to marry within the group, regardless of how broadly the group was defined. Their outmarriage rate, consequently, remained high and currently exceeds 80 percent (Kayal 1975:Chp. 11).

The Syrian-Lebanese Christians had only one major institution to keep their culture alive, and that was their churches. They created what we can call an operative "Arab-American culture religion" supported and maintained by their churches. Membership in the Syrian community meant activity and participation in the churches and vice versa. They formed an "ethno-religion" which fused ethnicity and religion (Sklare 1957). For a time, this protected their ethnicity, since it made ethnicity appear like a function of their religious beliefs and traditions.

What became a successful adaptation for the first and second generation up until World War II developed into a problem for the third and fourth generations. Syrian-American Christians were opting for an "ethnic-identity" at a time when most other American ethnic groups seemed to be "melting" into the three religious categories of Catholic, Protestant, and Jew. This meant that the Orthodox Syrians would also have to find a "religious pot" with which to identify. They did this with their Greek and Russian coreligionists. Obviously, however, such a step would draw the Orthodox Syrians out of their Arab ethnic identity and commitments. The Catholic Syrians faced a similar problem, since their affiliation with the Roman church brought them into close contact with other Catholics who placed the uniformity of the church above all else. Will Herberg (1960) also reminds us that all religions had to Americanize so as to keep the second and third generations faithful to them while general acculturation went on in the economic, educational, social, and cultural spheres.

What both the Catholic and Orthodox Syrians needed was a *raison d'etre*, something greater than simply keeping the "ethnic group" alive for its own sake. At the same time, the ethnic group needed a purpose, goal, and orientation which would keep people interested in its life without making the group members outsiders to American society. The ethno-religious solution worked for a while, but in time it became meaningless, as the ethnic culture it was supporting was too superficial to require the institutional support of the various rites and religions of the Syrians. Both the Orthodox and Catholic Syrians began to discover that their religious traditions could be appealing to Americans in general and that the real task of ethnic maintenance belonged to the family and the social clubs of the community. In this way the increasing numbers of non-Arab church members could participate in the life of the church without having to accept and identify with the culture that went along with it. The third- and fourth-generation Melkites and Orthodox could then participate in a legitimate religious life devoid of ethnicity, yet have access to ethnic events in contexts other than their religion. In a sense, the Americanization of the churches allowed the creation of an ethnic group whose interests could now be secular. Because they fused culture, religion, and nationality, this arrangement has been particularly difficult for the Maronites, especially the immigrant generation. Many of these people stress the Phoenician origin of the Lebanese and accept the French-inspired "Phalangist" philosophy that Lebanon belongs primarily to the Maronites and that it has a unique place in Middle Eastern history as an outpost of Christianity in a hostile Muslim world. Yet the typical Lebanese-American knows that Lebanon is an "Arab" nation and that Christianity in no way interferes with pan-Arabism or the Arab cause in general (Hagopian 1978). Their churches can no longer rely on tradition, family pressure, or even culture to retain their membership. Their out-marriage rate is very high and their third and fourth generations are generally assimilated and well-educated. Like their Melkite and Orthodox "cousins," the Maronites are no longer influenced by either the French, Latin, or even Western definition of their identity and purpose.

CONTEMPORARY
SYRIAN-LEBANESE-AMERICAN CONSCIOUSNESS

Until recently, the Syrian-Lebanese Christian community lacked a clear reason for maintaining itself. Their own socioreligious history was at the root of their divisiveness, while acculturation and economic success in America weakened the basis for sustaining a separate ethnic identity. The churches actually lost more members the more they tried to keep ethnicity alive. The Syrian-Lebanese were at the point of disappearing from the American scene even before they became a recognizable and noteworthy American ethnic group. It took the 1967 Arab-Israeli war to alter the complacent and ambivalent ethnic consciousness of Syrian Christians. Events outside their control were forcing them to identify more closely with their ethnic origins, and with the problems and political struggles of their homelands. Just as the second-, third-, and emerging fourth-generation Syrian Christians in America were settling into stable and relatively affluent middle-class communities, the Palestinian rights controversy erupted on the American political scene. Because this issue was framed as an Arab versus Jewish or Israeli problem, the Syrian Christians were forced to examine their history, ethnic identity, and social relationships with one another and the Arab world in general. The situation became even more complicated and pressing for them when the struggle for Palestinian rights recently shifted to Lebanon and became defined in religious terms. The fact that the Arab-American Christian community was ethnically both Syrian and Lebanese meant that a wedge might be driven into their communal life. Syria was defined as a Muslim enemy and Lebanon as a poor Christian state under Muslim attack. Pro-Israeli propagandists were busily at work trying to redefine the problems and issues of the Palestinians and their rights in terms of some recognizable Western language like that of religion. Fortunately, the third- and fourth-generation Syrian-Lebanese were not easily swayed by these arguments.

More important, the contemporary Syrian-Lebanese Christian population had come to be at peace with the designation "Arab" and were rather angered at the generally negative depiction of their culture and history. Even more galling to them was the fact that their patriotism was becoming suspect and their constitutional freedoms threatened. Their image in the mass media was foreign to their own experience and self-understanding. They became tired of being the victims of the "new racism" which blames all Arabs for the suffering of the Jews, when in fact, Arab nations sheltered the world's persecuted (Armenians, Circassians, Jews, and others) for centuries.

What the Syrian-Lebanese Christians in America began to realize was that it was their Arab culture which distinguished them from others and not necessarily their particular rites, religions, and nationalities. They were "Arabs" because they spoke Arabic and inherited an Arab cultural heritage. In examining their history and experiences in the U.S., they were proud of what they discovered—a culture which is family-centered and deeply religious. Known as hard workers and successful entrepreneurs, they have contributed much to American civilization. They have been characterized as frugal, industrious ethnic Americans with solidly middle-class aspirations, traditions, and moral consciences. Perhaps William Cole (1921:4) best described the Syrian Arab-Americans, whom he claimed were distinguished by their

> Pride of race, a high degree of native intelligence...shrewdness and cleverness in business, devotion to the institutions of this country, imaginativeness, religious loyalty, love of domestic life, courtesy, and hospitality, eagerness for education, fondness for music and poetry, temperance in the men and chastity in the women, self-respect and self-reliance...such are some of the more obvious traits of the Syrians.

Whether they like it or not, the Syrian-Lebanese in this country were forced by circumstances to identify themselves as Arabs since that had become the designation applied by the American mass media to all Middle-Easterners from Arabic-speaking countries. To be heard, understood, and reckoned with, the Syrian-Lebanese learned to identify with and positively interpret their Arab origins. Their desire to take pride in their heritage brought them into closer contact with other Arab-Americans of different religious and regional backgrounds who were likewise being handicapped by the pro-Israeli American media. Because the Middle East conflict was presented as an Arab-Jewish struggle, many third- and fourth-generation Syrian-Lebanese Christians found themselves accepting their identification as "Arabs." In order to be heard, one had to accept the designation imposed. This became easier as the Arab world gained greater unity, status, credibility, and importance.

While the Syrian-Lebanese Christians in America are beginning to identify with their Arab roots, they nevertheless have a particular perspective and viewpoint on the whole Palestinian/Lebanese question. Being Middle Eastern Christians gives them a special affinity toward the region, especially in the area of defending the right of the Palestinian and Lebanese people to live in peace. They argue that it is not the Muslims who are responsible for the turmoil in the region. Their concern over the fate of Christianity in the Holy Land (Fisher 1981) and the welfare of the Palestinians in Lebanon exists precisely because many of these refugees are, in fact, Christians.

It is shocking for the American Syrian-Lebanese to learn that since the "Six-Day War" in June of 1967, the Christians in the Holy Land now number less than ninety thousand, with those remaining in Israel preferring to leave for countries where religion or race has less influence on ordinary life and opportunities. In other words, the very seat of their religious origins is threatened with extinction. Messages received here, for example, from the Melkite patriarch are always desperate in their appeal for compassion and funds for all the refugees whether Christian or Muslim and regardless of nationality. Melkite, Maronite, and Orthodox children have been orphaned in increasing numbers, a matter of great concern to the American Syrian-Lebanese. Israel's forays into Lebanon and Syria have aroused interest and concern, and except for a small minority of American Maronites (Phalangists), have generally angered them.

While the Maronites in America want the security and peace of Lebanon reestablished, they also want justice. They know Lebanon is being bombed because it has harbored the innocent who have no shelter elsewhere. Moreover, the nearly eight hundred thousand third- and fourth-generation American Syrian-Lebanese can now learn the facts about their homeland not only from visiting prelates but also from the newly-arrived Arab intellectuals migrating to this county. This helps the assimilated Arab-Americans return to a closer understanding of their ethnicity and history, and as Americans, enables them to argue their point of view from the position of concerned American citizens. They realize that a prejudicial American approach is detrimental to this nation's welfare as well as to international peace, justice, and economic well-being (Kayal 1982:231).

A particular issue which has especially distressed the Syrian-Lebanese community in America has been Israel's change in the status of Jerusalem, a city sacred to Muslims and Christians alike. The Israeli annexation of East Jerusalem represented a radical distortion of the city's historical and spiritual significance. It has further confirmed the suspicion that Zionism set apart the Jews as "special people" with unique rights and privileges which would be exercised at the expense of other peoples. This realization helps explain why Arab Christians in America have uniformly supported the recent United Nations declaration that Zionism in its present form is synonymous with racism (Kayal 1982:232).

While all Arab Christians are united in their opposition to Israel's "control" of Lebanon and of the fate of the Palestinians, the most outspoken of the Christian Arab-Americans are the Antiochian (Syrian) Orthodox, who went on record urging the then United Nations Secretary General U-Thant to convene the Security Council to scrutinize breaches in the 1967 General Assembly resolution protesting the annexation of the Arab section of Jerusalem by Israel. This annexation, they argued, was forced in unilateral defiance of world opinion and international and moral law. The recent physical changes made in East Jerusalem by Israeli occupation forces were also condemned, since the changes were made arbitrarily and without regard for the wishes of the indigenous inhabitants. In June 1972, Dr. Frank Maria, chairman of the Department of Near East and Arab Refugee Problems of the Antiochian Orthodox Church in America, appeared before the Executive Committee of the National Council of Churches to present the Christian Arab perspective on the Middle East crisis. He was concerned over the reluctance of the American Christian establishment to tackle the "Jerusalem question" head on.

Moreover, the displacement of Christians from Lebanon and the Israeli-occupied West Bank and Gaza has affected the institutional and communal life of the Arab-American community directly. There are now thousands of Arabic-speaking refugees needing services and support from their coreligionists in America. The already assimilated members of the Melkite, Maronite, and Orthodox churches have now to accommodate immigrants some sixty years after they thought the immigration experience had ended. With the death of the early immigrants and old-timers, the churches are predominantly attended by English-speaking Americans who do not really know how to relate to the newly arrived. Parishes are again troubled with the ethnocultural problems that the grandparents faced.

There is a remarkable similarity between the experiences of the Syrian-Lebanese community and that of the emerging Egyptian-American community. Both Coptic Christian and Muslim Egyptians arriving here are well educated, politicized, and proud of their Arab origins. Consequently, they are similar to new immigrants in the adjustments they must make, but they are also very much like the American-born Arabs because of their education. They are now undergoing the same conflicts the Syrian-Lebanese underwent. The Copts among them use the rite of Alexandria and received the faith from St. Mark the Evangelist. They can be considered Orthodox. While being fully Egyptian, they are a minority within a minority—much like the Orthodox and Melkites before them. Since they have fused their faith and nationality, their experience will probably mirror that of the Orthodox Syrians.

More important, however, is the fact that regardless of particular national, or religious origins, all Arab-Americans are learning to join together to fight what they see as injustice and prejudice as it pertains to them as Arabs. After Israel shot down a Libyan airliner in 1973, for example, it was condemned by virtually all Arab Christian clerics throughout the United States. The most unified action to take place among the American Syrian-Lebanese, however, was in response to the bombing of the Lebanese consulate in Los Angeles. Claiming to represent sixty thousand Arab-Americans living in Southern California, every Muslim and Syrian Christian leader living in the area sent telegrams indicating their shock and dismay to Mayor Samuel Yorty, to the district attorney, and to the chief of police. On the other hand, even though the community was distressed over the issue, it was unable to help congressional candidate George Corey of San Mateo County, California win a seat in Congress when his Democratic opponent for the nomination accused the American-born Christian Corey of being an "Arab" candidate supported by the PLO. When county residents were given the facts, however, and learned the truth through Arab-American press releases, they refused to elect his opponent, who had launched the racist attack in the first place.

CONCLUSION

It has been our argument that the emergence of a unified Syrian-Lebanese community took several generations because of the original problems of identification and adjustment to American society. Over time and with Americanization and education, it became useful for the community to understand the Arab perspective on political issues affecting the well-being of the Arab states and the American economy. It also became easier for Syrian-Americans to take pride in their roots and heritage as the American nation began to accept and encourage the notion of cultural pluralism, that is, that it was acceptable to be an ethnic and an American at the same time. Thus, the Syrian-Lebanese eventually learned to view themselves as products of the Arab East, with roots in and relationships to the Arab world. Now we have an emerging Arab-American community with strong backing from the grandchildren of the Syrian-Lebanese immigrants. The special issue which has united them has been the mass media's negative portrayal of Arabs and their culture. Indeed, the Arab-American community was able to help effect the censure of Jimmy Carter's aide, Paul Rand Dixon, who called consumer advocate Ralph Nader a "dirty Arab" in a public address. Given the community's history, this is quite an accomplishment.

Another milestone in the evolution of an Arab-American ethno-political community consisting of Syrians, Lebanese, Palestinians, Egyptians, Jordanians, Muslims and Christians was the establishment of the Association of Arab-American University Graduates (AAUG) some fourteen years ago, which has attracted hundreds of American-born Syrian-Lebanese Christians. What the grandparents could not do and what the second generation was ashamed to do, the third generation, or grandchildren, accomplished, since they were able to fuse their patriotism, ethnic pride, history, and sense of fair play. Their objectives in forming the AAUG were mainly educational and informational.

More activist Syrian-Lebanese and other Arab-Americans, however, also established the National Association of Arab-Americans, which was incorporated in 1972 for the purpose of providing moral, financial, and political support to those Americans of Arab heritage who sought political or public office, regardless of party affiliation or faith. This indicates that the American-born Arab Christians are willing to transcend the old divisions and to join with their fellow Muslims to protect their rights and interests. The Muslim membership is significantly large enough in the association that the "religious" or nationality question is neutralized.

The most significant Arab-American political organization to emerge from the old Syrian-Lebanese Christian community is the American-Arab Anti-Discrimination Committee (ADC). By December 1982, its membership exceeded fifteen thousand. Since it was conceived by former United States Senator James Abourezk, a Lebanese Orthodox, and its Executive Director, Dr. James Zogby, a Lebanese Maronite, it has attracted national attention and a membership which not only spans the diverse Arab-American population but also many other individuals interested in civil liberties. The Christian presence in the organization indicates that the old provincialisms have finally died. There is recognition of the fact that one can be a member of a Christian tradition other than one of the dominant American ones and not be considered strange or "exotic." The old tendency to apologize for one's origins is all but gone and the desire to be completely assimilated has been lessened by the country's recent appreciation of its diverse ethnic and cultural heritage. Previously, the Syrian-Lebanese could not articulate their feelings about their past and their intended role in American society. They were disappearing and assimilating because the society did little to encourage either their religious or their secular distinctiveness.

Now American Syrian-Lebanese are realizing that America never really was a "melting pot" and that they have the right to maintain their own way of life both religiously and secularly. In all fairness, however, we must mention that this development of an ethnopolitical consciousness has had an effect on the religious institutions of the community. People cannot be in two places at the same time, nor can they afford to fund too many different social causes. The churches need members and funds and so do the community's nonreligious institutions. This might explain why no Arab-American religious institution has thrown its full weight into supporting any of the above-mentioned organizations. Of course, thousands of individuals from these communities have become members, but no religious leader has officially endorsed these organizations.

The problem, of course, varies according to tradition and generation. The Syrian Orthodox are the least troubled by the sociopolitics of their community and members. Indeed, they are the most directly supportive. The Melkites are the most assimilated and least likely to produce national Arab-American leaders because they are still struggling for independence and sociocultural maintenance. The more involved in the official life of the Melkite Church that one is, the less likely that person is to be politically active on behalf of the Palestinians, or in other causes. This does not mean, of course, that the Melkite hierarchy is not busily politicizing itself within the American Catholic hierarchy concerning questions of justice for the Lebanese and Palestinians as are the Orthodox bishops in the World Council of Churches. It is just that the church as a church is interested in surviving as a distinct American organization and not as an Arab-American institution. The old-timers see this church as a "Syrian church" with a cultural component while many of the grandchildren see it as either their grandparents' church, as a quaint artifact, or simply as an Eastern rite Catholic church. The problem is complicated by the fact that over half of the clergy in this rite are American-born or of non-Arab origin.

The Maronites, being a "national church," have the greatest problem, since they too are dispersed and uncertain as to where to make their commitments. Like the Melkites, they are understaffed, misinformed, and Americanized. The older generation see the church as a national-ethnic institution, and the young see it as an anachronism. The Maronites remain under Roman control to a greater degree than the Melkites and really do not know how to define the present Middle East crisis. They want a pluralistic Lebanon, and yet they want a pure Maronite rite; they want the Palestinians to be treated justly, but at the same time they cannot seem to understand how a free Lebanon can exist without a dominant Maronite presence. The American press would have them see the issue in religious terms, whereas knowledgeable people everywhere see it as a much more complex issue. The Maronite community's troubles in this country are very real and threatening. The fourth generation is not interested in maintaining the appearance of an ethno-religious tradition. Their out-marriage rates, like the generation before them, is over eighty percent, their liturgy is archaic, and their clergy is either very old, or very young and non-Arab. They may be able to survive as an ethno-religion, but most likely they eventually will become another American Eastern Catholic rite devoid of ethnicity and only Lebanese in historical origin. As we have noted, however, the American-born Maronites have been able to produce an informed activist generation working on behalf of the Arab cause.

Arab-Americans, then, evolved into an ethnic group which includes Syrians, Lebanese, and other Arab nationals, as well as Muslims and Christians because they recognize in each other values, traditions, and behaviors with which they can identify. While having transcended their past, they still find it relevant, useful, and rewarding in the present. No longer do they have to make a choice between being an American or an Arab, a Christian or a Muslim. In a sense, they have finally arrived on the American sociopolitical scene.

REFERENCES

Atwater, Donald
   1935   *Catholic Eastern Churches.* Wisconsin: Bruce.

Cahnman, Werner
   1944   Religion and Nationality. *American Journal of Sociology*
          49(6):524–529.

Cole, William I.
   1921   *Immigrant Races in Massachusetts.* Boston: Massachusetts
          Department of Education. (Pamphlet)

Fisher, Paul A.
   1981   Revivified Christian Presence Needed in Holy Land. *The
          Wanderer,* 17 December.

Hagopian, Elaine
   1978   Lebanon and the Arab Question. In *South Lebanon.* E.
          Hagopian and S. Farsoun, eds. Special Report No. 2. Bel-
          mont, Mass.: Association of Arab-American University
          Graduates.

Herberg, Will
   1960   *Protestant, Catholic, Jew.* New York: Doubleday & Co.

Hitti, Philip
   1924   *Syrians in America.* New York: Doran Co.

Jabara, Abdeen
   1979   *The History and Legal Status of Arab-Americans in the
          United States.* Unpublished document. Detroit.

Kayal, Philip
   1973   Religion and Assimilation: Catholic "Syrians" in America.
          International Migration Review 7(4):409–426.

   1974   Religion in the Christian "Syrian-American Community." In
          Arabic Speaking Communities in American Cities. B. Aswad,
          ed. pp. 111–136. New York: Center for Migration Studies.

   1979   The Sociology of Ecumenicism. *Diakonia* 14(2):101–107.

   1982   America's Arabs. In *Contemporary American Immigration.*
          D. Cuddy, ed. pp. 220–239. Boston: Twayne Publishers.

Kayal, Philip, and Joseph Kayal
    1975   *The Syrian-Lebanese in America: A Study in Religion and Assimilation.* Boston: Twayne Publishers.

Malik, Charles H.
    1964   The Near East. In *The Prospects of Christianity Throughout the World.* Minner Searle Bates and Welhelm Pauck, eds. New York: Charles Scribner.

Maloof, Alan
    1951   Catholics of the Byzantine-Rite in the United States of America. *Eastern Churches Quarterly.* No. 5 (Winter).

Maloof, Louis
    1958   A Sociological Study of Arabic Speaking People in Mexico. Ph.D. dissertation, University of Florida.

Sklare, Marshall
    1957   The Function of Ethnic Churches: Judaism in the United States. *Religion, Society and the Individual.* J. M. Yinger, ed. pp. 459–463. New York: MacMillan Co.

Tannous, Afif
    1942   Group Behavior in the Village Community of Lebanon. *American Journal of Sociology* 48(2):231–239.

Treudley, Mary Bosworth
    1953   The Ethnic Group as a Collectivity. *Social Forces* 31(3):261–265.

ABSTRACT

Muslim immigration to the United States occurred in several stages. Unlike their predecessors, Arab Muslims arriving after World War II tended to be better educated and identified themselves as professionals. Many of these later immigrants were students who played a leading role in the establishment of Islamic organizations and institutions in the United States. One of the largest and most active Islamic organizations in the United States today is the Muslim Student Association, founded in the early 1960s.

The establishment and growth of Islam in the United States has followed the familiar development patterns of other faiths which have been carried to a new country by immigrants. The initial growth period of Islam in North America witnessed the adaptation of Islamic practices to a new environment. This resulted in a distinct American influence on the mosque, its functions and administration; hence the role of the mosque in North America is closer to that of an "ethnic" church than to mosques in the Arab world. Since the early 1970s, however, there has been a return to normative Islam, sometimes referred to as "reform." The reform movement has been stimulated by the recent influx of new immigrants who have revived more traditional Islamic practices in America.

Arab Muslims and Islamic Institutions in America: Adaptation and Reform

by Yvonne Haddad

IMMIGRATION OF ARAB MUSLIMS[1]

Aside from the few individuals who crossed the ocean as explorers or unwilling slaves, early Muslim contact with the United States was minimal (Younis 1961). A few Yemenis came after the opening of the Suez Canal in 1869; others took advantage of the Homestead Act of 1862, especially in the West. Still others decided to remain in this country as traders after visiting the Centennial Exposition in Philadelphia in 1876.

Significant Arab Muslim migration to the United States occurred in several waves—1875 to 1912, 1918 to 1922 when Lebanese Muslims came to work in the Ford Rouge Plant in Dearborn (Wasfi 1971:132), 1930 to 1938, 1947 to 1960, and 1967 to the present. The two world wars and changes in the U.S. immigration laws were principally responsible for the lulls or interruptions in the flow of immigrants. The first permanent group arrived from what was then called Greater Syria, now the combined area of Syria, Lebanon, Palestine, and Jordan. Mostly uneducated, unskilled, and of peasant stock, this group left their homes in the mountain areas of Lebanon in response to favorable reports from Lebanese Christians who had worked as immigrants in the United States.

The economic situation in the Middle East from 1890 to World War I gave impetus to further immigration. Farming had become unprofitable because of a general decline in the price of agricultural products. Aggravating the situation was the opening of the Suez Canal in 1869, which destroyed the land route to India and resulted in the loss of income levied

---

[1] Portions of this article originally appeared in 1979 as "The Muslim Experience in the United States," *The Link* 2(4):1-11. It is reprinted here by permission of the author and publisher.

on transit shipments. The Japanese competition in silk production led to the flooding of Lebanon's traditional French market, cheapened prices, and practically eliminated the silk industry of Mount Lebanon. To further aggravate the situation, the vineyards of the area became infested with disease.

Around 1900, the number of Muslims who entered the United States increased, especially among the Shia and the Druze.[2] Apprehension about traveling to a non-Muslim country dampened the motivations of many, but continuing success stories of other immigrants provided the necessary incentive. Most of the early immigrants intended to return home after accumulating enough capital to build a house or start a business. Some who were successful did return, and offered proof of the wealth and vertical social mobility available in the United States to those who were willing to work hard.

In the United States, however, several factors worked to impede the flow of immigrants. Many were turned down by immigration officials at Ellis Island. Discrimination appeared in various localities where Arab immigrants settled. One court found persons from the Arab world ineligible for citizenship because they were neither Caucasian nor African. Although a higher court overruled that decision, the debate about the size of head and nose as determinants of race continued in the press (Younis 1961). The immigrants also faced new laws that restricted the number permitted into the United States. Preference was given to relatives of previous immigrants, as evidenced in the flow of immigration after World War II. Intermarriage and the influx of relatives from the Middle East helped to preserve old country ideals and customs and to slow down the process of acculturation and assimilation.

By the 1950s, most of the Arab countries had gained their independence and were undergoing radical change due to the failure of the institutions implanted by the colonial powers. This resulted in a new kind of immigrant arriving in this country. A growing number came from the capitalist classes, the landed gentry, and the influential urban-based families of various countries, who had been replaced by a new leadership. Many of them were Palestinians displaced by the creation of the state of Israel, Egyptians whose land had been appropriated by the Nasser regime, Syrians overthrown by revolutionaries, and Iraqi royalists fleeing the Republican regime.

---

[2]There are two main divisions in Islam: Sunnis, who follow the *Sunna*, the traditional practice of Muhammad as set forth in the *Hadith* ("Traditions"), and Shia. The Shia is a "faction" that held that only descendants of the Prophet Muhammad and his son-in-law Ali could legitimately head the Islamic community. Over the centuries these two groups have split into several sects, each of which has developed its distinctive teachings.

The Druze are another sectarian group which is an offshoot of the *Isma'iliyaa* which developed in the eleventh century around the figure of the Fatimid Caliph al-Hakim bi-Amr Illah, regarded by his followers as an incarnation of the divine spirit.

The majority of these post-World War II immigrants were westernized and fluent in English. They sought higher education, advanced technical training, and specialized work opportunities as well as ideological fulfillment. About two-thirds of the students married American women (Suleiman 1969:37) and pursued integration into the general society. Many of them now teach in colleges and universities and can be considered to have achieved intellectual as well as social integration.

Mainly from urban areas, most of this group arrived with the intention of settling permanently. They had attended western or westernized schools in their home countries. Some had experimented in representative government or remembered their frustrated efforts to institute freely elected governments in their countries. Their ethnic identities were thus influenced by national, rather than religious considerations. They were part of what could be called the "brain drain." It is estimated that about fifty thousand Arab Muslim intellectuals and professionals entered the United States in the decade between 1957 and 1967. Of these, 73% had received higher education in Europe and the United States (Elkholy 1969:15). Their impact on Islamic institutions in this country appears to be marginal, however. The majority were either "un-mosqued," i.e., did not attend the mosque, or were "Eid Muslims," those who participate in mosque services on the two main Islamic feasts, *Eid al-Adha* and *Eid al-Fitr.*

Studies of Islamic communities in the United States conducted by Muslim scholars emphasize a distinction between the early immigrants and those who arrived later. The distinction is usually based on status identification, with the later immigrants identifying as members (or aspirants) of a professional class. To a certain extent, this distinction has been exaggerated, as many later immigrants were not professionals. These studies tend to ignore the consistent flow of chain migration as relatives continued to join those who preceded them, swelling the number of Muslims from rural areas of the Arab world.

The new immigrants settled in various parts of the country. In places where a large number of Arab Muslims were already established, such as Dearborn, they built their own ethnic mosques. In smaller communities (e.g., Quincy, Massachusetts and Rochester, New York), the newly arrived Muslims joined the existing institutions. While this has brought added vitality to the group through an infusion of energetic and active members, it has created strain over leadership positions. Some of the tension between "new" and "old" immigrants is a result of the cultural differences between the two groups.

There are no reliable statistics on the number of Muslims, Arab and non-Arab, in the United States. Estimates have ranged from half a million to six million depending on the source and the purpose for which the number is being utilized. In 1979, there appeared to be a consensus among Muslim leaders that there were about three million Muslims (Haddad 1979:2). A more conservative estimate given to this author in the summer of 1982 by a leader of one of the umbrella organizations placed the number at a million and a half. It was suggested that inflated numbers are sometimes used to gain per capita aid for the organizations or to help enhance their political, economic, and spiritual influence.

THE DEVELOPMENT OF ISLAMIC INSTITUTIONS

The development of Islamic institutions in the United States came about slowly because the number of Muslims in proportion to the total population has been relatively small. Immigrants who came to amass wealth and then return to their homelands were not interested in establishing institutions; their allegiance remained with their families at home, which they helped support financially.

Those Muslims who decided to settle in this country, however, began to think of developing institutions and organizations to preserve their faith and to transmit it to their children. Individuals in different areas took the initiative: Abdullah Ingram in Cedar Rapids, Iowa; Muhammad Omar in Quincy, Massachusetts; J. Howar in Washington, D.C. In other cities, like Dearborn, Michigan, a small but determined group backed the effort.

The earliest recorded group who organized for communal prayer in private homes was in Ross, North Dakota in 1900 (Naff 1980:132). By 1920, they had built a mosque. Later, they became so integrated into the community that they assumed Christian names, and married Christians. By 1948, even the mosque was abandoned. In 1919, an Islamic association was established in Highland Park, Michigan, followed by another one in Detroit in 1922. A Young Men's Muslim Association (Arab) was established in Brooklyn in 1923; and the Arab Banner Society in Quincy in 1930. The first building designated as a mosque was in Cedar Rapids in 1934. The mosque founders also purchased the first Muslim cemetery (believed still to be the only one in the United States). In 1957, the Islamic Center of Washington, D.C. opened to serve an American congregation as well as members of the Muslim diplomatic corps residing in the capital. Today, there are over four hundred mosques and Islamic associations in the United States.

The increase in the number of Islamic associations appears to correspond to the increased number (and participation) of students from Muslim countries, and to the growing number of Muslim immigrants who are committed to an Islamic way of life. All of this has created the need for instructional material and for a more efficient organizational structure. The last fifteen years have seen the establishment of a number of national organizations to fill these needs. Because Islam does not have a hierarchical structure in which organization is imposed from above, these institutions were of necessity begun by individuals at the local level. Participation in them remains optional.

THE FEDERATION OF ISLAMIC ASSOCIATIONS

The Federation of Islamic Associations was established through the efforts of Abdullah Ingram of Cedar Rapids, Iowa. Through a personal request to President Eisenhower, Ingram gained religious recognition for American Muslims serving in the army. In 1952, he called for a meeting of Muslims from various centers in the United States and Canada with the aim of coordinating efforts to preserve Islam and Muslim culture, and to expound the teachings of Islam. Ingram was also interested in providing accurate information about Islam to non-Muslims. This meeting brought into being the International Muslim Society, whose members were mostly second- and third-generation Lebanese-Americans. Two years later, during its third meeting in Chicago, the Society adopted the name Federation of Islamic Associations (FIA).

The FIA (predominantly Arab in constituency, mostly American-born in leadership) continues to hold annual meetings and conventions. Unlike some of the more recently formed organizations, its character is American. Through the structure provided by the FIA, Muslims have an opportunity to meet and become acquainted within a common cultural and religious context. The organization also provides specific services to the Muslim community. It publishes *The Muslim Star* magazine, devoted to Islamic topics, and in 1970 produced selected readings from the Quran as well as a directory of Muslims in the United States. It has attempted to conduct a census of Muslims, to standardize Sunday school teaching materials, and to counteract the anti-Muslim and anti-Arab literature in the United States through an antidefamation office. Coordinated activities with United States and international Muslim groups have resulted in such projects as a joint *hajj* (pilgrimage) to Mecca (Saudi Arabia) in 1975 with the Muslim Student Association.

THE MUSLIM WORLD LEAGUE

In May of 1962, the Muslim World League was established in Mecca as an international body of Muslims dedicated to fostering the cause of Islam throughout the world. Included among its goals are the defense of Islam against those who seek to destroy it, the development of Muslim communities, and the provision of assistance where needed, especially in areas where Muslims are oppressed or where they are a minority. Its missionary outreach seeks the spread of Islam.

With offices in several nations, including one in the United States, the League has served since 1974 as a nongovernmental representative in the United Nations. It also has a consultative status with UNICEF and UNESCO. League activities in the United States include free distribution of the Quran and other Islamic material in English translation. The League also provides imams, twenty-six of whom are now functioning as leaders in various mosques. They are predominantly Arab in background and have received their Islamic education in Saudi Arabia, Egypt, or Lebanon.

The Muslim World League sponsored the first Islamic Conference of North America, which met in Newark, New Jersey in late April, 1977.

Representatives from more than two hundred mosques and Muslim associations were in attendance. The purpose of the conference, according to its published proceedings, was "to strengthen and help coordinate Islamic work and promote unity and cooperation among the large number of Muslim groups in the North American continent." The conference organized itself into the Islamic Coordinating Council of North America, which aims at harmonizing the various Islamic organizations and streamlining the efforts of the various communities in order to eliminate duplication.

The Muslim World League has recently helped form the Council of Masajid in the United States, with offices in New York City. Primarily concerned with encouraging the building, furnishing, and maintenance of mosques, the council fosters cooperation among mosques in the United States, between U.S. mosques and those in other parts of the Muslim world, and with its headquarters in Mecca. It attempts to protect all United States mosques from being taken over by "deviant" groups, while encouraging local mosques to secure funds for the care of buildings, salaries of imams, and general operating expenses. Like other Muslim organizations, it encourages the spread of an Islamic consciousness and supports the educational, social, and benevolent activities of local mosques. A substantial number of mosques built by Arab-Americans have opted to join the council. Membership in the council does not in any way jeopardize a mosque's membership in the FIA.

THE MUSLIM STUDENT ASSOCIATION

The most active of the Islamic organizations in the United States is the Muslim Student Association (MSA), established by twenty-five Muslim students from fifteen different universities on January 1, 1963, at the University of Illinois in Urbana. Its purpose is to unite Muslim students under one platform in order to provide Islamic understanding of problems besetting contemporary societies. The MSA affirms a spiritual approach to life which encompasses religious, social, economic, political, and moral perspectives.

In its early days, the MSA competed with the Organization of Arab Students (OAS) for the allegiance of Arab students on various American campuses. The OAS was supported by the Nasserite government in Egypt, which advocated nationalist and socialist goals. The MSA with its direct ties to the anti-Nasserite Muslim Brotherhood and the *Jamaati Islam,* rejected these ideologies as alien to the essence of Islam. The popularity of the OAS during the sixties reflected the prevalent ideology in the Arab world at the time. Its effectiveness appears to have waned, however, beginning in the mid-1970s and with the rise of Islamic identity in various Arab countries.

Prior to the 1970s, most of the Muslim students who came to the United States were enrolled in graduate programs. They considered the West as a source of knowledge and a guide towards development and progress. During the 1970s, however, Muslim students began to seek an alternative source of identity and purpose. The October 1973 Arab-Israeli war, followed by the Arab oil boycott, provided a new perspective on the future.

The dramatic rise in the income of the oil-producing countries increased the number of students being sent to the United States for training. Among them were a large number of undergraduates who were open to contending perspectives. In addition, many students began coming from parts of the Arab world that were not significantly represented before, and from families with less formal education. During the academic year 1981–82, for example, there were 9,540 students from Saudi Arabia, 1,000 from Egypt, and 1,000 from other North African countries enrolled on American campuses (American Council on Education 1982:9–12).

Many graduates from the universities who chose to remain in the United States felt uncomfortable with the Muslim institutions they found here. After joining the available mosques, they felt that Islam was not living up to its potential of molding the totality of life in accordance with the teachings of the Quran. Because of cultural differences, they were often unable to see the Muslims in this country with whom they came in contact as possessing what they felt to be "true" Islam.

All of these changes led the MSA to establish a new set of objectives in 1975. The original goals of the MSA, as stated in 1963, were to improve students' knowledge of Islam, to perpetuate the Islamic spirit, to guide life in a non-Muslim culture, to explain Islam to North America, and to restore Islam in the students' home countries. The priorities as reformulated by the planning and organizing committee of 1975 were changed to include: "producing and disseminating Islamic knowledge, establishing Islamic institutions, providing daily requirements, initiating *daawah* (the propagation of the faith), recruiting and training personnel, promoting and nourishing the unity of Muslims."

The dramatic increase in the number of Arab students in the U.S. has led to a steady "Arabization" of the leadership of the Muslim Student Association, whose world headquarters is located in Kuwait. This, plus the recently adopted policy of forming organizations based on regional linguistic distinctions (given the success of the Iranian Muslim Student Association in helping establish an Islamic government in Iran), has led to the formation of the Muslim Arab Youth Association, which focuses on Arab problems. It publishes its own Arabic magazine, *Al-Amal,* and has several chapters on various campuses. The president, Hassan Al-Banna Ibrahim, resides in Carbondale, Illinois.

Among the projects and activities of the MSA are the Islamic Books Service, a correspondence course on the principles of Islam, a fund for helping oppressed Muslims, a cooperative project for interest-free loans, printing and publishing Islamic literature, a prison project to teach Islam to inmates, an information bureau about Muslim festivities and duties, a slides and films project, and a program that provides tape recordings of the Quran and cards with Muslim greetings. Plans are also underway to construct a national headquarters in Plainfield, Indiana, where the central office is now located. The new buildings will include an Islamic center, mosque, library, gymnasium, auditorium, and administrative offices for the MSA and its subsidiary organizations such as the Islamic Teaching Center and the North American Trust.

ADAPTING ISLAMIC PRACTICE IN AMERICA

The establishment and growth of Islam in the United States has followed the familiar developmental patterns of a faith brought into a new country by immigrants. Such patterns exist in the penetration and spread of Islam to fringe areas of the Islamic empire, areas unconquered by Muslim armies, where individuals have maintained the faith without the support and supervision of an Islamic government.

A "portable" faith, Islam is not hampered by the necessity for clergy, sacraments, or specified structures. In the initial stage of its establishment in the United States, as in other areas, it remained a personal faith of the individual immigrant. As the community grew, immigrant groups began communal prayer to serve their spiritual needs. This was followed by efforts to recruit teachers in order to provide religious instruction for their children.

As in other areas of the world, the initial growth period of Islam in North America reflected "mixing" or acculturation. Severed from traditions accumulated over centuries, the immigrants attempted to create their own Islamic institutions. For this, they borrowed institutional forms from the local inhabitants. The role of the mosque in North America is closer to that of denominational churches than to mosques in the Arab world.

Historically, the mosque has functioned as a gathering place for the community, where Muslims expressed their religious and political allegiance during the Friday service. In the new country, it acquired a social and cultural meaning as the Arab Muslims struggled to maintain an Arab and Islamic identity in an alien culture. Not only are weddings and funerals conducted at the mosque, in keeping with American practices, but even fund-raising activities (primarily directed by women) such as mosque bazaars, bake sales, community dinners, and cultural events have been adopted as well. Occasionally, even folk dancing in the basement of a mosque has brought young people together in fellowship.

Women participate in other aspects of mosque life generally not open to them in the Middle East. These include attending the Sunday service and teaching Sunday school. Interviews with second- and third-generation Muslims indicate the very active role assumed by pioneering Arab Muslim women in the construction and maintenance of the mosque. This role has been curtailed in areas where more recently arrived immigrants predominate. A coalition between illiterate traditional rural men and highly educated young students or immigrants committed to a strict Islamic order has formed, and, as one third-generation Arab-American Muslim put it, appears to be operative in "wresting the leadership of the mosque" away from those who labored long to bring it into being. In an increasing number of Arab Muslim mosques where traditional imams have been installed, women have seen their participation in mosque functions reduced and restricted, a restructuring aimed at conforming to patterns idealized in the Arab world.

Also reminiscent of Christian practices is the passing of the collection plate (witnessed in Quincy, Massachusetts) during the Sunday meeting to supply funds for the maintenance of the mosque. Sunday services and Sunday schools have been adopted as a result of adjustment to North American realities. Most working members cannot attend the prayers on Friday, which is the designated day for communal worship in Islam.

The manner in which the mosque is administered also reveals a distinct American influence. There is a predominance of "congregational" control in the mosque, as elected committees have assumed the right to hire an imam or prayer leader. In the Arab world, most mosques are controlled by the ministry of endowments, giving local people no power in matters of administration. With the appointment of imams financed by outside sources, such as Al-Azhar in the 1960s and the Muslim World League at present, local congregations appear to have lost some of their powers. The bureaucratization of Islamic institutions under umbrella organizations appears to act as a deterrent to acculturation and Americanization. One of the "deviations" of acculturation has to do with the specific Quranic injunction against usury, generally interpreted as receiving or paying interest on money lent or borrowed. This is currently being rectified by the availability of financial aid from overseas organizations. Previously, the inability to finance mosque building required the congregation to obtain a mortgage. This accommodation to American practices is frowned upon by both the MSA and the MWL. Aid from foreign sources is now available for the construction of mosques and centers.

The role of the imam in the larger mosques has taken on added significance, given the new realities of the American milieu. The traditional duties of leading the community in prayer and providing guidance through preaching and Quranic exegesis have been expanded to include the administration and maintenance of the mosque. Moreover, the minority status of the Muslim community has added to the imam's duties, which now include attending to the community's general welfare as well as representing them in interreligious functions. He has become the spokesman for the group, the ambassador of the Muslims to the community, frequently lecturing about Islam in churches and schools.

Another feature of the imam's new role is his function as a family guide and counselor. With no training in counseling, the imam often reverts to providing Islamic answers based on theological law, which is not received favorably by some members of the second- and third-generation Arab Muslims.

The predominance of nuclear families among Arab Muslims has led to undue pressures on the spouses who are accustomed to the counsel of friends and relatives. Arab customs relegate problem-solving to parents or an inner family circle, who arbitrate conflicts and function as peacemakers. The absence of such help in the United States places great stress on the couple, allowing misunderstandings to fester and continue unresolved. Imams in various cities have reported that their help is generally sought as a last effort, given the tendency of Arabs to confine the knowledge about intimate affairs to the immediate family.

Imams are also pressed into upholding the traditional morality by the older generation, a demand that keeps a substantial number of Muslims away from the mosque. The freedom to choose from a multiplicity of lifestyles, with no clearcut societal definition of acceptable behavior, is upheld by second-, third-, and fourth-generation Arab Muslims as part of being American. In many ways, these lifestyles contradict the traditional Islamic legal and cultural patterns. The fact that imams are trained in the Arab world and have little understanding or tolerance for American customs leads to further alienation of the American-born.

Interfaith marriage, especially in cases where the woman does not convert to Islam, has led to deep strains in marital relationships. This is particularly true with regard to the religious education of children. The liberal Muslim father who advocates and practices permissiveness tends to become more inflexible when the religious instruction of his children is involved. The imam thus plays a primary role both in helping families resolve some of the problems attendant to these concerns, and in providing the kind of Islamic education desired by many Muslim parents.

In the smaller and more recently established societies, the role of imam is assumed by the most learned man in the congregation. Sometimes, he is the one most thoroughly versed in Islamic traditional learning; in other instances, he is often the person who has earned the highest academic degree. Both forms of leadership may exist in the same congregation, so that one leads the prayer while the other preaches the sermon or becomes the president of the executive committee.

THE MOVEMENT FOR "REFORM"

Since the beginning of the 1970s, there has been a return to normative Islam, sometimes referred to as "reform." Efforts are made to purge Islam of innovations which accumulated over the years and to eradicate unnecessary and un-Islamic patterns of acculturation. Reform has been heightened by the influx of new immigrants, from Lebanon (1975–82), many of whom are totally committed to Islam as a way of life. This commitment appears to be a result of the sectarian strife in that country and its influence in stimulating, if not crystallizing, confessionalism. The struggle against the Phalangists and their supporters, the Israelis, appears to have turned many Muslims in Lebanon inward, in search of identity and coherence in their religion. Reform is also advocated by the Muslim World League and the new imams who have recently arrived from the Middle East to head the mosques. They find the "Americanization" of

Islam unacceptable. Finally, the Muslim Student Association has consistently considered Arab-American Muslims to be un-Islamic. Generally, their efforts to convert them to a more Islamic way of life have not been very successful.

The dramatic increase in the number of Muslims in the United States during the last decade has heartened followers who remember a time when Muslim holidays went by scarcely noticed or observed. The celebrations in the various mosques and organizations have added a new dimension to the growing sense of dignity, identity, and purpose of the Muslims. Perhaps S.S. Mufassir best captured the change when, on the occasion of the American Bicentennial, he wrote in *Islamic Items:*

> But the technotronic cybernetic society which has put to death the false God of man's making has failed to render Islam irrelevant. Islam has survived in the very heart of the industrialized West, and has pushed forward with indomitable spirit without apology, compromise, assimilation or mutation.

This affirmation reflects the growing belief of Muslims that they have a purpose and a message for mankind. The sense of mission in the United States is nurtured by Muslim scholars from India, Pakistan, and Saudi Arabia, who travel throughout the country proclaiming normative Islam, and by various local Muslim organizations which are committed to *daawah* (mission) and supported by mission funds from Saudi Arabia, Kuwait, Qatar, Libya, and Pakistan. Islam's mission in America was further elaborated by Professor Ismail al Faruqi of Temple University, an internationally recognized Islamic leader in the United States. In introducing Wallace Muhammad to the Plenary Session of the American Academy of Religion in 1978, he restated the case for Islam in these words:

> In America, Islam is contending anew. It is contending for men's souls, as well as claiming that it supplies the answers to the very social and religious problems besetting America. The social problems of America are well known—racism, nationalism, the disintegrated family, promiscuity, alcoholism. Well, Islam contends that it has radical solutions for all of these evils.

This does not mean, however, that Islam has an easy task in the United States. Even among immigrant Muslims, mosque participation is limited. Community observers estimated that between one to five percent are active mosque participants. The number is higher in some areas where family chain migration is pervasive, or where the Arab Muslim group is relatively stable and there is no steady influx of new immigrants.

Social class, national origin, level of education, focus of identity (whether national or Islamic), and ability to integrate in the American society appear to have direct bearings on mosque attendance. These factors also affect conflict in the mosque. Arab Muslims reflect the political, ideological, and territorial differences of the countries from which they emigrated. These differences sometimes become a major focus of contention among individuals affirming exclusive claim to their view of the "true" Islam. A substantial number of un-mosqued are disaffected by the conflict. Others find the reforms to be irrelevant to life in America. Still others are well-integrated second-, third-, and fourth-generation Americans who resent outsiders telling them what to do. They are alienated from the recently arrived who take religion "very seriously," making themselves noticeable and open to possible discrimination by the host society. Among those in the un-mosqued ranks are the professional and intellectual Arab Muslims who arrived in the 1950s and 1960s. A majority of them were influenced by Arab nationalism which relegated religion to a personal relationship between the individual and God. The nationalists have generally directed their energies to Arab rather than Islamic causes. They exercise leadership in such institutions as the Association of Arab-American University Graduates (AAUG).

THE MUSLIM ENCOUNTER WITH AMERICA

The early immigrants faced grave problems establishing Islam. Mostly uneducated and unacquainted with American culture, they felt discrimination in their jobs as well as in their efforts to erect houses of prayer. Zoning laws sometimes obstructed them. They found themselves unable to teach Islam to their children for want of materials in English.

Muslims are also hampered in fulfilling their prayer obligations which require praying five times a day at prescribed times, including noon and early afternoon, because they often face ridicule or pressure from their peers. The author is aware of one Muslim who lost his job because he was performing ablutions (the necessary ritual cleansing of hands, feet, elbows, ears, face and head before prayer) in the men's room. Prayer also requires a clean area with no pictures or portraits hanging on the walls.

Muslims are expected to join other believers in the communal prayer on Friday, an impossibility for many. Consequently, communal prayer services held on Friday are often attended by the old and unemployed. Almost all mosques hold Sunday services, which serve only as alternative meetings and do not replace Friday worship.

The two most important holidays of Islam, *Eid al-Fitr* (celebrated at the end of the month of fasting) and *Eid al-Adha* (observed by Muslims worldwide at the end of the *Hajj*, the pilgrimage to Mecca where the whole community of Muslims renews its dedication to the worship of God) are not recognized the holidays in this country (except in Dearborn, Michigan where the holidays are recognized semi-officially). Muslim students are not excused from classes, nor are workers given a day off to participate in these celebrations.

The dietary laws of Islam forbid the consumption of alcohol, pork, and improperly slaughtered meat. Muslims are expected to eat *halal* (meat from an animal that is not stunned, but properly butchered and bled with the name of God recited at the time of slaughtering). Some urban areas have butchers who sell *halal* meat. Other Muslims use Kosher meat, reciting the proper phrase on it before consumption. But most Muslims have no access to *halal* butchers. The use of lard in most baked goods makes pious Muslims wary of consuming prepared goods. (Recently it has been revealed that buns used by McDonald hamburger chains are made with lard and therefore cannot be consumed by Muslims.) The recent discovery of pig enzymes in some processed cheese has made Muslims generally cautious of processed foods. Efforts have been made to isolate the brands that use these enzymes in order to guide Muslims in their choice of foods.

The practice of Islam in the United States is hampered by American civil laws which are different from Islamic laws governing divorce, alimony, child custody and support, marriage, inheritance, and adoption. Islamic law is derived from the teachings of the Quran, which defines God's way for mankind. Thus, by living in America and adhering to American law, the Muslim may be forced to accept judgments that contradict the will of God.

Muslims often see overindulgent, materialistic American culture as opposed to the Islamic ethos. The Quran teaches that man was placed on the earth to administer it for God. The emphasis on consumption and planned obsolescence is paramount to mismanagement of resources; the goals of individualism and personal gratification jeopardize the Muslim teaching of communal commitment and responsibility. Individual satisfaction leads to exclusiveness and discrimination which are contrary to the revelation of the Quran affirming that all people are brothers and sisters. The only way one human being can excel over another is in piety and devotion to God.

Islam has faced other problems in America. A logistical problem arose as Muslims scattered throughout the United States. Although the number of mosques and Islamic centers continues to increase, the dispersal speeds the process of acculturation and Americanization and leads to local innovations. Where chain migration has occurred in cities like Cedar Rapids, Detroit, Toledo, and Quincy, the Muslims were able to organize institutions early. Family ties, shared experiences, and common outlook helped weld the community together. The second and third generations, while committed to their Arab Islamic identity, are anxious to maintain their American roots. Thus, differences between the American-born Muslims and those who were raised overseas will continue to be a source of strain, each group fervently believing that their world view is ultimately better for the future of the community.

Many Muslims in the United States have little involvement with mosques which reflects the fact that they are mostly westernized and secularized. A great number of them have opted to live in this country, as one Muslim leader put it, "because they are dazzled by its affluence and want to participate in it." A great number of them would find better positions were they to return to their home countries, but the choice they have made leads them to seek integration into American life.

Political tensions between Muslims from different Arab countries surface occasionally in community gatherings. In the past, this led to a ban on discussions of political and doctrinal issues. With the reassertion of normativist Islam, emphasis is placed on the eternal nature of Islam. There is no American Islam, British Islam, or African Islam—only Islam as willed by God for humanity and as revealed in the Quran. Periodically, rivalries for position or influence lead to factions and schisms in communities. Various groups vie for power. A few have sought aid from overseas, thereby exaggerating their numbers and scope of their influence.

A great number of second- and third-generation Muslim women are alienated by attempts at reform. In some cases they feel that those Muslim men who insist on eliminating the social function of the mosque are not being true Muslims. They point to the equal status and role of women at the time of the Prophet. Efforts to keep them out of the "male-space" are seen as reactionary and old-fashioned. They point to the loss of a substantial number of third- and fourth-generation young people to Christianity (through intermarriage) or to secular society as a reaction to unnecessary strictures. These strictures, they believe, are un-Islamic, but, as one second-generation mother said, "are designed by men for the glory of men."

Finally, Muslims have experienced a considerable amount of prejudice in the United States. In addition to general public ignorance about the teachings of Islam, there is an accumulated heritage of mistrust that has lingered since the Crusades (Said 1978). Recently, the Arab-Israeli conflict has led to several myths about Islam and the Muslims. The late philosopher, Ayn Rand, on a Phil Donahue show aired June 12, 1979, dismissed the Arabs as a collection of "savages" who are "racist" and who oppose Israel because it brings industry, technology, and intelligence into the area.

A "Sixty Minutes" program on Arabs in England entitled "The Arabs are Coming, the Arabs are Coming" not only generated fear, but also portrayed the Arabs as spendthrifts and their women as "chattel." Other programs characterize Muslims and Arabs as cunning, cruel, weak, decadent, and untrustworthy (Shaheen 1982:89–96; Terry 1982:97–104). Still others show them as gluttonous, scheming, and crafty, with insatiable sexuality. None take note of the fact that the rate of divorce in Muslim countries is only a fraction of what it is in the United States. These stereotypes extend to social science textbooks as well as Sunday school materials (Aswad 1981:73–80).

CONCLUSION

Islam in the United States continues to grow through three means: immigration, conversion, and procreation. Conversion provides a cadre of Muslims committed to normative Islam, asserting the necessity of Islam's governing the totality of behavior in the social, economic, political, cultural, educational, and religious aspects of their lives. Historically, converts have provided the best advocates of the faith. For them, faith is not just the verbal affirmation of the believer's understanding of the teachings of Islam, but involves all aspects of the practice of the Islamic religion. These converts generally join MSA.

Among Arab-Americans, converts are generally American men who profess their Islam when they marry an Arab Muslim woman. In conversations with members of the community, it was surprising to find a carefree attitude toward this phenomenon. Community members perceive such conversions in terms of expediency, and think that they should not be taken too seriously. If the young man is willing to abandon the faith of his fathers for the sake of a woman, then his religious affiliation, it is believed by many, is not genuine. As one woman confided, "You know, for these Americans religion means nothing."

Non-westernized new immigrants have formerly functioned as conservative agents, maintaining the validity of the home culture and restraining others from innovative changes. The number of future immigrants, as well as the nature of their commitment to Islam, will no doubt influence the shape Islam will take in the United States. Should a substantial number immigrate from among those committed to national rather than Muslim identity, as in the most recent immigration from Iran, and should they be willing to subsidize the Islamic organizations, a shift to a less normative Islam may eventually appear.

REFERENCES

American Council on Education
   1982   *Foreign Students and Institutional Policy.* Washington, D.C.:
   American Council on Education.

Aswad, Barbara
   1981   Biases and Inaccuracies in Textbooks: Depictions of the Arab
   World. In *The Arab World and Arab-Americans: Understand-
   ing a Neglected Minority.* Sameer Y. Abraham and Nabeel
   Abraham, eds. Detroit, Michigan: Wayne State University,
   Center for Urban Studies.

Elkholy, Abdo
   1969   The Arab-Americans: Nationalism and Traditional Preservations. In *The Arab Americans: Studies in Assimilation.* Elaine
   C. Hagopian and Ann Paden, eds. Wilmette, Ill.: The Medina
   University Press International.

Flehan, Henry
   1981   History of the ADS. *Our Heritage* 1 (2):9–10.

Haddad, Yvonne
   1979   The Muslim Experience in the United States. *The Link* 2(4):1–11.

Naff, Alixa
   1980   Arabs. In *Harvard Encyclopedia of American Ethnic Groups.*
   Stephan Therstrom, ed. Cambridge, Mass.: Harvard University Press.

Said, Edward
   1978   *Orientalism.* New York: Pantheon.

Shaheen, Jack G.
   1982   The Arab Image in American Mass Media. *American-Arab
   Affairs,* No. 2 (Fall):89–96.

Suleiman, Michael W.
   1969   The New Arab American Community. In *The Arab Americans: Studies in Assimilation.* Elaine C. Hagopian and Ann
   Paden, eds. Wilmette, Ill.: The Medina University Press International.

Terry, Janice
   1982   The Arab-Israeli Conflict in Popular Literature. *American-
   Arab Affairs,* No. 2 (Fall):97–104.

Wasfi, Atif A.
 1971 *An Islamic Lebanese Community in the United States.* Beirut: Beirut Arab University.

Younis, Adele L.
 1961 The Coming of the Arabic-Speaking People to the United States. Ph.D. dissertation, Boston University.

Part Two

Case Studies
of Arab-American Communities
in Detroit

ABSTRACT

Detroit's Arab-American community numbers approximately 200,000 residents. It is an extremely diverse community, composed of four major nationality groups including Lebanese, Palestinians, Yemenis, and Iraqi-Chaldeans, with numerous religious affiliations present. A variety of "push-pull" factors have been responsible for Arab emigration to the Detroit area. The recent political conflicts in the Middle East and socioeconomic policies of some governments insure that Arab migration will continue to increase into the foreseeable future. The diversity of the community is further evidenced in the geographical areas that each group inhabits and the social and religious institutions which have emerged, resulting in a number of distinct and self-contained communities (or subcommunities). Even as social and political factors divide the community in significant ways, a shared language, cultural heritage, and identity serve as a basis for communication and a common purpose which is becoming increasingly more visible in the pan-community organizations which serve the community as a whole.

Detroit's Arab-American Community: A Survey of Diversity and Commonality

by Sameer Y. Abraham

The existing literature and research on Arab-Americans in the Detroit area is generally limited to the study of a particular nationality group or subgroup within it.[1] In general, these studies point to the social heterogeneity which characterizes the community and the many shared characteristics which continue to bind the community together. The purpose of this article is to survey the research literature and compile a general profile of the community with an emphasis on its diversity. The survey will be confined to six related topics, including: nationality and religion, population, migration patterns, residence, changing identity, and community. While the review produces a picture of a community which is rich in diversity, there are strong ties of commonality which bind the community.

NATIONALITY AND RELIGION

The Arab-American community in the Detroit area is composed of four principal nationality groups: Lebanese, Palestinian/Jordanian, Yemenis, and Iraqi-Chaldeans.[2] One of the problems associated with clarifying the

---

[1] This article is based in part on an earlier work which appeared in *The Arab World and Arab-Americans: Understanding a Neglected Minority* (Detroit: Wayne State University, Center for Urban Studies, 1981), pp. 23–33.

[2] A number of other Arab groups reside in the Detroit area and in other parts of the state including Jordanians, Egyptians, Kuwaitis, and Moroccans. Among these groups, the Egyptian Copts probably represent the largest number. Since our knowledge of these groups is extremely limited, they will not be discussed in this article.

national identity of many of these immigrants has to do with the time of arrival of the earliest immigrants and the changing political environment in the Middle East over the past century. For example, at the time of the first Lebanese arrivals in the late 19th century, Lebanon was still a province of Greater Syria under the tutelage of the Ottoman Empire. Although some of the earliest arrivals hail from cities in modern Syria (e.g., Damascus), the majority of early Lebanese arrivals had their homes in Mount Lebanon or, as in the case of the later Muslims, southern Lebanon. For our purposes, we shall simply designate all Syrians and Lebanese as "Lebanese" since the majority originate from the area of modern Lebanon and/or identify themselves as Lebanese.

In the case of the Palestinians, the majority of the group arrived in the United States after part of historic Palestine became Israel in 1948 and the West Bank came under Jordanian rule. Since 1967, the West Bank (and Gaza) have been under Israeli military occupation. Most of the Palestinians in the area originate from villages and towns in the West Bank and maintain Jordanian citizenship. It would be incorrect, however, to identify this group as Jordanians, as they continue to identify as Palestinians even though their homeland remains in dispute. (A small group of ethnic Jordanians also reside in the Detroit area.) It would be appropriate therefore to designate this group as "Palestinians" or "Palestinian/Jordanians."

As for the Yemenis, they immigrated from what is today the People's Democratic Republic of Yemen (or South Yemen) and the Yemen Arab Republic (or North Yemen). The northern Yemenis constitute the majority (approximately 90 percent) of all Yemeni immigrants in the area. And although a political boundary divides both countries today, almost all Yemenis identify themselves as "Yemeni" and are identified as such by other Arab immigrants. The acceptance of the national designation reflects the historical existence of a single Yemeni nation to which all Yemenis believe they belong and are desirous of establishing.

The national identity of the Chaldeans is Iraqi, although many Chaldeans who immigrated to the United States during the early decades of this century continue to identify themselves only as Chaldeans. The more recent arrivals, however, prefer an Iraqi or Arab identity (see the article by Sengstock in this volume for more on this point). Although the Chaldeans constitute a distinct ethnic minority in Iraq and are recognized as such, they are culturally indistinguishable from their Iraqi-Arab brethren. (A small group of non-Chaldean Iraqis can also be found residing in the area.) In this article, then, these identities will be joined and all Chaldeans referred to as "Iraqi-Chaldeans."

The religious identities of Arab-Americans are in many ways just as varied as their national identities. The community as a whole is divided into two distinct religious groups, Muslims and Christians. Even though the dominant religion in the Arab world is Islam, the Arab Christian minorities are heavily represented among Arab immigrants. In fact, the overwhelming majority of Arab immigrants in the United States are of the Christian faith. Similarly, the majority of Arab-Americans in the Detroit area are also Christians, although Muslims are represented in significant and growing numbers.

Table 1. Nationality by Predominant Religious Affiliation

Nationality Group	Predominant Religious Affiliation
Lebanese (includes Syrians)	Maronite,* Melkite (both Eastern rite Catholics) Greek Orthodox,* Syrian Orthodox Muslim (Sunni and Shia*)
Palestinian/Jordanian	Greek Orthodox,* Roman Catholic, Protestant Muslim (predominantly Sunni)
Yemenis	Muslim (Shafei and Zeidi; appear to be evenly divided.)
Iraqi-Chaldean	Chaldean (Eastern rite Catholics)

*Indicates largest groups.

Table 1 illustrates the religious affiliations among the different Arab nationality groups. While the major division between groups is that between Muslim and Christian, a considerable amount of variation can also be found within some groups. To a large extent, the religious divisions and affiliations represented in the Detroit area reflect the religious diversity in the immigrant's country of origin. As Table 1 indicates, the Lebanese and Palestinian/Jordanians include both Christian and Muslim representatives, whereas the Iraqi-Chaldeans and Yemenis are homogeneous. Within religious groups, subgroup affiliations also exist, as in the case of the Lebanese Muslims and Yemenis, where the division between Sunni and Shia and Shafei and Zeidi respectively prevail.[3] At one point, these schisms were active in the community and continue to play a restricted role among certain groups (see Elkholy 1966), particularly as pertains to choice of mosque and marriage patterns. Generally speaking, however, religious schisms are dormant and political schisms appear to play the leading role in intracommunity affairs.

[3]There are two main divisions in Islam: Sunni, who follow the *Sunna,* the traditional practice of Muhammad as set forth in the *Hadith* ("Traditions"), and Shia. The Shia is a "faction" that held that only descendants of the Prophet Muhammad and his son-in-law Ali could legitimately head the Islamic community. The Shafeis represent one of the four major schools which constitute the Sunni branch, whereas the Zeidis form a Shia following in Yemen.

POPULATION ESTIMATES

The tri-county (Wayne, Oakland, Macomb) Metropolitan Detroit area is generally recognized as the home of the largest Arab-American community in North America, numbering some 200,000 individuals. (In Michigan Arab-Americans number about 250,000, almost three percent of the state's population as of 1980.) Unfortunately, the lack of sound and reliable data has made it difficult to gauge the exact size of the population except with the crudest of measuring devices, a problem which has plagued many ethnic groups in the United States. The population estimates contained in Table 2 are based upon the projections of researchers in the field and the information supplied by community members and representatives who are intimately involved with each group. For each separate group and the community as a whole, these figures represent the closest estimation for those individuals and their offspring who were either born in an Arab League[4] country and/or identify themselves as being of Arabic-speaking origin. The population mainly consists of the immigrant-generation (or first-generation) members, a bountiful second generation, in some cases a flourishing third generation and even a youthful, although not very significant, fourth generation.

As Table 2 illustrates, the Lebanese constitute the largest group of Arab-Americans, contributing 50 percent of the total. The Iraqi-Chaldeans account for the next largest share (20 percent), whereas the Palestinians (12.5 percent) and Yemenis (5 percent) make up the balance of the four principal groups under consideration. Although relatively small and widely dispersed by some accounts, Arab-Americans in the Detroit area represent a rather significant and sizable population. Consider the following comparisons, for example: (1) the Arab-American community significantly outnumbers the entire populations of Livingston, Monroe, and St. Clair counties, while rivaling that of Washtenaw in size; (2) Arab-Americans represent one-fifth the size of Oakland county and roughly one-sixth the population of Wayne county; and (3) as of 1978, the community represents approximately one-sixth the population of the city of Detroit.

Two statistics in particular tend to reflect the increasing size of the community and the rate at which it is growing. For the 1981–1982 school year, the Detroit Public Schools reported that approximately 42 percent of the students enrolled in their bilingual program were Arabic/Chaldean speakers.[5] That is an increase of almost 10 percent in the past five years. Many more Arabic bilingual students should be enrolled in the program, which would substantially increase Arab enrollment. In either case, the

---

[4]The Arab League includes the following member states: Algeria, Bahrain, Djibouti, Egypt, Iraq, Jordan, Kuwait, Lebanon, Libya, Mauritania, Morocco, Oman, Palestine, Qatar, Saudi Arabia, Somalia, Sudan, Syria, Tunisia, United Arab Emirates, Yemen Arab Republic, People's Democratic Republic of Yemen.

[5]Source: Detroit Public Schools Bilingual Education Department, November 1, 1982.

Table 2
SEMCOG Regional Population and Metropolitan Detroit Arab-Americans

County	Population*	Nationality Group	Population Estimate**	Percent Distribution
Livingston	86,900	Lebanese	100,000	50%
Monroe	127,300	Iraqi-Chaldean	40,000	20%
St. Clair	129,000	Palestinian/Jordanian	25,000	12.5%
Washtenaw	258,800	Yemeni	10,000	5%
Macomb	694,400	Egyptians, Kuwaitis, etc.	25,000	12.5%
Oakland	1,005,900			
Wayne	2,394,500	(Outside Metropolitan area)	(50,000)	
(Detroit)	(1,231,500)		200,000	100%
	4,696,800			

*Source: South East Michigan Council of Governments (SEMCOG), estimated 1978.

**Source: Based on a review of the existing research literature and information provided by knowledgeable professionals combined with projected population growth rates.

Arabic student population has steadily increased in a number of school districts over the last two decades (cf. Doctoroff 1978). In the state of Michigan, Arabic bilingual students constitute the second largest student population with "limited English-speaking ability."[6] The increase has forced Detroit and Dearborn to institute bilingual/bicultural programs for Arab students.

Another measure of population growth (albeit an indirect one) can be gleaned from the work of the community social service organizations. One such organization located in the heart of Dearborn's "Southend" community, the Arab American Community Center for Social Services (ACCESS), reported an increase in its case load from 175 client services in 1971, when the organization first opened its doors, to 5,166 cases in 1979. Table 3 illustrates the annual distribution of client services during the past decade. These figures represent a phenomenal increase in immigrant services. In less than a decade these services increased 3,000 percent. That is the equivalent of an (average) annual increase of 300 percent. What is even more striking is the case load for 1980: in the first six months alone ACCESS recorded 4,471 cases, a figure which is equivalent to 86 percent of 1979. At this rate, ACCESS is expected to *double* its case load within a year's time.

While these measures are admittedly indirect, they do nevertheless point to substantial growth in the size of the population and to an increasing number of immigrant-related problems. Most observers are convinced that Arab-Americans constitute *the* fastest-growing immigrant-

[6]Source: Michigan Department of Education, Foreign Languages and International Studies, April 22, 1981.

ethnic community in the metropolitan area.

Table 3. ACCESS Social Service Case Load, 1971–1980

Year	Case Load Total
1971	175
1972	290
1973	400
1974	635
1975	1,350
1976	2,028
1977	3,612
1978	3,937
1979	5,166
1980 (first 6 months)	4,471

Source: ACCESS Statement, published March 26, 1980; amended July 10, 1980.

PATTERNS OF ARAB IMMIGRATION

Arab immigration to Detroit (and the United States) can be divided into four broad periods: 1890–1912, 1930–1938, 1947–1960 and 1967 to the present (Elkholy 1969:3). The Lebanese (Christians) were the first to arrive in Detroit in the 1890s, even though members of this group had already made their way to other parts of the country a decade or two earlier (Houghton 1911; Hitti 1924). According to one report, by 1900 there were about fifty Arabs located in the city, consisting mostly of unmarried Lebanese men (Rankin 1939:245). While the Christians were among the first arrivals, their Muslim counterparts were not long in following. The first Muslims, in this case Lebanese, arrived between 1900 and 1915, settling in Highland Park near the Ford Motor Company's first factory (United Community Services 1975:5). Between 1908 and 1913, the first Palestinians (reportedly Muslims) are also reported to have settled in the city, while the first Yemenis made their appearance at about the same time, somewhere between 1920 and 1925, although some reports record their presence as early as 1900 (Mayer 1951:27; N. Abraham, this volume). The earliest Iraqi-Chaldean immigrants arrived between 1910 and 1912 (Sengstock 1970:299). Palestinian Christians had already settled in other urban centers as early as 1920 (Kassess 1970; Zaghel 1976).

With few exceptions, it is difficult to estimate the size of any particular group of early immigrants. A recent analysis of the Ford Sociological Department archives found in the Henry Ford Museum revealed 555 Arabic men—classified as Syrians—among factory employees in 1916 (Schwartz 1974:256). The size of each nationality group and the community as a whole had to be large enough, however, to support the religious institutions which were established during these early years. The first Lebanese Maronite church, for example, was erected on East Congress Street in 1916 (Semaan 1979). Likewise, the first Islamic mosque in America was established in Highland Park in 1919 (Elkholy 1966). Both of these institutions testify to the existence of a sizeable Arab population following the first wave of Arab immigration in 1890 to 1912.

The second immigration influx between 1930 and 1938 is best characterized as a period of primary growth mainly among Lebanese immigrants. The first official United States Census which documented the number of Arabic-speaking people in Detroit was conducted in 1930. At that time, the Arab community was largely confined to the city of Detroit and totaled nearly 9,000 inhabitants. It is assumed that the overwhelming majority of these immigrants were Lebanese of humble peasant origins. With little formal education, many of the early Arabs did not fare well in Detroit during the Depression years of the 1930s. Some reports contend that there was a visible movement of Arabs from urban areas into southern states where farm labor was welcome (Semaan 1979; Tannous 1943). Although the other nationality groups were also present and increasing in number during this period, their growth appears less dramatic.

The third period, 1948–1960, appears to be a primary growth period for all Arab nationality groups, with a marked increase in Muslim immigrants and the entry of Palestinians following the Palestine War of 1948 (Elkholy 1969; Arif-Ghayur 1981). It is difficult to say with any certainty which group(s) contributed the most to the community increase given the paucity of reliable data. Unlike the two previous migratory waves, this third wave tended—at least on a national level—to include immigrants who were better educated and more politicized (Suleiman 1969; Jaafari 1973). It is more than likely, however, that even as the Palestinians and Muslims arrived in increasing numbers, the community patterns established in the first two waves of immigration remained generally unchanged.

With the liberalization of the immigration laws in 1965, post-1967 immigration takes a quantitative leap for all nationality groups. Prior to 1965, immigration from the "Asia-Pacific Triangle" (stretching from Pakistan and India to Japan and the Pacific Islands, and including the Arab countries) had been limited to 2,000 persons annually. The abolition of the national origins quota system gave Asian nationals (including Arabs) a more than equal chance to immigrate, although each country was limited to 20,000 persons exclusive of immediate relatives in the United States (Keely 1982). The new law took effect on June 30, 1968. Since then Arab immigrants have been arriving into the Detroit area in large numbers, making Arabic-speaking immigrants the fastest-growing immigrant-ethnic community in the area. Arab immigration now spans almost a century; the reasons behind this immigration have changed dramatically for some groups, while for others the causes remain unchanged.

PUSH-PULL FACTORS IN MIGRATION

Like earlier groups, pre-World War II Arabs migrated to the United States for a combination of reasons, some of which acted as "push" factors whereas others operated to "pull" them in a specific direction. For the earliest immigrants, Hitti suggests that the Syrian-Lebanese immigrated chiefly for economically-related reasons: the destruction of the once prosperous silk industry, limited landholdings on an inhospitable soil, heavy taxation, and occasional drought worked to push the peasantry from the land (1924:48–49). On the other side, an expanding American economy was the principal pull force for most early Arab immigrants, whether they were Lebanese, Yemenis, Iraqi-Chaldeans, or Palestinians. Generally speaking, the bulk of Arab immigrants who arrived in Detroit prior to World War II were economically motivated. Their chief objective was to make as much money in as short a period as possible and then return home. The fact that some early immigrants continue to speak of "returning" to their homelands once they have realized their economic objectives is testimony to the fact that many viewed their migration as a *temporary* sojourn and not as a permanent venture.

Economic considerations continued to predominate in the decision to immigrate for Arabs in the post-World War II period as well. As soon as some arrivals established themselves, they sent away for family members and relatives and began a process of "family chain migration" which is still very much in evidence today. With time, it became clear to many immigrants that their temporary status was becoming transformed into a permanent one, either by design or by forces outside their control. Rather than remain alone as single males, they decided to return to their countries to marry or, if married, to send for their wives and children. Assisting family members in immigrating also allowed families to reestablish themselves in North America. Other immigrants aided family members and kinsmen to migrate in order to assist them in family stores and other economic ventures (cf. Sengstock 1982:32–40).

The reasons for the post-1967 migration differ markedly from those of earlier periods. While economic objectives remain a major cause for migration, a number of related political factors have intermingled to increase the immigration of all nationality groups during this period. Political and social instability resulting from *coups d'etat,* revolutions, war, and military occupation appear to have accelerated the economic push-pull forces at work. In other words, had these events *not* occurred, it is unlikely that so many Arab immigrants would have decided to immigrate for economic reasons alone.

The two Arab-Israeli wars—1967 and 1973—coupled with the booming oil economies of the Middle East have had a dramatic and far-reaching effect throughout the region and world. These and other events have acted to push immigrants from each nationality group to participate in the largest immigration wave ever to the Detroit area.[7] For the Palestinians, for

---

[7] The fact that a sizeable Arab community has existed in the area since the turn of the century permits a large number of immigrants to enter under the U.S. immigration family preference system. A "snowball" effect eventually develops; one relative sponsors another, and they in turn sponsor others, and so on until entire villages and towns are transplanted to the United States.

example, the Israeli military occupation since 1967 has produced a new set of political, economic, and social forces with which the West Bank-Gaza population has had to contend (cf. Ryan 1974; Hilal 1976; Ryan 1979; Graham-Brown 1979). Major social dislocations have occurred, forcing villagers to quit their lands and homes and travel to other countries in search of education and work. The pressures are increasing on many Palestinians to continue their flight out of the country. While the majority of Palestinians emigrate to nearby Arab countries, a growing number of Palestinians from the West Bank towns of Ramallah, El Bireh, and Beit Hanina are reuniting with kinsmen in the Detroit area.

The Lebanese population has faced a similar set of forces, particularly in southern Lebanon. Already economically underdeveloped through decades of neglect, southern Lebanon (and later all Lebanon) became a battleground where the Palestinian-Israeli conflict was fought (Sharif 1978). Unlike the Palestinians, the Arab-Israeli wars of 1967 and 1973 did not have as momentous an impact on the Lebanese population. Rather, it was the chain of events which followed which produced a major immigrant influx to the United States and other countries of the world (e.g., Greece, France, Jordan). The continuing border skirmishes between Palestinians and Israelis forced many Lebanese to flee to the major urban centers of Lebanon, especially Beirut. Border conflict was soon followed by the Lebanese civil war (1975–1978) which divided the country and further debilitated the economy. In the spring of 1978, Israel launched a major military invasion of southern Lebanon against Palestinian guerillas which culminated in the mass exodus of over 300,000 Lebanese to other parts of the country. While the civil war raged intermittently, inhabitants were fleeing the country in growing numbers. The recent Israeli invasion of Lebanon (June 1982) and the continuing military occupation of southern Lebanon has exacerbated the situation. Without a resolution to the serious problems of Lebanon and the Palestinians, it is safe to assume that Lebanese emigration will continue unabated. As in the past, some of this emigration will be channeled directly into the Detroit area. In fact, a substantial part of all Arab immigration to the Detroit area can be attributed to the Lebanese situation.

In the case of the Yemenis, continuing internal unrest after the Republican revolution of 1962 and border conflict between the two Yemens have generated a situation of political and social instability. Most of the Yemeni immigrants in the Detroit area originate from the *al-Montaqah al-Wustah* (the Central Region) in northern Yemen. It is precisely that area of the country—an area which borders both Yemens—that much of the border conflict is occurring and where the internal opposition to the existing regime appears most visible (N. Abraham, this volume; 1978). While political factors alone are not sufficient as an explanation for continuing immigration to Detroit, these factors coupled with the economic dislocations both Yemens have faced since the 1960s have acted to insure that a steady stream of inhabitants would embark in search of a livelihood elsewhere (Swanson 1979).

As for the Iraqi-Chaldeans, their country faced a revolution in 1958 and a radical change in government in 1968. The new Baathist government ushered in a set of economic and political policies which set the country on an entirely new course. Perhaps the most directly destabilizing event for the Chaldeans has been the attempt by the Kurdish minority in their area of northern Iraq to win autonomy from the central government. The war between the government and the Kurds had raged for well over a decade, until in 1970 a limited form of "autonomy" was granted to the Kurds. Fighting continued intermittently but was significantly forestalled in 1975 when the shah of Iran discontinued his support for the Kurdish insurgents after reaching an agreement with the Baghdad government over the division of the Shatt al-Arab waterway. Added to this are the disastrous effects of the Iran-Iraq war which began in September 1980 and continues to become increasingly destructive with each succeeding battle. Even with Iraq's newly acquired oil wealth, many Chaldeans have preferred to emigrate to the United States rather than confront the risks of internal instability and a raging war which threatens their area.

All in all, it is more than likely that Arab immigration to the Detroit area will continue to increase as long as political stability and sufficient economic opportunity are not present in the countries of Iraq, Yemen, Lebanon, and the occupied West Bank of Jordan. The fact that family members and kinsmen are in the Detroit area both facilitates and provides added incentive for their immigration. One factor which may intervene to significantly reduce or halt continuing Arab immigration to this area is the recent legislation which has been introduced in the U.S. Congress to make it more difficult for certain categories of family members to enter the country under the existing preference system (Keely 1982:28–65).

RESIDENTIAL PATTERNS

The residential patterns of Arab-Americans in the Detroit area are just as varied as their history of migration. Historically, the earliest Arab settlements tended to mirror those of other immigrant groups. There was a tendency to locate either in the center of the city, near the major points of commerce and residence, or to reside in ethnically mixed working-class neighborhoods near the vicinity of one's place of employment. This pattern is clearly revealed in the three earliest Arab settlements which were formed in: (1) downtown Detroit along the streets of Lafayette and East Congress; (2) near the first Ford Motor Company plant in Highland Park; and (3) near the Ford Rouge Complex in southeast Dearborn. Only one of these settlements, the "Southend" community in southeast Dearborn remains a residential area for Arab immigrants today.[8] Like other immigrants, Arabs had aspirations for upward mobility which led them to locate in other parts of the city or in the suburbs once they realized the

---

[8] For a discussion of the Southend community see the article by Abraham et al. in this volume.

necessary economic wherewithal.

Figure 1 identifies the general localities within the metropolitan area in which the largest concentrations of Arab-Americans currently reside. Several observations are apparent in the Arab-American population distribution. First, the residential settlements tend to vary greatly in density, with some communities heavily populated whereas others are widely dispersed. With the exception of the Iraqi-Chaldeans in Detroit, three of the four densest concentrations are populated by Muslims. The density of these areas is best exemplified in the case of the Southend community in Dearborn where almost 75 percent of the inhabitants are Arab-Americans, according to a recent survey (Bowker 1979). Conversely, those communities which are widely dispersed over large tracts are almost entirely composed of Arab Christians, including Lebanese, Palestinians, and Iraqi-Chaldeans, who inhabit the distant eastern, western, and northwestern suburbs of Detroit. Households in these areas are widely scattered throughout these cities and townships without central points of concentration. Some blocks may have one or two Arab-American residents; others may include dozens of Arab households. Physical dispersal should not, however, be equated with social isolation, as interaction and daily exchange continues to occur between households through a variety of other means, be it daily visiting, telephone contact, or church and club meetings (cf. Ahdab-Yehia 1970).

Second, with the exception of the Southend community of Dearborn, all of the residential areas are composed of a single nationality-religious group and exhibit a marked degree of social homogeneity. In some cases, the degree of social homogeneity extends beyond nationality and religion to include religious sect, village (or town) of origin, and social class. For example, the Palestinians located in the western suburbs are almost all from the West Bank town of Ramallah and, although of mixed religious denominations, all are Christians and consider themselves members of the "middle class" (cf. Saba 1971; Swan and Saba 1974). The Lebanese Maronites residing in Detroit's eastern suburbs are of the same sect and emigrated from the northern mountain villages of Tourza, Hasroun, Serhel, and Nahir. They, too, consider themselves solid members of the "middle class." A similar set of identifying characteristics has over the years given rise to a form of residential community consciousness. In other words, each group in a specifically delimited geographic area tends to view itself as a distinct "community." (This point will be discussed presently at greater length.)

Third, while there is very little contiguous connection between residential areas, some communities function as "primary" receiving areas for new immigrants and feed into the development of other areas. This pattern is most apparent in Dearborn, where the continuing influx of new immigrants into the Southend has created a "spillover effect" evident in new residential growth in northeastern Dearborn, southwest Detroit, and the downriver suburbs. In a recent study of northeastern Dearborn, for example, Katarsky (1980) found that almost half of his respondents had moved to

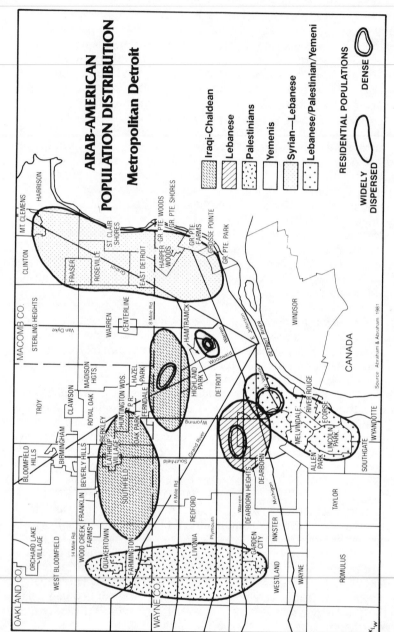

ARAB-AMERICAN POPULATION DISTRIBUTION

Metropolitan Detroit

Iraqi-Chaldean

Lebanese

Palestinians

Yemenis

Syrian—Lebanese

Lebanese/Palestinian/Yemeni

RESIDENTIAL POPULATIONS

WIDELY DISPERSED   DENSE

Source: Abraham & Abraham 1981

Figure 1

the area from the Southend, whereas the other half had arrived directly from Lebanon. These findings tend to suggest that not only is the Southend community outgrowing its current location, but that "family chain migration" remains a key means of entry for new immigrants. A similar pattern also appears to be in evidence among the two Iraqi-Chaldean communities in Detroit and Southfield (Sengstock 1982).

A detailed overview of each group's residential patterns follows.

Lebanese. The residential patterns of the Lebanese can be clearly demarcated on the basis of religion and degree of residential concentration, with the Muslims densely populating a western suburb and the Lebanese Christians widely dispersed over a number of eastern suburbs. When they first arrived in Detroit, the Lebanese Christians tended to settle residentially in the center of Detroit along the streets of Lafayette and East Congress and later on the east side of Detroit (Ahdab-Yehia 1974). As they became upwardly mobile, they located in the Grosse Pointes, St. Clair Shores, East Detroit, and Harper Woods, although they can still be found in the eastern reaches of Detroit. Recently, there has been a renewed push into the more distant suburbs of Mt. Clemens, Roseville, and Sterling Heights (Semaan 1979). The fact that the Maronite church located at Kercheval and St. Jean was recently sold and that plans are currently underway to construct a new church in northern St. Clair Shores near Sterling Heights is testimony to the wide dispersal of this group over the past 100 years, and to the establishment of a new residential center outside Detroit.

The Lebanese Muslims, on the other hand, are predominantly located in Dearborn (a suburb adjacent to Detroit), both in the "Southend" community and in a newly burgeoning community in northeastern Dearborn. Unlike their Christian counterparts, the Lebanese Muslims are densely concentrated in these two localities, although there appears to be some new movement into southwest Detroit, Dearborn Heights, as well as the downriver suburbs of Allen Park, Lincoln Park, Wyandotte and elsewhere. So densely populated is the Southend community, for example, that it is considered the most highly concentrated Arab Muslim community in North America.

Iraqi-Chaldeans. The residential patterns of the Iraqi-Chaldean community are quite similar to those of the Lebanese. Some early Chaldean immigrants resided among the Lebanese Christian counterparts in downtown Detroit during the interwar years (Sengstock 1974). As the community increased in number in the post-World War II period, a westward shift took place, with new residential growth in the vicinity of Boston and Chicago Boulevards between Woodward and Hamilton Avenues. Other residential centers were also being established during this time in the Seven Mile Road and Livernois area and near the Woodward-State Fair grounds area (Sengstock 1967; 1974). Today the majority of Chaldeans can be found in two distinct localities: (1) in the vicinity of the Woodward-State Fair grounds area; and (2) in the northern and northwestern suburbs of Southfield and Oak Park, with new developments emerging in the surrounding communities of Bloomfield Hills, Sterling Heights, Warren, and Troy.

Palestinians. Like the Lebanese, the Palestinian community can also be easily differentiated internally on the basis of religion and residential density. The Palestinian residents of the "Southend" community in Dearborn are overwhelmingly Muslim and highly concentrated in this small physical enclave. They originate from two villages in the West Bank, El-Bireh and Beit Hanina, and most are solidly situated within the working class. As of late, this group has been moving into southwestern Detroit, that area bounded by Michigan Avenue to the north, Jefferson Avenue to the south, West Grand Boulevard to the east and the city of Dearborn to the west.

Unlike their Southend counterparts, the Palestinian Christians are predominantly located (and widely dispersed) in the western suburbs of Farmington, Farmington Hills, Livonia, Westland, and Garden City. They originate from a single town in the West Bank, namely, Ramallah, and are predominantly members of the middle class. Recently there has been some movement into other surrounding communities (e.g., Bloomfield Hills), although no clearly established trends are as yet discernable.

Yemenis. Generally speaking, the Yemeni immigrants tend to reside near their places of employment. Two major residential centers have emerged over the years which constitute approximately 80 percent of the Yemeni population, according to a recent study (N. Abraham, this volume). A large part of the community is located in the Southend along with the Lebanese and Palestinians. The Southend community is, of course, within walking distance of the vast Ford Rouge Complex. A second small community has emerged in the vicinity of Chrysler's Dodge Main Plant along the Hamtramck/Detroit boundary. Other small enclaves of Yemeni workers can be found near Carl's Chop House (a well-known local restaurant) along Grand River and the John C. Lodge Expressway, near the Ford plant in Flatrock and near a foundry in Coldwater, Michigan. Over the past decade or so, movement from the Southend community into southwest Detroit has been growing.

CHANGING ARAB IDENTITY

The identity of Arab immigrants and their offspring has evolved over the course of this century in keeping with the changing political realities of the Arab world. Those immigrants who arrived prior to World War I from the Ottoman province of Greater Syria (including Lebanon, Syria, Jordan, and Palestine) tended to identify themselves as Syrians.[9] As the Arab countries gained independence, incoming immigrants would identify themselves according to the nation-state from which they originated.

[9] Immigration officials at Ellis Island and other entry points would classify these same individuals as "Turks," "Syrians," "Arabs," and sometimes mistakenly as "Armenians" (Naff, this volume).

Hence, the former Syrian immigrants now became "Lebanese," "Jordanians," and so on in accordance with the division of the Middle Eastern states into separate political entities. This tendency is still very much in evidence today.

Changes in identity have also occurred from time to time to transcend identities and broaden them. During the Nasserite era (1952–1970), for example, many Arab immigrants identified with the pan-Arab nationalist movement (Elkholy 1966). The 1950s and 1960s were years of intense nationalist sentiment, a period during which identifying as Arabs first took precedence over one's identification with country of origin (Wigle and Abraham 1974). An individual owed his/her primary allegiance to the larger Arab nation, toward the unity of the Arab countries and not to his/her home government. As Nasser's plans for Arab unity floundered with the break-up of the United Arab Republic between Syria and Egypt (1958–1961), pan-Arab identity weakened and all but vanished following the defeat of the Arab states in the 1967 Arab-Israeli war. Most Arab immigrants have returned to identifying solely with their home countries while verbally indicating their approval of notions of greater Arab unity.

While pan-Arabism remains latent among most Arab immigrants, three distinct identities have recently surfaced (or resurfaced) to characterize the community. These include: Palestinian nationalism, pan-Islam and certain, for lack of a better term, provincial identities. Palestinian nationalism is perhaps the best known because of the constant media attention given to the Palestine problem. The revival of Palestinian nationalism is generally predicated on the failure of pan-Arabism in the 1967 Arab-Israeli war and the emergence of the Palestinian guerillas and PLO (Quandt, et al. 1973). After the dismemberment of Palestine in 1948, many Palestinians began to identify with the country in which they were residing or with pan-Arab (or other nationalist) tendencies. Palestinians became Jordanians in some instances, or Lebanese-Palestinians, Kuwaiti-Palestinians, and so on. The rise of the Palestine resistance movement transformed the situation radically. Palestinians today identify first as Palestinians even while holding the citizenship and passport of another state. Detroit's Palestinian community has followed the pattern of Palestinians all over the world. In this way, Palestinian nationalism is very similar to other resurgent nationalisms (e.g., Irish, Eritrean) of oppressed peoples striving for national self-determination.

Pan-Islam is another tendency which surfaced recently and appears to be gaining strength in some quarters of the community. While a pan-Islamic tendency has always been present to some degree, its renewed vitality emerged during the struggle to overthrow the shah of Iran (1978). Muslims throughout the world identified with the popular movement of the Iranian people, although many disagreed vehemently with the Khomeini regime's excesses. Some newly arrived Arab immigrants tend to identify as Muslims first and only secondarily as Arabs. To a great extent this phenomenon is limited to recent immigrants and has not taken hold among second- or third-generation members of the community. Pan-Islamic adherents have been active in reviving mosques, their memberships, and activities as a focal point of community life (Haddad 1979).

Finally, there remains in some cases a long-standing tendency for some members of the community to continue to identify in a provincial manner, according to the religious minority or ethnic group of which they were members in the Arab world. The Chaldeans are a good example of this tendency. They are a distinct ethnic group in Iraq and are recognized as such by the Iraqi government and society. While many newly arrived immigrants have been influenced by pan-Arab nationalist currents, many of the early immigrants and their offspring continue to cling to their Chaldean-*only* identity (Sengstock 1982:105–116). The Lebanese Maronites tend to follow a similar pattern even though the Maronites constitute the dominant economic and political group in Lebanon, while the Muslims remain the majority in numbers. The Lebanese civil war (1975–1978) and intermittent conflict between sectarian groups has divided the Lebanese and re-ignited a Maronite identity and in some cases even a "Phoenician" identity. Generally speaking, most Lebanese, whether Muslim or Christian, tend to identify as Lebanese first. The extent to which any of these provincial identities will remain intact, gain greater force, or vanish will depend to a large extent on events in the Arab world, and the manner in which local community leaders respond to those events. In cases where the leadership has taken sides, leaders have attempted to impose their views on the institutions and organizations they control or influence (e.g., church, mosque, social club, etc.).

Notwithstanding the diverse number of identities among Arab immigrants and their offspring, there continues to exist a general tendency to identify with the Arab world and Arab culture. The emergence of an "Arab-American" (or "American-Arab") identity is a recent phenomenon and one with which most Arab immigrants and their offspring appear comfortable. This identity allows its members to emphasize the common features of their Arab history, culture, and language, on the one side, and those common threads which bind them in their American experience on the other. The emergence of a number of Arab-American organizations at the national level has also acted to reinforce shared characteristics as well as a common identity.[10] Added to this is an *imposed* identity, oftentimes negative and stereotypic, which tends to cast all Arabs in the same category without distinction.[11] Hence, a number of forces are currently at work unifying the diverse group of Arabs into a single community irrespective of their many differences and occasionally contending identities.

---

[10]These organizations include: The Association of Arab-American University Graduates, formed in 1967; the National Association of Arab-Americans, established in 1972; the Palestine Congress of North America, founded in 1979; and the American-Arab Anti-Discrimination Committee, established in 1980.

[11]For a review of the Arab stereotype and its impact on Arab-Americans, see Shaheen 1980a; 1980b; 1982; Slade 1981.

A MONOLITHIC COMMUNITY?

To a certain extent, it is possible and even convenient to speak of a single and nearly monolithic Arab-American community. In other respects, particularly from a sociological perspective, such a designation may appear premature, or as an attempt to simplify a very complex social reality through overgeneralization. While all Arab-Americans share a common cultural heritage, language, and history, they have not developed into a *single* community in the strict sense of the word. Rather, it would be more accurate to speak of *several* almost self-contained and thriving Arab communities (or subcommunities) in the Detroit area. These communities are separated by geography, by their religious institutions (e.g., churches, mosques) and formal organizations (e.g., social clubs, service organizations, etc.) and identify as separate communities. Hence one can speak of an Iraqi-Chaldean community, a Palestinian, Lebanese, and Yemeni community. Further distinctions can be made within these national communities on the basis of religion and occasionally social class. Frequently reference is made to a Lebanese Christian community and similarly to a Lebanese Muslim community for instance. Each community inhabits a different geographical area (see Figure 1), the Christians the eastern suburbs and the Muslims the western suburbs of Detroit. Each group also maintains separate institutions and organizations which rarely bring the two communities into direct contact with each other. A similar distinction can be made with reference to the Palestinians, although the points of demarcation are not as rigid. While geography is a critical variable in defining a community, it alone is not sufficient. Even though communities are isolated geographically and tend to establish separate institutions which promote a distinct set of social interaction patterns, overlap and exchange does exist between communities. Other forces are at work moving communities toward greater cooperation and unity.

Greater community cohesiveness and unity among Arab-Americans is emerging at two distinct levels: self-awareness and organization. Notwithstanding the real differences between segments of the community a number of objective factors have acted to fuse the community. A common cultural heritage, language, and history have already been mentioned as shared characteristics. More importantly, the members of the separate communities or subcommunities tend to identify as part of the larger Arab-American community of Detroit even while maintaining narrower lines of distinction among themselves. This community-wide identification provides many with a sense of pride and even power as the size of the community grows and Arab-Americans become more visible in the larger society. Recognition that Arab-Americans can no longer be neglected as in the past has provided the community with a sense of belonging to a group with common interests and goals. How those interests and goals are defined is another matter altogether. The fact remains, however, that Arab-Americans throughout the area tend to respond favorably to the concept of a larger Arab-American community to which all belong and

102 Sameer Y. Abraham

are desirous of promoting through shared institutions and organizations.

Three local organizations have emerged over the past decade in an attempt to merge resources and energies, and meet the needs of the community as a whole. These organizations include: ACCESS (the Arab Community Center for Economic and Social Services), ACSSC (the Arab-Chaldean Social Services Council), and ADC (the American-Arab Anti-Discrimination Committee).[12] As their names suggest, both ACCESS and ACSSC are social service organizations dedicated to providing assistance to needy community members and newly arrived immigrants and their families. Both organizations have received community-wide acceptance and make their services available to all sectors of the Arab-American population throughout the metropolitan area. In each case, support and recognition has also been forthcoming from the larger society. Owing to the nature of their missions, these organizations have been able to transcend national, religious, and provincial differences between Arab subcommunities. The ADC has followed a similar pattern of development, although it is dedicated solely to defending the rights of Arab-Americans and combatting the negative and often derogatory stereotypes and prejudice directed at Arabs and their cultural heritage.[13] What all three organizations share in common is their concern for all Arab-Americans and the common interests which bind them together. In a real sense, these three organizations can be considered *supra-organizations* (or pan-community organizations) which tend to give expression to the larger identity and interests of the community as a whole. As these organizations have developed over the years, a complementary development has occurred at the level of community leadership. While each subcommunity has its own leaders (e.g., religious, business, political), there is a growing tendency for these and other leaders to play a wider role in coping with events and problems which affect the larger community. And although no single leader or leadership is readily identifiable, the fact is that a number of leaders are widely recognized as spokesmen for the community and its interests.

CONCLUSION

Detroit's Arab-American community is extremely diverse in character. Unlike other Arab-American communities in the United States,[14] Detroit's community is socially heterogeneous in many respects. Contrary to expectation, it does not consist of a single nationality or religious group but is composed of four major nationality groups with a multitude of

---

[12] ADC is a national organization with a regional office and Greater Detroit Chapter located in downtown Detroit.

[13] ADC's official statement of purpose is found in "Arabs: The Convenient Scapegoat" presented by former Senator James Abourezk at the founding meeting of ADC on May 3, 1980 in Washington, D.C.

[14] Examples of communities which appear more homogeneous in character are given by Smith (1981:141–176), Aruri (1969:50–66), and Kassess (1970).

religious affiliations. Differences also appear with regard to each group's time of arrival as well as the size each group has attained. Recent events in the Middle East have greatly complicated the migratory picture and have given newly arrived immigrants a wide assortment of reasons for migrating. Even the downturn in the state and local economies does not appear to be decreasing the flow of Arab immigration into the Detroit area. Indications are that the community will continue to grow at an accelerated rate into the forseeable future. As these immigrants arrive they tend to settle with or near established kinsmen, co-villagers, and countrymen, in distinct geographic areas. The geographic distance between nationality/religious groups has given rise to a corresponding set of separate social institutions and organizations throughout the area. Consequently, it is possible to point to a number of distinct and oftentimes close-knit Arab subcommunities which are basically self-contained. The separation between groups appears in the form of estrangement and occasionally is manifested in competition and rivalry. Counterpressures also exist toward greater cooperation, unity, and fusion between groups, especially at the level of identity and organization building. It is in this context that the diversity of the community exists within—and is undergirded by—a sense of unity and commonality.

A shared language, history, and cultural heritage binds the various Arab subcommunities together in a very broad way. These elements constitute the basis for a common identification and understanding. They allow Arab immigrants from different parts of the Arab world (and their American-born descendants) to empathize with one another, to communicate easily about the past, present, and future. Much of the communication today is over the events in the Arab world and how those events impinge on the lives of Arab-Americans here. To a great extent the fate of the Arab world is mixed in with the fate of Arab-Americans. As the Arab world emerges as a region of influence or falters, the extent of one's identification, pride, and self-esteem will vary correspondingly. Other factors have also surfaced to draw Arab-Americans closer together. There is a growing attempt to transcend differences and to work for common goals and interests. The organization of social service organizations and local chapters of national organizations (ADC, AAUG, etc.) concerned with the treatment of Arab-Americans is a case in point. It is likely that these trends toward unification will continue and that eventually Arab-Americans will take concerted action at the local level to express more forcefully their interests in the political arena. While the community remains diverse in character, a deeper structural unity has developed, built on a common cultural heritage, that has significant social and political implications for the future.

REFERENCES

Abraham, Nabeel
1977 Detroit's Yemeni Workers. *MERIP Reports* 57:3-9.

1978 National and Local Politics: A Study of Political Conflict in
      the Yemeni Immigrant Community of Detroit, Michigan.
      Ph.D. dissertation, University of Michigan, Ann Arbor.

Abraham, Sameer Y.
1975 Arabic Speaking Communities of Southeastern Dearborn: A
      General Overview. Mimeo. University of Wisconsin, Madison.

1981 A Survey of the Arab-American Community in Metropolitan
      Detroit. In *The Arab World and Arab-Americans: Understand-
      ing a Neglected Minority.* Sameer Y. Abraham and Nabeel
      Abraham, eds. pp. 23-24. Detroit: Wayne State University,
      Center for Urban Studies.

Ahdab-Yehia, May
1970 Some General Characteristics of the Lebanese Maronite Com-
      munity in Detroit. M.A. thesis, Wayne State University,
      Detroit.

Arif-Ghayur, M.
1981 Muslims in the United States: Settlers and Visitors. *The Annals
      of the American Academy of Political and Social Science* 454
      (March):150-163.

Aruri, Naseer
1969 The Arab-American Community of Springfield, Massachu-
      setts. In *The Arab Americans: Studies in Assimilation.* Elaine
      C. Hagopian and Ann Paden, eds. pp. 50-66. Wilmette, Ill.:
      Medina University Press International.

Aswad, Barbara C., ed.
1974 *Arabic Speaking Communities in American Cities.* New York:
      Center for Migration Studies and the Association of Arab-
      American University Graduates, Inc.

Bowker, Joan P.
1979 Health and Social Service Needs Assessment Survey. Mimeo.
      Dearborn: University of Michigan, Dearborn.

Doctoroff, A. M.
1978 The Chaldeans: A New Ethnic Group in Detroit's Suburban
      High Schools. Ph.D. dissertation, University of Michigan,
      Ann Arbor.

Elkholy, Abdo A.
1966 *The Arab Moslems in the United States: Religion and Assimilation.* New Haven: College and University Press.

1969 The Arab-Americans: Nationalism and Traditional Preservations. In *The Arab Americans: Studies in Assimilation.* Elaine C. Hagopian and Ann Paden, eds. pp. 3-17. Wilmette, Ill.: Medina University Press International.

Graham-Brown, Sarah
1979 The Structural Impact of Israeli Colonization. *MERIP Reports* 74 (January):9-20.

Haddad, Yvonne
1979 The Muslim Experience in the United States. *The Link* 2(4):1-11.

Hilal, Jamil
1976 Class Transformation in the West Bank and Gaza. *MERIP Reports* 53 (December):3-15.

Hitti, Philip
1924 *Syrians in America.* New York: George H. Doran.

Houghton, Louise S.
1911 The Syrians in the United States. *Survey.* No. 1 (July):480-495; no. 2 (August):647-665; no. 3 (September):786-802; and no. 4 (October):957-968.

Jaafari, Lafi Ibrahim
1973 The Brain Drain to the United States: The Migration of Jordanian and Palestinian Professionals and Students. *Journal of Palestine Studies* 3(1):119-131.

Kassess, Assad S.
1970 The People of Ramallah: A People of Christian Arab Heritage. Ph.D. dissertation, Florida State University, Tallahassee.

Katarsky, Anthony P.
1980 Family Ties and the Growth of an Arabic Community in Northeast Dearborn, Michigan. M.A. thesis, Wayne State University, Detroit.

Keely, Charles
1982 Immigration and the American Future. In *Ethnic Relations in America.* Lance Liebman, ed. pp. 28-65. Englewood Cliffs, N.J.: Prentice-Hall.

Mayer, Albert J.
   1951 Ethnic Groups in Detroit: 1951. Unpublished paper, Department of Sociology and Anthropology, Wayne State University, Detroit.

Mehdi, Beverlee T.
   1978 *The Arabs in America.* Dobbs Ferry, N.Y.: Oceana Publications, Inc.

Naff, Alixa
   1980 Arabs. In *Harvard Encyclopedia of American Ethnic Groups.* Stephan Thernstrom, ed. pp. 128-136. Cambridge, Mass.: The Belknap Press of Harvard University Press.

Quandt, William, Fuad Jabber, and Ann Mosley Lesch
   1973 *The Politics of Palestinian Nationalism.* Berkeley: University of California Press.

Rankin, Lois
   1939 Detroit Nationality Groups. *Michigan History Magazine* 29 (Spring):240-246.

Ryan, Sheila
   1974 Israeli Economic Policy in the Occupied Areas: Foundations of a New Imperialism. *MERIP Reports.* No. 24 (January):3-24.

   1979 Political Consequences of Occupation. *MERIP Reports.* No. 74 (January):3-8.

Saba, Leila
   1971 The Social Assimilation of the Ramallah Community Residing in Detroit. M.A. thesis, Wayne State University, Detroit.

Schwartz, Jonathan
   1974 Henry Ford's Melting Pot. In *Immigrants and Migrants: The Detroit Ethnic Experience.* David W. Hartman, ed. pp. 252-260. Detroit: New University Thought Publishing.

Semaan, Anthony
   1979 The Patterns and Processes of Settlement of Detroit's East Side Lebanese-Maronite Community, 1896-1979. Mimeo. Wayne State University, Detroit.

Sengstock, Mary C.
   1967 Maintenance of Social Interaction Patterns in an Ethnic Group. Ph.D. dissertation, Washington University, St. Louis.

1970   Telkaif, Baghdad, Detroit: Chaldeans Blend Three Cultures. *Michigan History* 54:293–310.

1974   Iraqi Christians in Detroit: An Analysis of an Ethnic Occupation. In *Arabic Speaking Communities in American Cities.* Barbara C. Aswad, ed. pp. 21–38. New York: Center for Migration Studies and AAUG, Inc.

1982   *Chaldean Americans: Changing Conceptions of Ethnic Identity.* New York: Center for Migration Studies.

Shaheen, Jack G.
1980   The Arab Stereotype on Television. *The Link* 13 (2:April-May):1–13.

1981   The Influence of the Arab Stereotype on American Children. In *The Arab World and Arab-Americans: Understanding a Neglected Minority.* Sameer Y. Abraham and Nabeel Abraham, eds. pp. 53–58. Detroit: Wayne State University, Center for Urban Studies.

1982   The Arab Image in the American Mass Media. *American-Arab Affairs.* No. 2(Fall):89–96.

Sharif, Hasan
1978   South Lebanon: Its History and Geopolitics. *Special Report,* No. 2, pp. 9–34. Belmont, Mass.: Association of Arab-American University Graduates, Inc.

Slade, Shelley
1981   The Image of the Arab in America: Analysis of a Poll on American Attitudes. *The Middle East Journal* 35 (2:Spring): 143–160.

Smith, Marlene K.
1981   The Arabic-Speaking Communities in Rhode Island: A Survey of the Syrian and Lebanese Communities. In *Hidden Minorities: The Persistence of Ethnicity in American Life.* Joan H. Rollins, ed. pp. 141–176. Washington, D.C.: University Press of America.

Suleiman, Michael
1969   The New Arab-American Community. In *The Arab Americans: Studies in Assimilation.* Elaine C. Hagopian and Ann Paden, eds. pp. 37–49. Wilmette, Ill.: Medina University Press International.

Swan, Charles, and Leila Saba
    1974 The Migration of a Minority. In *Arabic Speaking Communities in American Cities.* Barbara C. Aswad, ed. pp. 85–110. New York: Center for Migration Studies and AAUG, Inc.

Swanson, Jon
    1979 *Emigration and Economic Development: The Case of the Yemen Arab Republic.* Boulder, Colo.: Westview Press.

Tannous, Afif
    1943 Acculturation of an Arab-Syrian Community in the Deep South. *American Sociological Review* 8 (3):264–271.

United Community Services
    1975 Arabic-Speaking Peoples of Metropolitan Detroit: A Community Profile. Mimeo. Detroit: Research Department, United Community Services of Metropolitan Detroit.

Wasfi, Atif A.
    1964 Dearborn Arab-Moslem Community: A Study of Acculturation. Ph.D. dissertation, Michigan State University, East Lansing.

Wigle, Laurel, and Sameer Y. Abraham
    1974 Arab Nationalism in America: The Dearborn Arab Community. In *Immigrants and Migrants: The Detroit Ethnic Experience.* David W. Hartman, ed. pp. 279–302. Detroit: New University Thought Publishing Co.

Zaghel, Ali S.
    1976 Changing Patterns of Identification Among Arab-Americans: The Palestinian Ramallites and the Christian Syrian-Lebanese. Ph.D. dissertation, Northwestern University, Evanston, Ill.

ABSTRACT

The small but growing community of Yemeni immigrants in the Detroit metropolitan area arrived mainly during the 1960s and 1970s. The community is, for the most part, composed of unaccompanied males who emigrated primarily for economic reasons. This population divides into two basic types —settlers and non-settlers. The settlers intend to establish a permanent residence in the United States. Many of them came from the city of Aden in South Yemen. They are in the minority. The majority of Yemeni immigrants are non-settlers with rural backgrounds. After working in the United States a number of years and accumulating funds, these immigrants plan to re-establish permanent residence in Yemen and enjoy social mobility and prosperity there. The non-settlers consciously minimize their interaction with the host society and maintain strong social and economic links with the home society.

The Yemeni Immigrant Community of Detroit: Background, Emigration, and Community Life

by Nabeel Abraham

This study provides an ethnographic account of the Yemeni immigrant community of Detroit, Michigan. Data used in this paper are derived from field research undertaken by the author in the eighteen-month period extending from September 1975 to March 1977.[1] The account begins with a description of Yemeni immigrants in Detroit, their occupational patterns, residential distribution, and social environment. Discussion then turns to the immigrants' background in Yemen—areas of origin, socioeconomic status, emigration patterns, and motivations. Finally, a description of immigrant lifestyles and community life is presented within the context of the immigrants' overall goals and their attitudes toward the host society.

As the discussion reveals, there are, in general, two types of Yemeni immigrants in Detroit: a minority which favors permanency and assimilation in the host society, and a majority which opposes assimilation in favor of permanent return to Yemen. This study demonstrates that each perspective leads to radically different attitudes and behaviors toward the host society as well as toward the home country. In the case of the assimilationist minority, their perspective sets them apart from the immigrant community. The perspective of the non-assimilationist majority, on the other hand, leads to a preoccupation with events in Yemen, as opposed to events in the host society.

There are an estimated 5,000 to 6,000 Yemeni immigrants in the Detroit metropolitan area.[2] A small Yemeni immigrant community has existed in

---

[1] This article is excerpted from the author's doctoral dissertation (1978:16-55).

[2] Unless otherwise stated, all estimates given in this paper are the researcher's own

the area since the early 1900s. The bulk of today's community, however, is composed of first-generation immigrants who arrived during the late 1960s and early 1970s. While most immigrants are married, unaccompanied males represent over 90 percent of the population, as married immigrants tend to immigrate without their families. Most immigrants are in their twenties and thirties, although boys as young as twelve years old and many men over forty can also be found among the immigrants. With notable exceptions, the population is generally illiterate or semiliterate, unskilled peasants, who have little or no knowledge of English.

OCCUPATIONS

Over 90 percent of the immigrants are unskilled manual workers; the remainder includes a dozen or so grocers, some landlords and skilled workers, and a handful of functionaries. The latter two groups are mostly British-trained Adenis (see below). The unskilled manual laborers are primarily employed in the auto plants and related industrial and manufacturing enterprises as production-line workers. The largest concentration of Yemeni workers in any single factory is probably that of Chrysler's Hamtramck Assembly Plant (known locally as "Dodge Main"), where they are estimated to number 1,000–1,500 out of a total work force of 10,000 (Figure 1). Several hundred Yemenis are also employed at the Ford River Rouge Complex in Dearborn (Figure 1), where an estimated 2,000 Arab workers are employed (Georgakas and Surkin 1975:78). Smaller concentrations of Yemeni workers are employed at Chrysler's Jefferson Assembly, Mack Avenue Stamping, and Lynch Road Assembly Plants, all located on Detroit's east side (Figure 1).[3]

A growing number of Yemenis work as busboys, dishwashers, and janitors in numerous restaurants and hotels scattered throughout the Detroit area. These workers are for the most part recent arrivals and young boys, two groups who find it difficult to obtain jobs in the better paying, but economically hard-pressed auto industry. Another 150–200 Yemenis work as seafarers on Great Lakes cargo ships. According to one estimate, Yemenis account for one-fifth of all seafarers on the Great Lakes (Morse 1977). Finally, there exists a very small number of Yemeni skilled workers in Detroit, most of whom have encountered great difficulty in gaining

---

for 1976. The estimates were made in consultation with the heads of the three Yemeni immigrant associations then in existence, and with other persons having extensive contact with the Yemeni community (e.g., union and company officials, community social workers).

[3]The distribution of Yemenis in the auto plants has changed considerably since the field research was undertaken. For example, the Dodge Main Plant is no longer operating, and other factories mentioned here (e.g., Mack Avenue Stamping and sections of the Ford River Rouge Complex) have been reorganized and restructured to take advantage of newly introduced capital-intensive technology (cf. N. Abraham 1977).

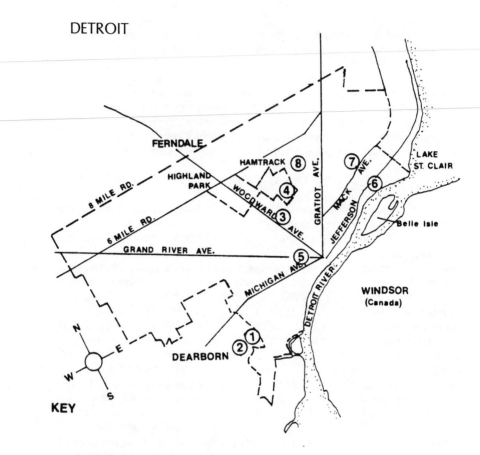

DETROIT

1. The Southend/Dearborn Yemeni Community
2. Ford River Rouge Complex
3. Detroit Yemeni Community
4. Dodge Main Complex
5. Carl's Chop House '
6. Chrysler's Jefferson Assembly Plant
7. Chrysler's Mack Avenue Stamping Plant
8. Chrysler's Eldon Avenue Complex

Figure 1. Location Map of Yemeni Residential Areas and Places of Employment in Detroit (Modified from Georgakas and Surkin 1975:vi).

admittance into their respective trades.

RESIDENTIAL PATTERNS

As a general rule, Yemeni immigrants tend to reside near their place of employment, which permits them to walk to work. Consequently, two large Yemeni residential concentrations have sprung up in the Detroit area. One is located in the Southend area of Dearborn in the vicinity of the Ford River Rouge Complex, and the other in the vicinity of the Chrysler Dodge Main Plant (see Figure 1). These two residential settlements account for the bulk of the Yemeni population. In addition, several smaller residential concentrations, ranging from 30 to 100 persons, are found in the environs of several Chrysler auto plants on Detroit's east side, and of a major restaurant in downtown Detroit (Figure 1). During the past few years, two new Yemeni residential groups have sprung up outside Detroit near a Ford auto plant in Flatrock, Michigan, and a foundry in Coldwater, Michigan. Both groups number no more than 50–100 individuals. This study focuses on the two large Yemeni residential settlements (hereinafter known as the "Dearborn" and the "Detroit" communities).

THE DEARBORN YEMENI COMMUNITY

The largest concentration of Yemeni immigrants in Detroit is located in the Southend of Dearborn, a suburb of Detroit (see the article by Abraham, et al. in this volume). The Southend is a heterogeneous neighborhood of predominantly Arab immigrants (Lebanese, Palestinians, Yemenis), southern whites, and the remnants of an older community of Italian and Eastern European immigrants (Aswad 1974:55). The Southend is reputedly the largest and oldest Arab Muslim community in North America (Elkholy 1966:28). In total, some 5,000–7,000 persons dwell in this ghetto-like enclave, which is situated between the mammoth Ford River Rouge Complex on the west, railroad tracks and a large gravel and asphalt complex to the north, and a cemetery and park to the south and east. Aswad has described the neighborhood in the following terms:

> The houses are of varying styles, most are of frame, brick or stucko [sic] in the thirty and forty year age bracket. They are primarily one or two family houses. Most have neat lawns and many have gardens. There are also a few multiple dwellings. Commercial establishments consisting largely of Middle Eastern restaurants and coffeehouses, small grocery stores and other small businesses line Dix Road, a road which serves as a north-south division for the community. (1974:56, 58)

Until the late 1960s, the Southend was dominated by the Lebanese, and to a lesser extent the Palestinians. In 1959, Elkholy (1966:27) found the majority of Detroit's estimated 6,000 Arab Muslims (mostly Lebanese) residing in the Southend. Over a decade later, the Lebanese population in the neighborhood seems to have decreased as a result of an exodus of second- and third-generation Lebanese Americans. In a 1971 survey of the Southend, Aswad (1974:61) found the Lebanese constituting only one quarter of the total Southend population (estimated at 5,000 persons), and just below half of the Arabic-speaking population. The decline of the Lebanese and other well-established Southend ethnic populations was further exacerbated by the city of Dearborn's attempts to raze the neighborhood under the guise of urban renewal.[4] This out-migration coupled with a steady rise in Yemeni immigration into Detroit in the late 1960s and early 1970s radically altered the ethnic composition of the Southend. By the late 1970s, the Yemenis, who numbered 2,000–3,000 persons, became the most visible group in the Southend. On any given day tens of Yemenis could be found standing in front of the coffeehouses and restaurants that line Dix Avenue.

The emerging predominance of Yemenis in the Southend is reflected in their growing control of many local businesses which were once owned by Lebanese and Palestinian immigrants. For example, out of the twenty grocery stores and coffeehouses found in the Southend, half are now owned by Yemenis. Another sign of Yemeni influence in the neighborhood is found in the Islamic (Sunni) Mosque, the oldest Arab community institution in the Southend. Built by Lebanese immigrants in the late 1930s, the Dearborn Islamic Mosque is today frequented by a mostly Yemeni congregation. Yemeni control of the mosque was consolidated in autumn 1976, when a Yemeni religious sheikh, trained and sponsored by Saudi Arabia, arrived in Detroit to assume the leadership of the congregation. In recent years Lebanese Muslims of both Shia and Sunni Islamic sects have tended to affiliate with the (Shia) Islamic Center of Detroit, located several miles outside the Southend in East Dearborn.[5] Home ownership is the only area in which Yemenis have not made major inroads, preferring instead to be renters. Nevertheless, it is possible to discern a small but growing trend of home purchases by Yemenis, especially over the past few years. These houses are usually multiple dwelling units which are rented to other Yemenis.

---

[4]For a detailed discussion of this subject see Aswad 1974.

The decline of the Lebanese population in the Southend appears to have been reversed in the past several years as a result of the Lebanese civil war (1975–76), which brought a new wave of Lebanese immigrants to the Southend.

[5]A Shia Islamic mosque, the Hashmite Club, located on Dix Avenue several blocks from the Sunni mosque, no longer functions as a place of worship. Built by Lebanese immigrants in 1933, the Hashmite Club was replaced as a Shia place of worship in 1964 by the Islamic Center in East Dearborn (cf., Elkholy 1966; S. Abraham 1975, 1981). The Hashmite Club continued to function as a community meeting hall until it was partially destroyed by fire in early 1977. It was razed several years later.

THE DETROIT YEMENI COMMUNITY

There are approximately 1,000 to 2,000 Yemeni immigrants living in the vicinity of Chrysler's Dodge Main Plant on Detroit's near east side.[6] The majority work at the Chrysler plant, while several hundred are employed at other auto plants and restaurants scattered throughout the east side and downtown areas. The Detroit Yemeni community was established in the late 1960s, when a small group of Yemenis from the Dearborn community started working at Dodge Main. Part of the impetus to reside in the neighborhood stemmed from the desire to avoid commuting back and forth to work from the Southend, a distance of some ten miles. Nearby residence also provided many Yemenis seeking employment with ready access to jobs which were becoming increasingly available at Dodge Main in the late 1960s.

The majority of Yemenis in the Detroit community live within walking distance of the Chrysler plant. The plant itself is located in the city of Hamtramck, a heavily Polish-American enclave situated within the city of Detroit. The largest number of Yemenis live immediately south of the plant in a predominantly black neighborhood, which is in Detroit. Many other Yemenis also live in the area immediately north of the plant in the city of Hamtramck. Unlike the Dearborn Yemeni community, which is part of a larger Arabic-speaking community, the Detroit Yemenis are in a number of ways culturally isolated. There are no mosques, Arabic restaurants, or coffeehouses in the neighborhood. Instead, the Yemeni Arab Association of Detroit (YAA), located a half-mile south of the Chrysler plant, doubles as a coffeehouse and meeting hall for the entire Yemeni community.[7] Individual Yemenis also own and operate four grocery stores in Hamtramck. During the five year period of 1971–1976 Yemenis purchased 75 to 100 homes, mostly in Hamtramck. The majority, however, tend to be renters like their counterparts in Dearborn.

IMMIGRANT BACKGROUND IN YEMEN

Detroit's Yemeni immigrants come from the Yemen Arab Republic (North Yemen) and the People's Democratic Republic of Yemen (South Yemen), which are both located in the southwest corner of the Arabian Peninsula (see Figure 2). Over 90 percent of the immigrant population is

---

[6]Since the recent closing of Chrysler's Dodge Main Plant, it is supposed that the Detroit Yemeni community described below has suffered a serious loss of numbers. Exact data on recent demographic shifts in the community are not available.

[7]At the time of field research, a prayer-room annex was under construction on the second floor of the YAA building. This building was subsequently destroyed in the razing of the Poletown neighborhood to make way for a new General Motors automotive plant in 1982. The Yemeni Arab Association has subsequently relocated to another building in the town of Hamtramck, several miles north of its former location.

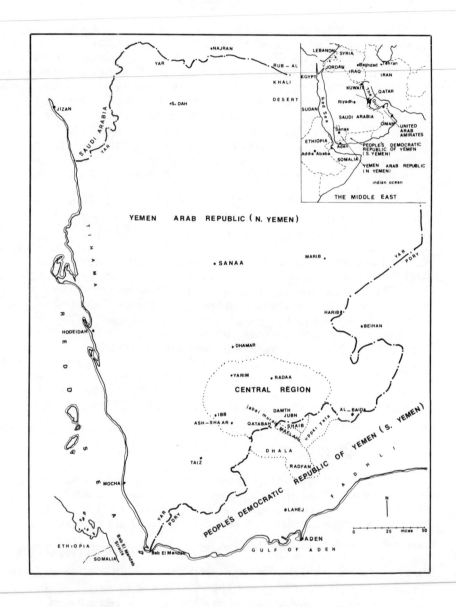

Figure 2. Map of North and South Yemen (Modified from Schmidt, 1968:10–11; Inset modified from Halliday, 1975:2).

of rural origin. The majority are said to come from middle and small land-owning peasant families. The former group is defined by the immigrants as those owning enough land to provide subsistence all year long, while members of the latter are said to own only enough land for about four months of subsistence. There are, in addition, a small number of immigrants from large landowning families. They are said to own more land than is required for subsistence. In such cases, surplus lands are rented to small peasants, who retain half of the harvest. In addition to the land-owning peasants, there exist a very small number of immigrants from the landless class. This group comes from the "service class" (i.e., barbers, butchers, musicians) who are considered to be of inferior social rank to the landowning peasantry.

Immigrants with urban backgrounds come exclusively from the South Yemeni city of Aden. In contrast to their rural northern and southern counterparts, the Adenis are a relatively small group, numbering 150 to 200 persons. Before emigrating to Detroit, the Adenis worked as skilled laborers, technicians, merchants, teachers, and government functionaries.

The Northerners account for 70–80 percent of the Yemeni immigrant population in Detroit. They come almost exclusively from an area known as the "Central Region" (*al-Montaqah al-Wustah*), located in the south central part of North Yemen (Figure 2). There are two provinces in the Central Region from which the immigrants originate—Liwa Ibb and Liwa al-Baida. Those immigrants from Liwa Ibb come mostly from ash-Shaar, al-Oud, Baadan, Ammar, and Murais.[8] Those immigrants from Liwa al-Baida come mostly from al-Hagagh, al-Reyashiyah, al-Rubaatein, al-Hubayshiya, and Malah. The Central Region is a predominantly Shafei (Sunni Muslim) area, though many Zeidis (Shia Muslims) are also found living there.[9] In general, more Shafeis are found in Liwa Ibb, while more

---

[8] I have refrained from calling these areas "villages," as the immigrants employ political categories that denote units larger than villages when referring to their place of origin in Yemen. As far as can be determined, these names designate the category *mikhlaf* (pl. *makhalif*). A *mikhlaf* is an administrative unit headed by a "tribal sheikh." A *mikhlaf* embraces a number of *izal* (sing. *izla*), which are said to be a number of villages that act as a mutual defense unit. A number of *makhalif* form a *nahiyah* (pl. *nawahin*) or "subdistrict," and a number of *nawahin* in turn form a *qadaa* (pl. *aqdiya*) or "district"; an unknown number of *aqdiya* in turn form a *liwa* or "province."

[9] Sunni Muslims accept the principle of nonhereditary elections to the caliphate, and therefore support the line of caliphs that followed Muhammad's death. Shia Muslims trace the line of succession from Muhammad along hereditary lines start-ing with Ali Abi Talib, the Prophet's nephew and son-in-law. (For more informa-tion see Gibb, et al. 1954.)

Zeidism is one of the many offshoots of Shiaism. There are three major doctrinal differences separating Zeidism from other Shia sects. (1) Zeidis are "Fivers"; that is, they recognize "Zayd as the fifth Imam rather than his brother Muhammad al-Baqir" (Wenner 1967:31). (2) Whereas most Shia sects consider Ali's claim to the caliphate mainly a hereditary one, Zeidis hold Ali's claim was founded on his

Zeidis are found in Liwa al-Baida. In some areas such as ash-Shaar in Liwa Ibb the two religious groups live side by side and frequently inter-marry.[10]

In contrast to the Northerners, who number 4,000–5,000 persons, the Southerners constitute a relatively small minority of about 800–1,000 persons in the immigrant community. Unlike the Northerners, the South-erners are all affiliated with the Sunni religious sect. Southerners from rural backgrounds, numbering approximately 500–800 persons, come mostly from three neighboring provinces—Shaib, Dhala, and Upper Yafa (Figure 2).[11] All three provinces border North Yemen's Central Region. The close geographic proximity of these two border areas appears to have resulted in long-established social and kinship ties between them, especially between the Dhala/Shaib areas and the Central Region. Many Southerners, for example, trace their origins to parts of the Central Region, while others have married women from across the border. In fact, the North-South Yemeni border in this area remained undemarcated until very recently (Wenner 1967:44–45).

There is a consensus among Yemenis that the Northerners from ash-Shaar form the largest single group of Yemenis in Detroit. They are preva-lent in both the Detroit and Dearborn residential communities. The other Yemeni groups are distributed between the two residential communities in the following manner. Except for the Adenis, the majority of South-erners reside in the Dearborn residential community. The Adenis tend to avoid the ghetto-like residential concentrations of their rural countrymen in favor of residential dispersion throughout low- and middle-income suburbs like Ecorse, Lincoln Park, Taylor, and Melvindale. Three North Yemeni groups constitute the bulk of the Detroit community—ash-Shaar, al-Oud, and Baadan. With the exception of immigrants from al-Oud and Baadan, virtually every North Yemeni group cited above is represented in Dearborn's Southend. Thus, whereas the Dearborn community is com-

---

particular merits, not on his relationship to the Prophet. Accordingly, Zeidi imams are theoretically elected, even though they may have hereditary claims to the imam-ate (Wenner 1967:31). (3) The Zeidi imam is considered by his followers to have special and unique powers, unlike those of any other spiritual ruler in other Shia sects or in Sunni Islam (Wenner 1967:32).

[10]Data on the Zeidi-Shafei breakdown in the immigrant community were extremely difficult to obtain in the field owing to the immigrants' sensitivity to this issue. They considered all inquiries about the religious cleavage to be divisive. In defer-ence to the immigrants' feelings, the subject was avoided.

[11]Like their Northern counterparts, the Southerners do not identify themselves according to village origin, and instead refer to the regions cited above. Conse-quently it is impossible to give a more detailed account of the immigrants' areas of origin other than to cite the official designations currently in use by the South Yemeni government. The immigrants from the Shaib/Dhala areas are from the Northern County, Second Governorate; those from the Upper Yafa area are from the Western County, Third Governorate.

posed of Northerners as well as Southerners, the Detroit community is made up entirely of Northerners.

EMIGRATION PATTERNS

Emigration from Yemen[12] to Detroit follows the classic "chain migration" pattern, whereby one kinsman or co-villager sponsors another's migration. Many of the early immigrants of the late 1960s and early 1970s arrived in Detroit after having migrated elsewhere first. Some worked in the oil-rich countries of the Arabian Peninsula (e.g., Saudi Arabia, Kuwait, and the Arabian Gulf states); others migrated to Britain, where the largest Yemeni immigrant community outside Saudi Arabia is located.[13] Still others migrated to already established Yemeni communities in California, Brooklyn and Buffalo, New York, and Dayton, Ohio before migrating to Detroit.[14] In recent years Yemeni immigration to Detroit has tended to be less secondary, as migrants travel directly to Detroit from Yemen.

Whatever the case, direct or indirect migration, Yemeni immigration to Detroit is a selective process which tends to reproduce kinship and village units in the host society. As indicated, the various Yemeni groups represented in the immigrant community are limited to certain regions in the two Yemens. There are two factors contributing to the selective nature of Yemeni immigration to the United States and Detroit. First, United States immigration laws give preference to "immediate relatives" (i.e., unmarried sons and daughters, spouses, parents) of American citizens and residents (United States Department of Justice 1972). Second, the costs of emigrating to the United States are prohibitive for the average Yemeni, unless he has close kinsmen and co-villagers who can either provide him with financial assistance or assist him in securing a loan. This second factor deserves further elaboration, as it serves to indicate the economic basis underlying Yemeni emigration to the United States.

It is not unusual for a newly arrived Yemeni to have accumulated a debt of several thousand dollars in emigrating to the United States. Aside from purchasing his airfare to the United States, a prospective emigrant often encounters rampant corruption in the North Yemeni governmental bureau-

---

[12]Unless modified, the term "Yemen" is used in this study to denote the cultural/ geographic area that embraces the two Yemeni political entities. In this sense, the concept is in keeping with the immigrants' own use of the term.

[13]The major Yemeni immigrant communities in Britain are in Cardiff, Birmingham, South Shields (Halliday 1975:111; Serjeant 1944; Dahaya 1964). Yemeni immigrants in Saudi Arabia are estimated to number at least one million (Halliday 1977:9).

[14]Aside from a short article on Yemeni farm workers in Kern County, California (Bisharat 1975), very little is known about these communities.

cracy.[15] All the documents (birth, marriage, "good conduct" certificates) required to obtain a United States immigrant visa, as well as the passport and exit papers, are secured through bribery. This situation is often compounded further in North Yemen by periodic governmental decrees banning emigration from the country.[16] When this occurs, "bribe inflation" sets in, as corrupt governmental officials demand even larger sums of money from the emigrants for the required documents, especially passports. Finally, an emigrant must also have enough money to support himself and his family until he secures his first job abroad, a task which may take anywhere from several weeks to several months, depending on local economic conditions.

In most cases kinsmen in Detroit can afford to pay only part of the costs of emigration, and a prospective emigrant must out of necessity seek the assistance of a *wakeel al-mughtaribeen* (an "emigrant agent"). The *wukulaa* (plural) function like a lending institution, offering funds to prospective emigrants, especially if they have immigrant visas in hand, or their prospects of getting one are good. If an emigrant lacks social and kinship ties to the *wakeel* he may have to put up part of his lands as collateral in order to obtain a loan.

The *wakeel*'s services go beyond mere lending to include acquisition of documents, passports, airplane tickets, and the like. When an emigrant begins to remit his earnings, it is the *wakeel* who will receive the monies and deliver them to the emigrant's family in the countryside. The importance of this service cannot be overstated, since most Yemeni villages are still remote and difficult to reach. As the emigrant begins to accumulate larger sums of money, he will often turn to the *wakeel* and his business acumen to help him invest and manage his monies and supervise the various construction projects that the emigrant undertakes (see below). In return for the loan and his services, the *wakeel* collects a service charge called *ghwah* ("coffee money") from the emigrant in lieu of interest, since the latter is prohibited under Islam. The amount of "coffee money" varies from one individual to another depending on the type of services rendered and the closeness of the emigrant's ties to the *wakeel*.

IMMIGRANT MOTIVATIONS, OBJECTIVES, AND PRACTICES

The overwhelming majority of Yemeni immigrants in Detroit are economically motivated migrants. They have been driven into emigration by

---

[15] A discussion of governmental corruption is beyond the scope of this study; the reader is referred to Halliday (1975:146), and Stookey (1974:413–414) for more information.

[16] Such decrees are rarely enforced, however, especially for those emigrating to the United States. In contrast, South Yemen banned new emigration from the country several years ago. Unlike the North Yemeni "bans," the South Yemeni ban on emigration seems to be effective.

a host of factors including drought, crop failure, inheritance disputes over land, heavy taxation by the state and its tax farmers, and social and economic pressures created by past emigrations from the Yemeni country-side.[17] Although political oppression is sometimes cited by the immigrants as a reason for emigrating, it is not the type of political oppression commonly associated with the disenfranchisement of political and civil rights. That is, the immigrants were not driven from their country by an occupying army, nor were they the victims of political and social oppression meted out to national and religious minorities, as has occurred in other parts of the world. By political oppression many Yemenis mean oppression by the tribal sheikhs, who continue to wield considerable political and military power in the countryside (Stookey 1974, 1978). Nevertheless, most Yemeni immigrants still identify with their native country, to which they desire to return some day.

The economic motivation underlying Yemeni immigration to Detroit is expressed in the immigrants' overall goals—to make as much money as possible in the shortest period of time, after which they plan to return to Yemen permanently to enjoy the fruits of their labor. Immigration to the United States is perceived by the immigrants as a means to a livelihood (*talib al-raziqh*), while social mobility and material gratification are to take place in the home country, not in the United States. This determination on the part of the immigrants to return home permanently is reinforced by several practices which contribute to the maintenance of their familial and material ties to Yemen. First, most Yemenis leave their families behind in the villages when they emigrate to the United States. An estimated 70–80 percent of the immigrants are married, yet only a small fraction bring their families to live with them in Detroit. Although they advance a host of reasons, religious, cultural, or economic, for not bringing their families to the United States, the determining factor seems to be whether a person believes his return to Yemen is imminent or not. Those who tend to believe their return is imminent hesitate to bring their families to the United States, and thereby avoid the necessity of confronting the various "ideological" proscriptions against family emigration. On the other hand, those immigrants who have resigned themselves to a long-term stay in the United States tend to favor the emigration of their families to

---

[17]Needless to say, these factors do not hold for North and South Yemen equally, especially in light of the great social and economic upheavals that swept the South Yemeni countryside in the late 1960s and 1970s. For a discussion of these changes see Peterson 1981, 1982; Schmidt 1968; Halliday 1975, 1979.

A detailed discussion of the factors behind Yemeni emigration is beyond the scope of this study. The tax system in North Yemen is briefly discussed in Halliday (1975); the continuation of tax-farming in North Yemen is discussed in Stookey (1974, 1978). There is only one study to my knowledge which attempts to assess the effects of emigration on the North Yemeni countryside; see Swanson (1979a, 1979b). For a general discussion of this subject see Philpott (1970); Lowenthal and Comitas (1962); Böhning (1976); Miracle and Berry (1970).

Detroit.

A second practice strengthening Yemeni ties to the home country is the retention of farm land. Yemeni immigrants rarely, if ever, sell their lands, even though the value of those lands has increased enormously over the years.[18] If anything, Yemeni immigrants want to increase their land holdings in Yemen, which accounts for the dramatic rise in land prices. Several informants could not recall a single instance in which a Yemeni immigrant had sold his lands in Yemen. On the contrary, Yemeni immigrants will often engage in long and costly legal battles in order to retain title to lands disputed in inheritance claims.

A third factor contributing to the maintenance of the immigrants' ties to the home country is the practice of "recurrent migration." Recurrent migrations involve periodic visits to the home country, undertaken once every two to five years in the Yemeni case. The extent of these return visits can be appreciated from the results of a sample of Yemeni medical files taken at a physician's office in the Detroit Yemeni community. A random sample of 100 medical files out of a total of 500 revealed that about one-third of the Yemeni clients had made at least one return visit to Yemen during the two-year period from October 1974 to October 1976. In all probability this rate of recurrent migrations would be even higher were it not for the large costs involved in traveling between Yemen and the United States, and the desire of many Yemenis not to jeopardize their jobs by repeated leaves to Yemen. Consequently, most immigrants content themselves with making brief return visits, usually three to four months long, once every couple of years. However, immigrants in possession of United States citizenship are more willing to sacrifice their jobs in order to take extended visits of one year or more, since they have no fear of jeopardizing their status in the United States. In fact, the greatest spur behind a recent trend by Yemeni immigrants to acquire United States citizenship is that it enables them to remain in Yemen for longer periods of time, in contrast to noncitizens (i.e., permanent residents) who must limit themselves to short visits (less than one year), lest they lose their right to reenter the United States.

Perhaps the clearest indication of the immigrants' ties to Yemen lies in the great sums of money which they remit. A survey of four bank branches

---

[18]Swanson, who studied three villages in the Central Region of North Yemen, from where some of Detroit's Yemeni immigrants originate, made the following observations concerning land prices:

In the early 1960s good land was selling for between 100 and 200 Yemeni rials [4 YR equals 1 U.S. Dollar] per *shaakla* or *qasaba*, a unit of land approximately 18.5 feet on a side. In 1974–75 similar land was usually quoted at 1000 YR per *shaakla* or about $221 for .8 of one percent of an acre or slightly in excess of $28,000 per acre.... In October of 1976 a friend of the author's ... paid 75,000 YR for 30 *shaakla* of prime irrigated land, that is, nearly $70,000 per acre. (1979a:39) (two in the Dearborn Yemeni community and two in the Detroit community) having extensive business dealings with the immigrants revealed an estimated $1 million a month was being sent to Yemen from Detroit in 1976.[19] Assuming a total population of 5,000 persons, this amounts to an average of $200 per immigrant per month or $2,400 a year for every immigrant. For an average laborer, this sum comprises anywhere from one-sixth to one-fourth of his gross monthly earnings. However, it is not unusual to hear some Yemeni auto workers, who earned about $15,000 a year before taxes in 1976, boasting that they remitted $10,000 to their families in a single year.

The use of these remittances reveals the extent of the immigrants' determination to achieve social mobility and material gratification in the home country. After reimbursing their creditors (the *wakeel* and/or kinsmen), the immigrants give first priority to the construction of a large multistory stone house in their home village. These houses often cost $30,000–$40,000 or more to construct, and naturally serve to enhance their owners' social standing in the village. Once the house is finished, the immigrants, depending on their individual goals and resources, will undertake one or more projects and investments, which further enhance their prestige. Some invest their money in modern farm equipment (plows, tractors, irrigation pumps, flour-grinding mills) with the aim of increasing the agricultural productivity of their lands. Others use their funds to marry for the first time, or, as in the case of some older immigrants, divorce their wives and marry younger women. In either case, inflated "bride prices" make such ventures extremely costly. Another common practice is to engage in land speculation and/or buy and lease buildings and other properties in the rapidly expanding urban areas of North Yemen. (Such practices are prohibited in socialist-run South Yemen.) Finally, some of the more business-minded immigrants may invest their money in a truck-farming business in the countryside or open a commercial establishment in the city. These enterprises are usually left in the care of close kinsmen while the immigrant is abroad.

TRANSIENCY VERSUS PERMANENCY

The strong familial and material ties maintained by the immigrants with the home country serve as an affirmation of their desire to return home permanently. Belief in the "return" forms the cornerstone of immigrant thought and action in Detroit. A person's patriotism is often measured by

---

[19]This estimate is based on information provided by four bank managers. They based their estimates on average weekly sales of New York bank draft checks which were payable to persons in Yemen. The largest estimate from any single bank was $100,000 per week, and the smallest was $25,000 per week. It is likely that Yemeni remittances from Detroit are greater than $12 million a year, since Yemenis use other banks which were not surveyed, and, more importantly, many Yemenis prefer to remit money through unofficial channels (i.e., via personal carrier).

the degree of his attachment to this goal. Although there are many trends that point to the consolidation of a Yemeni colony in Detroit (increasing home purchases, increasing family immigration to Detroit, growing concern with job seniority and retirement pensions), most Yemenis will not tolerate any suggestions that they are destined to settle permanently in the United States. This was evident in their unfavorable reaction to a statement made by Joe Davis, then-president of UAW Local 3 at Dodge Main. In a public address before a large gathering of Yemenis, Davis offered a six-month leave of absence (instead of the customary four-month leave) to anyone at Dodge Main willing to return to Yemen for the purpose of relocating his family in Detroit.[20] Many Yemenis were angered by the offer which they felt was an insult to their nationalist sensibilities and patriotic aspirations toward Yemen. As far as can be determined, no one accepted Davis' offer.

Yemenis are acutely aware of the "plight" of other Arab immigrant groups in Detroit (e.g., Lebanese, Palestinians, Iraqis), who, notwithstanding declarations to the contrary, are considered to have forsaken their native countries and settled permanently in America. Yemenis argue that their own situation differs markedly from that of other Arab immigrant groups, and point to a Yemeni "specificity" in order to substantiate their claim. In myth-like fashion, they trace the historical origins of Yemeni emigration to the collapse of the legendary dam at Marib (see Figure 2), circa A.D. 542–570. The dam's collapse is said to have brought about the demise of Yemen's cultural and economic prosperity, and plunged the country into a centuries-long darkness, from which it is only recently beginning to emerge.[21] Since emigration from Yemen is the by-product of the demise of Yemeni prosperity, logic dictates that its termination will come about once Yemeni cultural and economic prosperity is restored. Advocates of this thesis believe that the rebirth of Yemeni society has already begun and it is only a matter of time before conditions favorable for their return to Yemen will arise. They differ only over which politico-economic model existing in Yemen—"capitalist" North Yemen or "socialist" South Yemen—will bring about Yemen's renaissance. In this context, the reunification of "historic" Yemen is considered an indispensable precondition for the full restoration of Yemen's past greatness.

There is a very small group of recent arrivals, who, unlike the majority of their compatriots, have resigned themselves to a more or less permanent existence in the United States. Although these immigrants (hereinafter referred to as "settlers") pay lip service to the notion of the "return," an

---

[20]The offer was made before several hundred Yemenis in the Dearborn community during ceremonies held to commemorate the 26th September and 14th October Yemeni revolutions in autumn 1976.

[21]This is more symbolic than factual since in all likelihood the dam's collapse was the *result* of cultural and economic decay rather than the cause (cf. MacMichael 1967; Brice 1966; Dayton 1975).

idea they too consider to be patriotic and noble, they nevertheless call for a "realistic" appraisal of the immigrants' situation. The settlers argue that permanent return to Yemen for all but a few is an unrealistic goal since neither Yemeni state can offer a viable economic and employment alternative to that found in the United States. Implicit in this argument is the assumption that Yemen is not on the threshold of a major cultural and economic rebirth, and probably will not witness such a rebirth for some time to come.

The settler group includes persons from both urban and rural backgrounds. Common to the entire group is a shared conclusion that social mobility is either totally unattainable in Yemen, or is more easily attainable (and desirable) in the United States than in Yemen. Settlers from rural backgrounds constitute a small number of the settler group. Typically they are found to be successful merchants and/or to have married American women in Detroit. Their decision to become settlers seems to have arisen gradually, in step with developments surrounding their personal lives (marriage, business success, failure to achieve social mobility in Yemen) and not as a result of an original determination to settle permanently in the United States. This is not the case with the majority of settlers who, significantly, are urban-based Adenis.

The factors underlying Adeni attitudes toward life in the United States are more social and political than personal as in the case of the rural-based settlers. Unlike other Yemeni immigrants, the Adenis were relatively better off than their rural counterparts before emigration, partially owing to the particular character of British colonial rule in South Yemen. On the whole, they enjoyed educational and employment opportunities and a higher standard of living unknown to other Yemenis living in the depressed rural areas of both North and South Yemen. However, this state of affairs abruptly changed after South Yemen's independence in 1967, when a radical and predominantly rural-based political movement rose to power in the country. This development came on the heels of the defeat of a more moderate, rival nationalist movement which many Adenis had backed during the war of independence (1963–67). As a consequence, the Adenis found themselves stripped of their former privileges and social positions. In addition, many middle-class Adenis suffered from the economic devastations brought about by the war.[22] These developments have naturally led many Adenis to conclude, as other settlers have, that social mobility is unattainable in Yemen. In the case of the Adenis this conclusion resulted from the loss of social privileges and status, and not from an inability to achieve them as in the case of settlers from rural backgrounds. For the Adenis, then, emigration to the United States was from the outset viewed as a chance at starting a new life.

Be that as it may, acceptance of permanency in the United States is

---

[22]These events are described in Halliday (1975, 1979); Rouleau (1973); Peterson (1981); Stookey (1982).

basic to all settlers, Adeni and non-Adeni, and it is precisely this acceptance which sets the settlers off from the nonsettlers in the immigrant community. For the settlers, acceptance of permanency leads to the adoption
of an assimilationist attitude toward the host society. For the nonsettlers,
belief in the "return" results in a transient, nonassimilationist attitude
toward the host society. Each perspective leads to different practices
which serve to widen the gap between the two groups. Thus, whereas the
nonsettlers are reluctant to bring their wives and children to Detroit, the
settlers favor family immigration. Over half of the Adenis, for example,
have brought their families to live with them in Detroit.[23] Another area
of major divergence between the two groups is in the maintenance of
material ties with the home country. Whereas virtually all Yemeni immigrants remit money to Yemen, the settlers do so only for purposes of assisting kinsmen. Since the settlers have no intention of achieving social mobility in Yemen, they do not undertake the construction and investment
projects that were discussed in the example of nonsettlers above. In fact,
the settlers chide their compatriots for engaging in "decadent" and "fool-
ish" practices like expensive court battles over land inheritance claims
and the payment of enormous bride prices.

Perhaps the area of greatest divergence between the two groups lies in
their attitude toward immigrant community life in Detroit. The assimila-
tionist-minded settlers reject the ghetto-like residential concentrations of
the nonsettlers in favor of residence in the various lower- and middle-
income suburbs that ring the city of Detroit. In so doing, they shun involvement in the highly volatile politics of the immigrant community and
its basic nonassimilationist orientation (cf. N. Abraham 1978). The settlers
rationalize their aloofness from the Yemeni community by denouncing
the nonsettlers as "ignorant" and "backward" people; the Adenis call all
rural-based Yemenis *Jabaleyeen* ("mountain people"). The nonsettlers,
in turn, dismiss the settlers as a "reactionary" and "unpatriotic" minority,
and even go so far as to characterize the Adenis as "bastardized Arabs."
(This is a reference to the large non-Arab Asiatic population that flour-
ished in Aden during the long years of British colonial rule in South
Yemen.) The nonsettlers defend their nonassimilationist lifestyle and
closed community life on the basis that they are transients here in the
United States and only desire to earn a livelihood. Since they constitute
the overwhelming majority of Detroit's Yemeni community, it is only appropriate that we turn our attention to their community organization and
lifestyle.

COMMUNITY LIFE AND ORGANIZATION

The transient attitude of the nonsettlers toward their existence in Detroit

---

[23] In all likelihood more Adeni families would have emigrated were it not for South
Yemeni governmental restrictions on emigration.

lends itself to a particular lifestyle which eschews participation and assimilation in the host society. Moreover, such an attitude leads to the formation of a closed community social organization that serves as a buffer between the immigrants and the host society. The net result of the immigrants' transient, antiassimilationist attitude is a preoccupation with events taking place in the home country as opposed to events in the host society. This basic orientation toward Yemen is formalized in the community's only pan-Yemeni institution—the immigrant fraternal associations.

On the individual level, the immigrants lead a spartan existence which is characterized by hard and diligent work, preference for overtime work, frugality and savings, and the fulfillment of economic obligations toward one's family in Yemen. Material wants and social activities are kept to the barest minimum, while social mobility and material gratification are postponed until after the return to Yemen. Nonworking hours are spent within the narrow confines of the immigrant community among kinsmen and co-villagers, either in the residential household watching television or in the coffeehouse socializing and playing cards. A small number of pious immigrants attend the Dearborn mosque several times a week for communal prayer and religious meditation.

Not everyone, of course, adheres to this model of behavior. In fact, there is a sizeable number of immigrants, mostly in their teens and early twenties, who openly flout the behavioral norms of the immigrant community. Known as "hippies," or al-ṭaesheen (the "frivolous ones"), this group has adopted many of the mannerisms, behavior, and dress codes of lower working-class American youth. The hippies' involvement with women, alcohol, drugs, and gambling is a constant source of irritation to the rest of the immigrant community. This by no means implies that the "nonhippies" do not occasionally engage in such activities, for they do. The problem arises because the so-called hippies conduct their affairs in the open, rather than discreetly, as is the case with many older immigrants. In addition, the older immigrants fear the younger hippies will become so corrupted by the host society that they will be unable to reintegrate into Yemeni society and thus will eventually sever their ties with the home country. Even though the hippies are stigmatized and harshly criticized by the older immigrants, they are not ostracized from the immigrant community so long as they continue to fulfill their economic obligations toward their families in Yemen. However, those who fail to meet their obligations because of having become "corrupted" (i.e., alcoholics, drug addicts, compulsive gamblers) are dubbed bummieen ("bums"), and it is they who are "disowned" by kinsmen and co-villagers and ostracized by the community. Thus, so long as a person continues to fulfill his obligations to the home country, his personal behavior is tolerated, even though it may conflict with the norms established by the majority.

On the whole, social interaction with the host society is kept to an absolute minimum, or, in the case of the "hippies," to the realm of leisure time activities. The immigrants display a marked indifference toward wider social and political issues which directly or indirectly affect their social

and economic well-being as immigrant workers in Detroit, such as municipal elections, civic and neighborhood action, and union-related issues. In
the Southend, for example, the Yemenis remained largely apathetic
toward the city of Dearborn's urban renewal plans to raze the neighborhood, while other residents banded together in the Southeast Dearborn
Community Council to oppose the city administration (Aswad 1974). Sim
ilarly, the many Yemenis possessing United States citizenship did not
participate in the 1976 municipal elections, even though several Arab-
American political candidates actively courted their support.[24]

Perhaps a more accurate gauge of Yemeni attitudes toward the host
society and its institutions is their attitude toward the labor unions to
which the majority belong. Most Yemeni union members recognize that
the unions play an important role in protecting their rights as workers.
Nevertheless, they remain largely indifferent to the unions and especially
to union-management conflicts. A good case in point occurred during a
UAW strike against the Ford Motor Company. The union staged a month-
long strike in September-October 1976 in order to bolster its demands for
higher wages and other benefits during the contract negotiations. With
the exception of an extremely small number who openly supported the
strike and the demands of some radical American leftist groups, the vast
majority of Yemenis affected by the strike took a negative view of it. They
opposed the strike not because they were content with the wage scale and
benefits of the old contract, but because they felt the strike was an obstacle
curtailing earnings and preventing an early return to Yemen. From their
standpoint, the relatively moderate gains won by the union as a result of
the strike were outweighed by the short-term losses incurred during the
strike.

Yemeni participation in and interaction with the host society is in part
precluded by their illiteracy in English. Aside from a small number who
are able to conduct a conversation in halting English, most Yemenis can
express themselves in English only with great difficulty. But even this limi-
tation in their ability to interact with the host society is in large measure a
result of the immigrants' transient status in the United States. When asked
why they do not take greater advantage of the various English language
instructional facilities available to them in their communities, the immigrants typically cite the long hours at work and the physical and mental
fatigue resulting from work as the reasons. One could also add the obvious
difficulty of learning a foreign language for a person who is at best semiliterate in his native language. While these reasons are valid, they are secondary to a more basic reason behind the immigrants' failure to learn

---

[24]In fact, some of the more politically-minded Yemenis attempted to rally Yemeni
electoral support for the candidates after they were personally approached by the
latter. By all accounts, however, the Yemeni turnout was far below what had been
expected, given that there are probably 1,000 Yemenis in Detroit holding United
States citizenship. Some fifty Yemenis, for example, attended a reception for one
Arab-American candidate at a Yemeni meeting hall in the Dearborn community.

English. Yemeni seafarers, for example, are idle for three to four months at a time during the winter, as icy conditions on the Great Lakes bring shipping to a standstill. During this period the seafarers will either undertake a return visit to Yemen, or spend their time watching television at home and playing cards in a coffeehouse. Rarely are they ever found taking advantage of the English language courses being offered only a short walking distance from their place of residence. The attitude of the seafarers in this regard is indicative of a basic utilitarian reasoning toward the study of English common to the immigrants as a whole. This reasoning can be summarized in the following manner: "Since I shall return to Yemen in the near future, I need only learn enough English so as to obtain and retain a job; anything beyond that minimum is superfluous."

Cut off from the rest of society by their own volition, the immigrants live within the closed confines of a predominantly male community. There are three levels of social organization in the immigrant community: the residential household, the coffeehouse group, and the immigrant fraternal association. The residential household forms the basic organizational unit in the community. It is at this level that the immigrants spend the greatest part of their nonworking hours. The size of the residential household can range from a single individual living alone to the more common group of two or more single males, the maximum number being determined by spatial capacity. In the latter case, the residential group usually consists of a number of kinsmen and/or co-villagers who have banded together to share expenses for rent and food in order to minimize the cost of subsistence. Although the household units sometimes play a social role by virtue of their kinship composition, their primary function is to provide shelter and basic subsistence. Personal crises (e.g., death, injury, unemployment, financial need, etc.) fall in the domain of the wider kin/village units, which are normally dispersed over a number of residential households.

Above the residential household in the community organizational hierarchy is the coffeehouse group. Coffeehouses are individually owned and operated commercial establishments that serve as the immigrants' main locus of entertainment outside the residential unit. Although the decision to patronize a coffeehouse is largely a personal one, coffeehouse affiliation follows village group lines. A coffeehouse may be identified with one or more village groupings; the latter usually share a common geographic area in Yemen. In the case of one particular coffeehouse, which also serves as the headquarters of the Yemeni Benevolent Association, affiliation is along regional (i.e., Southerners) as well as political lines (i.e., supporters of the association). In general, coffeehouse groups are informal arrangements in which the immigrants exchange news and information, and engage in recreational activities such as card playing. As such, coffeehouse units do not function as organized or corporate bodies, nor do they have any decision-making power or representative authority.

At the highest level of the community organizational structure are the immigrant fraternal associations. As of 1976, there were three such organizations in the Yemeni community, two in the Dearborn community and one in the Detroit community. These voluntary associations are at the center of Yemeni community life by virtue of their status as the only formal pan-Yemeni institutions in the community. In 1976, the combined paid membership of the three associations was about 1,000 persons, approximately one-sixth to one-fifth of the total immigrant population. Ostensibly mutual aid societies, the associations command very few material resources with which to assist their members and the community at large. Their primary function is to provide a structure in which the immigrants can coalesce along national (pan-Yemeni) lines and preserve their national identity in the host society. In this respect, the fraternal associations are a logical outgrowth of the immigrants' antiassimilationist attitude and their desire to return permanently to Yemen.

Aside from an elected executive committee, internal structure in the loosely organized fraternal associations is virtually nonexistent. At the core of each association is found a group of politically active members who seek to influence policy. Membership in the associations is voluntary and open to all Yemenis. In practice, however, affiliation is largely along Yemeni regional lines (Northerners/Southerners). Members have virtually no obligations or duties other than the payment of nominal membership dues ($2 per month) and compliance with the general rules laid down in the association's constitution. Membership in a fraternal association entitles a person to vote in elections and run for elected office. With the exception of general election meetings, which are held regularly once a year, general body meetings are held infrequently, once every two or three months.

By virtue of their voluntary nature, the fraternal associations have very limited authority over their members and the community at large. They cannot, for example, interfere in the personal lives of members, and therefore must limit themselves to vague admonishments about a person's duty to family and country. The associations can impose punitive sanctions on a member only when he has committed a serious infraction, such as bodily assault on another member; they cannot impose or enforce social norms (e.g., dress codes, hair length, personal behavior, etc.) on members. Consequently, the associations have tended to concentrate their activities on promoting immigrant solidarity, the area where the greatest consensus exists. This is done through the staging of parties, meetings, lectures, and the like which are aimed at reaffirming the immigrants' national identity. In so doing, the associations have become the focal point for political contention in the immigrant community.

CONCLUSION

The Yemeni immigrant community of Detroit exhibits the following salient characteristics. In general, the population is composed of economically motivated, recent immigrants, who are for the most part unaccompanied males. The population is divided into two broad types: those who have for various reasons resigned themselves to permanent residency in the United States (the settlers), and those who are intent on returning permanently to Yemen in the near future (the nonsettlers). The nonsettlers constitute the overwhelming majority of the immigrant population.

The chief characteristics of the nonsettler group can be summarized as follows: in general, these immigrants share a common rural background and socioeconomic status in Yemen, albeit with some important differences. They also share a similar socioeconomic status in Detroit, as the majority are unskilled manual laborers who have little or no command of the English language. The immigrants view their presence in the United States as transitory and exhibit a deep-seated belief in the eventuality of their permanent return to Yemen, where they expect to attain social mobility and material gratification. This conviction is reinforced by the maintenance of strong familial and material ties with the home country. The immigrants' antiassimilationist attitude toward the host society is reflected in their individual lifestyles and community institutions, which serve to minimize immigrant interaction with the host society. Community life centers on the fraternal associations, whose primary objective is to preserve the immigrants' national identity and foster immigrant solidarity.

The predominant behavior and attitudes of the nonsettlers can be attributed to the relative recency of their arrival in the United States, the majority of whom immigrated in the late 1960s and early 1970s. By the mid-1970s, however, a tendency toward permanency among the nonsettler group was already becoming evident, as some Yemenis began to purchase homes and brought their families to live with them in Detroit. Ironically, even some of the prominent community leaders, persons with the greatest stake in preserving the immigrants' attachment to the homeland, were in the forefront of the emerging tendency toward permanent settlement. Undoubtedly, the struggle between transience and permanence among the nonsettler group will be determined by several factors, such as the immigrants' belief in the eventuality of their permanent return to Yemen, their strong familial and material ties to their home country, and their closeknit community life and institutions in the host society. These factors tend to color the immigrants' perceptions of themselves and their new environment. The ultimate direction of the community will be influenced by the manner in which these factors coalesce in the coming years.

REFERENCES

Abraham, Nabeel
1977   Detroit's Yemeni Workers. *MERIP Reports* 57:3-9.

1978   National and Local Politics: A Study of Political Conflict in the Yemeni Immigrant Community of Detroit, Michigan. Ph.D. dissertation, University of Michigan, Ann Arbor.

Abraham, Sameer Y.
1975   The Arab Muslim Community of Southeastern Dearborn: A General Overview. Mimeo. Madison: University of Wisconsin.

1981   A Survey of the Arab-American Community in Metropolitan Detroit. In *The Arab World and Arab-Americans: Understanding a Neglected Minority.* Sameer Y. Abraham and Nabeel Abraham, eds. pp. 23-33. Detroit, Mich.: Wayne State University, Center for Urban Studies.

Ahmed, Ismael
1975   Organizing an Arab Workers Caucus. *MERIP Reports* 34: 17-22.

Al-Khameri, Shakib M.
1979   Yemeni Immigrants in Detroit, Michigan: Characteristics and Correlates. M.A. thesis, Department of Geography, Western Michigan University, Kalamazoo.

Aswad, Barbara C.
1974   The Southeast Dearborn Arab Community Struggles for Survival Against Urban "Renewal." In *Arabic Speaking Communities in American Cities.* Barbara C. Aswad, ed. pp. 53-83. New York: Center for Migration Studies and Association of Arab-American University Graduates, Inc.

Bisharat, Mary
1975   Yemeni Farmworkers in California. *MERIP Reports* 34: 22-26.

Böhning, W. R.
1976   Basic Aspects of Migration from Poor to Rich Countries: Facts, Problems, Policies. *World Employment Programme* (WEP) 2-26:WP 6. Geneva: International Labour Organization.

Brice, William C.
1966   *A Systematic Regional Geography.* Vol. 3: *Southwest Asia.* London: University of London Press.

Dahaya, B.
1964   Yemenis in Britain: An Arab Migrant Community. *Race* 6(1):177–190.

Dayton, John
1975   The Problem of Climatic Change in the Arabian Peninsula. *Proceedings of the Seminar for Arabian Studies* 5:33–76.

Elkholy, Abdo A.
1966   *The Arab Moslems in the United States: Religion and Assimilation.* New Haven: College and University Press.

Georgakas, Dan, and Marvin Surkin
1975   *Detroit: I Do Mind Dying.* New York: St. Martin's Press.

Gibb, H. A. R., E. L. Provencal, and J. Schacht, eds.
1954   *The Encyclopedia of Islam.* Leiden: Brill.

Halliday, Fred
1975   *Arabia Without Sultans.* New York: Vintage.

1977   Labor Migration in the Middle East. *MERIP Reports* 59:3–17.

1979   Yemen's Unfinished Revolution: Socialism in the South. *MERIP Reports* 81:3–20.

Lowenthal, David, and Lambros Comitas
1962   Emigration and Depopulation: Some Neglected Aspects of Population Geography. *Geographical Review* 52:195–210.

MacMichael H. A.
1967   *A History of Arabian Sudan.* London: Frank Cass and Co.

Miracle, P. P., and S. S. Berry
1970   Migrant Labour and Economic Development. *Oxford Economic Papers* 22(1):86–108.

Morse, Susan
1977   Dearborn Seaman Awarded $750,000 for Ship Accident. *Detroit Free Press,* 16 January.

Peterson, J. E.
1981   *Conflict in the Yemens and Superpower Involvement.* Occasional Papers Series. Georgetown University, Center for Contemporary Arab Studies.

1982   *Yemen: The Search for a Modern State.* Baltimore: Johns

Hopkins University Press.

Philpott, Stuart B.
1970   The Implications of Migration for Sending Societies: Some Theoretical Considerations. In *Migration and Anthropology: Proceedings of the 1970 Annual Spring Meeting of the American Ethnological Society.* Robert F. Spencer, ed. pp. 9–20. Seattle: University of Washington Press.

Rouleau, Eric
1973   Revolutionary Southern Yemen. *Monthly Review* 25(1): 25–42.

Schmidt, Dana Adams
1968   *Yemen: The Unknown War.* New York: Holt, Rinehart and Winston.

Serjeant, R. B.
1944   Yemeni Arabs in Britain. *The Geographical Magazine* 17(4): 143–147.

Stookey, Robert
1974   Social Structure and Politics in the Yemen Arab Republic. *Middle East Journal* 28:248–260, 409–418.

1978   *Yemen: The Politics of the Yemen Arab Republic.* Boulder, Colo.: Westview Press.

1982   *South Yemen: A Marxist Republic in Arabia.* Boulder, Colo.: Westview Press.

Swanson, Jon C.
1979a Some Consequences of Emigration for Rural Economic Development in the Yemen Arab Republic. *Middle East Journal* 33(1):34–43.

1979b *Emigration and Economic Development: The Case of the Yemen Arab Republic.* Boulder, Colo.: Westview Press.

U.S. Department of Justice
1972   United States Immigration Laws: General Information. Pamphlet. Washington, D.C.: U.S. Government Printing Office.

Wenner, Manfred
1967   *Modern Yemen: 1918–1966.* Baltimore: Johns Hopkins University Press.

ABSTRACT

Chaldeans are immigrants from Iraq who differ from other immigrants from Arab nations in several ways: they are Roman Catholic, not Muslim; their mother tongue is Assyrian-Chaldean, not Arabic; they come from a rural village, Telkaif; and many feel that they have been the object of discrimination in Iraq. Consequently, Chaldean-Americans are reluctant to identify with the Arab community. This sense of identity in the United States, however, is also affected by American perceptions of Chaldeans and Arabs. On the one hand, American antipathy toward Arabs reenforces the Chaldean aversion to an Arab identity. On the other hand, the ready equation of "Arab" with "Chaldean" made by many Americans, as well as the general sense of power ascribed to Arabs creates a tendency in some Chaldeans to identify themselves as Arabs.

135

Detroit's Iraqi-Chaldeans: A Conflicting Conception of Identity

by Mary C. Sengstock

Chaldeans are Iraqi immigrants, the majority of whom reside in the Detroit Metropolitan area. Chaldean people are commonly identified as part of the Arabic community, but many Chaldeans do not readily accept this identity. In an effort to explain this divergence of self- and other-identification, this article will focus on two major issues: 1) a history of the Chaldean community, both in the country of origin and in the United States; and 2) a discussion of some of the similarities and differences between the Chaldean community and its culture, and the social patterns and culture of the Arab community.

HISTORICAL CONTEXT OF DETROIT'S CHALDEAN COMMUNITY

The Chaldeans trace their origins to what is now the modern nation of Iraq. The earliest Chaldean migrants came to the United States prior to the establishment of Iraq as a separate nation, however (Haddad and Nijim 1978; Sengstock 1982:43–45, 107). Most Chaldeans in Detroit are descendants of Telkaif, a northern Iraqi village near the ruins of the ancient city of Niniveh. Niniveh was the home of the ancient Assyrians and Babylonians, whom the modern day Chaldeans claim as their ancestors (Olmstead 1923:1; Perrot and Chipiez 1884, 1:18).

The two major respects in which Chaldeans have historically differed from other Iraqis are in language and religion. The traditional language of the Chaldeans is a modern day dialect of ancient Aramaic, which early Chaldean immigrants proudly identified as the language spoken by Jesus Christ (Sengstock 1982:15). The Chaldeans also take pride in the fact that their ancestors in the vicinity of northern Iraq trace their line of Christianity to the beginning of the Christian era. Legend states that this area was converted by the Apostle Paul on one of his missionary journeys (Attwater 1947; Sengstock 1982:14). Hence, Chaldeans are set apart from other residents of the Arab world both by their ancestral language and by their religion, both of which are sources of great pride to the community.

Today, Chaldeans are a part of the Roman Catholic Church, with designation as a separate "Chaldean rite" (Rabban 1967). In former years, however, they had been followers of Nestorius, an Eastern bishop of the early Christian era who differed from the Western church on several doctrinal points (Adeney 1965). Some followers of Nestorius remain today, both in Iraq and in the United States, notably in Chicago. The Catholic Chaldean rite, to which Detroit's Chaldeans belong, shares the major doctrinal points with the Roman Catholic Church; however, many of the rituals, as well as the traditional ritual language, Aramaic, are very similar to those of the Nestorians (Sengstock 1982:14–15).

MIGRATION TO THE UNITED STATES

The first Chaldean to arrive in the United States settled in Philadelphia in 1889; he later returned to his homeland. Chaldeans began to establish themselves in the Detroit area around 1910 (Sengstock 1982:42–43). The earliest migrants came to Detroit directly from Telkaif. Following World War II, most migrants have been Chaldeans who were born, or lived at least a portion of their lives, in Baghdad or one of the other Iraqi cities. Since 1965, migrants are again arriving directly from the village of Telkaif, largely to escape the political turmoil in the northern part of Iraq, manifested in conflicts between the Iraqi government and the Kurdish people who also live in that area (Sengstock 1982:50).

Migration into the Chaldean community has escalated steadily over the past two decades, especially since the change in United States immigration laws in the mid-1960s, which permitted a greater number of persons from Iraq to enter the United States (Sengstock 1982:50). In 1960, there were approximately 3,000 persons of Chaldean ancestry living in the Detroit area. By 1980, there were over 20,000 Chaldeans, representing a growth rate of 600 percent.[1] Most migration into the Chaldean community has been family-based chain migration (Sengstock 1982:52–53). That is, the first migrant, usually a male, will emigrate to the United States alone. Once he has established himself, he will send for other members of the family, first his wife and children, later brothers, sisters, in-laws, and other relatives. These in turn bring their relations in an ever widening circle (Sengstock 1982:47).

The Detroit Chaldean community is the largest community of Chaldeans in North America. Other Chaldean communities are in Chicago, Illinois, and San Diego and Turlock, California (Sengstock 1982:114–115). The phenomenal growth of the community has produced a population which is quite diverse. Some members are from the original rural village,

---

[1] There is considerable dispute over the size of the community. Some estimates range as high as 40,000. My estimate of 20,000 to 25,000 is based on an analysis of available data on the size of Chaldean parishes and a projection of growth rates.

others from a cosmopolitan urban background. Some speak the original Chaldean-Aramaic language and know no Arabic; others speak Arabic and know no Chaldean (Doctoroff 1978). Still others have been born and reared in America, perhaps even of American-born parents, and many of these know neither ethnic language. Members range from third-generation American-born persons to those who arrived from Telkaif within the past few weeks (Sengstock 1982:71–80). Community leaders have been faced with the difficulty of integrating so diverse a population into a single group.

RESIDENTIAL PATTERNS IN THE DETROIT AREA

The earliest Chaldean migrants in the Detroit area lived in the vicinity of Jefferson Avenue, from the downtown area to East Grand Boulevard. In this area, they were close to St. Maron's Church of Detroit, a Lebanese Maronite church, which is another Eastern rite of the Catholic church and similar to the Chaldean rite in many ways. As the community grew, it gradually moved westward. During the 1940s and 1950s, the major population center was in the vicinity of Boston and Chicago Boulevards, between Woodward and Hamilton Avenues. The first Chaldean parish, called Mother of God, was established during this period. During the 1960s, it was located in the center of the community on Hamilton Avenue near Glynn Court. At that time, there were smaller concentrations of Chaldean families living in Detroit near Seven Mile Road and Livernois, and near Woodward and State Fair; there was also a growing suburban community in Southfield (Sengstock 1970).

In the past twenty-five years, community residential patterns have changed considerably. Few, if any, Chaldeans remain in the Hamilton-Boston Boulevard area, and Chaldeans have also left the Seven Mile Road-Livernois area. But the Southfield settlement of the early 1960s has formed the core of a large suburban Chaldean community in Oakland County. This community includes persons residing in the affluent suburbs of Oak Park, Birmingham, Bloomfield Hills, and Troy, as well as Southfield (Doctoroff 1978). The growth of this suburban-based community and the decline of Chaldean population in the central city resulted in the relocation of Mother of God Church from Hamilton Avenue to a location near Ten Mile Road and Telegraph in 1973 (Sengstock 1982:18–19).

The small concentration of Chaldeans in the Woodward-State Fair area has also grown considerably, to represent the major central city community of Chaldeans. This segment of the community also has its own church, called Sacred Heart Chaldean Parish, which is located on Seven Mile Road near John R. Two additional Chaldean parishes have also been established, one in 1980 and another in 1981, to serve the growing Chaldean population in Oakland and Macomb counties. Mar Addai Parish is located in the city of Oak Park, and St. Joseph Chaldean Parish, located in Troy, serves Macomb County and eastern Oakland County. A bishop of the Chaldean rite has recently been appointed to oversee the Chaldean Church in America, with headquarters in the Detroit area.

SOCIOECONOMIC STATUS

It is to be expected that a population which includes both recent immigrants and third-generation Americans would be quite diverse in economic and social status. This is indeed the case with the Chaldeans. The suburban Chaldeans tend to include those who are American-born, as well as those immigrants who have been in the United States an extended period of time and have had the opportunity to establish themselves financially. The Sacred Heart Chaldean Parish area, in counterdistinction, tends to include relatively recent immigrants for whom the problems of economic and cultural adaptation to life in America predominate.

The Chaldean community is among those ethnic communities which are bound together by strong economic ties. A large percentage of the Chaldean population is engaged in a single occupation—the retail grocery business and its related wholesale supply industries. Over four hundred Chaldean-owned retail grocery stores were located in the Detroit area in 1980.[2] Most Chaldean businesses are family operations, owned and operated by father and son, several brothers, or uncle and nephew, and often including in-laws. With the extremely large number of stores in the Detroit area, coupled with the prevalence of grocery suppliers, the Chaldeans could develop a network which could rival the chain stores in controlling the retail grocery trade in the metropolitan area. Chaldean stores, however, all tend to be operated independently, and there is little cooperation between owners (Sengstock 1974).[3]

The grocery business has served as the major avenue of upward mobility for those Chaldeans who have been here a considerable period of time. Many immigrants have begun their life in America as employees in a relative's grocery store, often lacking even a knowledge of the English language. As they gained knowledge of the language and the grocery business and were able to save some money, they bought stores of their own. Today, many of the earlier immigrants and their children are owners of large supermarkets or of wholesale supply companies which cater to the grocery trade (Sengstock 1974:27).

These patterns in immigration and business have resulted in major discrepancies in income between the recent immigrants, who are relatively poor, and the earlier immigrants and American-born, who may be quite prosperous. This economic disparity is also reflected in the character of the parishes which have been established, with the suburban parishes, primarily Mother of God, serving the more affluent and acculturated Chaldeans, and the central city parish, Sacred Heart, serving primarily

---

[2]A number of well-informed Chaldean businessmen place the figure at well over 1,000. —The Editors

[3]Efforts are currently under way to remedy this situation. Attempts have been made to advertise collectively and to contribute to political campaigns and legal defense funds in order to protect and enhance the interests of *all* Chaldean store owners. —The Editors

the less prosperous, recent immigrants. This distinction between rich and poor is often felt in the community, with many recent immigrants feeling that their predecessors have little sympathy for their plight (Sengstock 1982:130).

The natural antagonism between rich and poor is tempered somewhat by the fact that extended families often include both prosperous suburbanites and recent arrivals with little money (Sengstock 1982:135). It is also mediated by the common occupation which all Chaldeans share or aspire to. Prosperous Chaldeans continue to have more in common with the entrepreneurial grocery trade than with other upper-middle-class Americans, who are usually more educated professionals. Wealthy Chaldeans have been economically successful in spite of the fact that most have little formal education. They tend to feel that education is of little importance. This attitude toward education has created some conflicts between Chaldeans and their neighbors in several wealthy suburban school districts (Doctoroff 1978).

SIMILARITIES AND DIFFERENCES BETWEEN CHALDEANS AND ARABS

In an earlier section it was suggested that the Chaldeans exhibit two major differences from the Arabs and their culture. The differences have to do with the Chaldeans' ancestral language and their religion. Two additional factors which distinguish Chaldean and Arab should also be mentioned. These are the village and regional distinctions which existed in Iraq, and the perception shared by many Chaldeans that they have suffered discrimination at the hands of Arabs. Each of these points will be discussed, together with its possible consequences for the relationships between the two communities. Finally, patterns of similarity between Chaldean and Arab will be discussed.

With regard to religious differences, one should not underestimate the importance of the Christian religion in the lives of Chaldeans. Chaldeans in Detroit take extreme pride in their status as Christians, as Catholics, and as members of the Chaldean Rite of the Catholic Church. The church has been a focal point for the Chaldean community almost from its beginning in the early decades of the 20th century, as the early immigrants planned for the establishment of a Chaldean rite parish in the Detroit area (Sengstock 1970).

Christians in Arab countries are often referred to as "Christian Arabs." Some Chaldeans, particularly those who have lived and worked for some time in major Iraqi cities, have come to view themselves in this way. The majority, however, view the Arabic tradition as intricately bound together with the Muslim religion, and see no way in which they can be allied with the Arabic tradition without compromising their Chaldean Christian heritage and beliefs (Sengstock 1982:117–118).

Similarly with the issue of language, Chaldeans often express pride in their ancestral language, Aramaic, which was spoken in the village of

Telkaif until the last few decades and was the mother tongue of Detroit's older Chaldean immigrants. Chaldeans share this linguistic heritage with the Nestorian community in Chicago, as well as with Protestant immigrants of Assyrian background, such as those living in Turlock, California. Chaldeans view the Assyrian language with great pride, particularly because of its tie to their early Christian origins and because it is the language of their traditional religious rituals. Attempts have been made to unite Assyrian immigrants throughout the United States on the basis of their common linguistic background (Sengstock 1982:112–115). In the Detroit community, there is considerable disagreement, some of it quite intense, with regard to the degree to which they should allow their traditional Assyrian tongue to be supplanted by Arabic. For some Chaldeans, there is lingering resentment over the fact that they had to learn Arabic in order to carry out their daily lives in Iraq.

In addition to the linguistic and religious differences, Chaldean reluctance to identify as Arabs has been generated by the distinct character of the region of Iraq in which Chaldeans lived prior to their emigration. Iraq has existed as an independent nation for a little more than half a century; its sense of unity as a nation undoubtedly covers a much shorter period, since it takes considerable time to weld a group of people into a single society (Berger 1962; Sharabi 1966). When Detroit's early immigrants left their homeland, Iraq as a nation-state did not exist. Their village was basically self-contained and isolated, offering little opportunity to become acquainted with others of different religious, linguistic, or regional backgrounds (Sengstock 1982:110–111).

It is only recently that people of divergent backgrounds have come together in the major urban centers of Iraq, where they can live and work together and begin to develop a sense of unity as Iraqis or Arabs by transcending the historic barriers which have existed between them (Sengstock 1977). In fact, those Chaldeans most likely to identify themselves as Arabs are those who have lived for considerable periods of time in major Iraqi cities, received an education in Iraqi schools, and worked in professional occupations (Sengstock 1982:118).

Finally, Chaldean reluctance to identify with Arabs is also affected by the fact that many Chaldeans believe they have been the target of discrimination by Arabs (Hourani 1946:126). Chaldeans in Iraq were a religious and linguistic minority and lived in a region of the country which was commonly considered to be ignorant and backward (Sengstock 1982:109–111). In fact, the term, "Telkeffee," was used in Baghdad as a term of derision, applied to anyone from the Mosul region, and indicated an ignorant, small-town hick, a term somewhat akin to the American term, "hillbilly." Some immigrants in the Detroit community express keen memories of such degrading attitudes in their country of origin. Most ascribed such prejudice, rightly or wrongly, to discrimination on the basis of their religious beliefs. While Chaldeans' perceptions of discrimination may or may not be accurate, the fact remains that many Chaldeans feel that their people have been the object of unfair treatment. This too affects their likelihood of identifying with their Muslim Arab countrymen.

Division between Chaldeans and Arabs has been shown to have four principal bases: religion, language, regional origin, and perceived discrimination. Any one of these factors could be sufficient to prevent the development of a sense of unity between the two groups. It should not be surprising, then, if we find that groups which are divided by all of these factors have difficulty developing a common identification. It should be recognized, however, that there are also a number of factors which Arabs and Chaldeans share.

If many Chaldeans fail to identify as Arabs, it is nonetheless true that their social patterns and especially their culture are similar to those of the Arabs in many ways. Family patterns constitute one of the major areas of similarity between Chaldeans and Arabs. In both groups the family patterns have been characterized as patrilineal, extended, and endogamous (Prothro and Diab 1974:61–62; Sengstock 1982:23).

Both Chaldean and Arab have historically placed a strong emphasis upon endogamy. Many Arab villages of the Middle East are endogamous (Prothro and Diab 1974:64–65). Similarly, most of Detroit's Chaldeans originate from a single village which was almost entirely endogamous, and which has retained a fairly strong emphasis upon endogamy even after emigration from the village (Sengstock 1975; 1982:25). Another respect in which Chaldean family patterns closely resemble those of their Arab neighbors is the strong emphasis placed on the patriarchal lineage in both family systems. The line of descent for Chaldeans as well as for Arabs, and the line of inheritance for land and other possessions, is from father to son (Prothro and Diab 1974; Sengstock 1975, 1982:23). Furthermore, the customs of both Chaldean and Arab culture impose a strict sexual division of labor upon the household, and establish the father as unquestioned head of the family, with his wife subject to his authority (Al-Nouri 1964:1–9, 200–206; Sengstock 1975, 1982:23–25).

Perhaps the most important similarity between Arab and Chaldean family patterns is the fact that ties with extended kin remain strong and encompass many aspects of life. In both groups, extended family households are common, at least for a portion of a married couple's life (Prothro and Diab 1974:62–68; Farsoun 1974:257–258; Sengstock 1982:23–25). Where extended kin do not share the same household, they often locate their households in close proximity to each other (Williams 1968:15; Sengstock 1982:24). Arab families have been described as "functionally extended families," in which members who do not share the same household still engage in many activities which are commonly household based (Farsoun 1974:257). Hence, property may be held in the name of the extended family rather than the individual or the nuclear unit, and other economic activities may involve the extended family (Aswad 1971). Similarly in the Chaldean community, economic production and business ventures are often extended-family based (Sengstock 1974; 1975; 1982:24, 33–34). Hence, Chaldeans share with their Arab neighbors a strong extended family system, which may in fact have been developed through

several centuries of contact with each other in their common homeland.
The similarity of family patterns between Arabs and Chaldeans is a
commonality which the two peoples have shared for several generations.
In recent years, however, as both groups have begun to live and work
more closely together in major urban centers of their common homeland,
a new commonality of culture has developed. Earlier it was noted that
the traditional Chaldean language is Assyrian, not Arabic. In recent years,
however, this language distinction has become more of a nostalgic allegiance than practical reality. Chaldeans may still profess a preference for
their ancestral language, but the fact is that most Iraqi-born Chaldeans
today know Arabic better than they know Aramaic (Sengstock 1982:76–77).
Aramaic still appears in some families as the spoken language, but increasing numbers of Chaldeans in Iraq have grown up speaking the national
language, and many younger immigrants speak only Arabic. Consequently,
Arabic has come to function as the language of the Chaldean community.
Often Arabic can be heard when Chaldeans meet each other, and all of
the Chaldean parishes now conduct services in Arabic for their recent immigrant members.

This dominance of the Arabic language is even more pronounced when
one analyzes the written, as opposed to the spoken, language. Virtually
no Chaldeans other than the clergy can read and understand Aramaic.
Signs in Chaldean stores are often printed in Arabic, as are the newsletters
published by the Chaldean parishes. Chaldean mass booklets published
by one of the parishes contain Aramaic prayers printed phonetically in
English and in Arabic characters. So few Chaldeans read the Aramaic
language that no Aramaic writing was used (Bazzi 1981).

FUTURE PROSPECTS

One might conclude that Chaldeans increasingly resemble Arabs in
their social patterns and culture, although few identify as Arabs as yet.
However, the tendency to identify as Arabs may also increase since recent
immigrants are more likely to be from the urban centers of Iraq, and these
are the Chaldeans most likely to identify with the Arab culture.

It should also be recognized, however, that the identification patterns
of immigrants are influenced by factors existing in this country as well as
by factors which existed in the country of origin (Sengstock 1982:105).
The attitudes and reactions of non-Chaldeans and non-Arabs encountered
by Chaldeans in their new homeland will also affect Chaldean identification as Arabs.

Consequently, whether the Chaldeans continue to maintain their own
religious/linguistic identity or become affiliated with the larger Arab
community is, in part, not a matter of choice. Rather, it is dependent
upon how other Americans choose to view them. To the average American, there is little to distinguish a Chaldean from an Arab. They both tend
to have dark hair and fairly dark complexions; they both come from the
same part of the world, even from the same nation. Both groups speak

languages which sound "strange" and, to the unlearned, are indistinguishable from each other; some Chaldeans even speak the Arabic language. In the unlikely event an American should happen to see the two languages in written form, they would not look very different to him. Hence it is unlikely that most Americans would bother to make the distinction between Chaldean and Arab.

In conclusion, while the identification of Chaldeans with Arabs is not strong at the present time, this identification may increase in the future for a variety of reasons. One is the fact that the more recent Chaldean immigrants are more likely to have developed ties with their Iraqi countrymen in their homeland. Also promoting the Arab identification is the tendency of Americans to associate Chaldeans with Arabs, a tendency which is associated with the vastly increased number of Arab immigrants, which makes them even more visible and noticeable to Americans. It is also heightened by the increasing attention given to the Arabs and the Middle East in international news. For all of these reasons, an increase in Chaldean identification with Arabs may tend to increase in future decades.

REFERENCES

Adeney, Walter F.
1965 *The Greek and Eastern Churches.* Clifton, N.J.: Reference Book Publishers.

Al-Nouri, Qais Naima
1964 Conflict and Persistence in the Iraqi-Chaldean Acculturation. Ph.D. dissertation, University of Washington.

Aswad, Barbara
1971 *Property Control and Social Strategies: Settlers in a Middle Eastern Plain.* Ann Arbor: University of Michigan, Museum of Anthropology.

Attwater, David
1947 *The Christian Churches of the East.* Rev. ed., 2 vols. Milwaukee, Wisc.: Brace.

Bazzi, Michael
1969 *Bladt Telkaif Matheka wa Hathereha* (The City of Telkaif Past and Present). Mosul, Iraq: Publications Bureau of the Province of Mosul.

1981 *Chaldean Mass Booklet.* Troy, Mich.: St. Joseph's Chaldean Parish.

Berger, M.
1962 *The Arab World Today.* Garden City, N.Y.: Doubleday.

Doctoroff, A. M.
1978 The Chaldeans: A New Ethnic Group in Detroit's Suburban High Schools. Ph.D. dissertation, University of Michigan. Ann Arbor: University Microfilms.

Farsoun, S. K.
1974 Family Structure and Society in Modern Lebanon. In *Peoples and Cultures of the Middle East,* Vol. 2. L. E. Sweet, ed. Garden City, N.Y.: Natural History Press.

Haddad, H. S., and B. K. Nijim
1978 *The Arab World: A Handbook.* Wilmette, Ill.: Medina.

Hourani, A. H.
1946 *Syria and Lebanon.* London: Oxford University Press.

Olmstead, A. T.
1923   *History of Assyria.* New York: Charles Scribner's Sons.

Perrot, C., and C. Chipiez
1884   *A History of Art in Chaldea and Assyria.* 2 vols. Walter Armstrong, transl. London: Chapman and Hall, Ltd.

Prothro, E. T., and L. N. Diab
1974   *Changing Family Patterns in the Arab East.* Beirut, Lebanon: American University of Beirut.

Rabban, R.
1967   Chaldean Rite. In *New Catholic Encyclopedia* 3:427–430. New York: McGraw-Hill.

Sengstock, M. C.
1970   Telkaif, Baghdad, Detroit: Chaldeans Blend Three Cultures. *Michigan History* 54:293–310.

1974   Iraqi Christians in Detroit: An Analysis of an Ethnic Occupation. In *Arabic-Speaking Communities in American Cities.* B. C. Aswad, ed. New York: Center for Migration Studies and Association of Arab-American University Graduates.

1975   Kinship in a Roman Catholic Ethnic Group. *Ethnicity* 2:134–152.

1976   Importing an Ethnic Community. In *Culture, Community, and Identity.* Judith Gardner and Richard McMann, eds. Detroit: Wayne State University Weekend College.

1977   Social Change in the Country of Origin as a Factor in Immigrant Conceptions of Nationality. *Ethnicity* 4:54–70.

1982   *Chaldean-Americans: Changing Conceptions of Ethnic Identity.* Staten Island, N.Y.: Center for Migration Studies.

Sharabi, Hisham
1966   *Nationalism and Revolution in the Arab World.* Princeton, N.J.: Van Nostrand.

Williams, J. R.
1968   *The Youth of Haouch el Harimi.* Harvard Middle East Monographs. Cambridge, Mass.: Harvard University Press.

ABSTRACT

Christian Maronite Lebanese have, since the inception of their sect in the 5th century A.D., maintained close theological and cultural ties with the Roman Catholic church. Concurrent with this openness to the West, Maronites historically have manifested a sense of alienation from both Byzantine Christian sects and Muslim religion and culture. Political alliance with France increased the Maronite tendency to identify with the West. When economic crisis in Mount Lebanon led to a gradually increasing flow of Maronite immigrants to the United States in the late 19th and early 20th centuries, established Maronite links with Western culture provided further impetus. Early Lebanese Maronite immigrants were mainly peddlers and small shop owners. In Detroit, they settled near the center of the city and later moved eastward. The very elements in the Maronite tradition that facilitated identification with American culture also led to rapid assimilation and ultimately a significantly weakened Maronite community structure. The recent influx of Lebanese Christians into the Detroit area as a result of the Lebanese civil war may have the effect of reinvigorating a growing sense of cultural awareness and renewed Arab identity.

The Lebanese Maronites: Patterns of Continuity and Change

by May Ahdab-Yehia

This study explores the role of various factors in the acquisition of individual modernity in a migrant community.[1] Of major interest are the problems of adaptation, integration, and assimilation encountered by a group of Lebanese Maronites in their migration from a traditional agricultural environment to an urban-industrial one. Specific attention is focused on the history and social background of the group, their motivations for emigrating, early settlement patterns, and assimilation characteristics. While the group is highly diverse in character, it is possible to isolate key patterns of change (i.e., modernity) as well as continuity.

For the purposes of this paper, first-generation Maronites are defined as individuals who were born in Lebanon and emigrated to the United States of their own volition. The children of these immigrants, and those who arrived with their parents before the age of twelve and who were reared and educated in the United States constitute the second generation of respondents. The third generation consists of the children of the second generation. First- and second-generation residents constitute the majority of respondents even though all three generations are present in Detroit's Maronite community.

HISTORICAL BACKGROUND

Lebanon is a small Middle Eastern republic stretching approximately one hundred miles along the Mediterranean coast, with a total area of

---

[1]This paper is based on research conducted in Detroit by the author in 1970. It consisted of a random sample of fifty Maronite respondents and their families (Ahdab-Yehia 1970). A supplementary investigation was conducted in 1971 and updated in 1982.

4,105 square miles and a population scarcely exceeding three million inhabitants (Salibi 1965:XI). The country is said to be as old as the human race. Among its first inhabitants, the Phoenicians were also the first who contributed greatly to the welfare of the area. Being essentially navigators, they carried the products of the land of the Euphrates to North Africa and Europe, building on their way some of the most famous trade centers of the time (Hitti 1967:6).

Because of its location at the crossroads of three continents, Lebanon has been invaded by different nations, including the Assyrians, Chaldeans, Egyptians, Greeks, Romans, Byzantines, Arabs, Turks, and French. Recently, the country has reappeared in the news as a nation torn by internal political and military upheavals, and by the broader Arab-Israeli conflict. Through all this turmoil, the people have managed to maintain their national identity and traditions while continuing to build their nation even in the face of great adversity.

Coming from different places, and established in the country under various circumstances, Lebanon's religious communities grew as distinct groups, characterized by special norms. The leading sect among the Christians of the country has been the Maronites. Their church, which may be described as a Lebanese Catholic church, traces its ancestry to the converts of St. Peter who settled in Antioch in the first century and who were among the first to be called Christians (Maloof 1962:6). It was not until the 5th century, however, that the foundations of the Maronite rite were established by the Syrian priest, St. Maron. Historians note that Maron was born in the year A.D. 350 in northern Syria, not far from the city of Aleppo. He studied religion in Antioch with another great saint, John Chrysostom. Early in life, Maron retired to the Ansaryah mountains in Syria, where he converted a pagan temple to a Christian monastery. At the time of his death in A.D. 433, St. Maron was so widely known and admired for his actions and preachings that his disciples founded the Maronite rite by educating their monks according to his legacy (Hitti 1967:248). The abbey of St. Maron became powerful, and in the year A.D. 555 was considered the most important religious center in Syria, capable of dispatching as many as eight hundred monks on any one missionary journey (Maloof 1962:8).

Even with its historical legacy, it is sometimes difficult to determine the religious beliefs which distinguish the Maronite sect from other rites. It has often been argued that the Maronites, while following the Syrian liturgy, were among the very few Near Eastern Christian groups who remained faithful to the church of Rome at a time when the other Christians of the region were attracted by the Monophysite doctrine. This theory rejected the doctrine of the two natures of Christ (divine and human) formulated by the Council of Chalcedon in A.D. 451, advocating instead that Christ had only one will (Hitti 1967:254). Because of this difference in belief, the Maronites separated from the Byzantine church and were forced by some of the Christians of the region to flee from Syria and seek refuge in the mountains of Lebanon in the year A.D. 694 (Dib

1962:70–72). Isolation for the Maronite sect was further intensified by the spread of Islam, which was introduced into the area by the Arab conquests in the year A.D. 638.

In their traditional way of life, the Maronites were typical Middle Eastern people whose culture was very similar to that of the Muslim population of the area. What distinguished them, however, was an acute consciousness of their religious indentity, and through it an affiliation with and openness to the Christian civilization of the West. Accordingly, the Maronites have consistently welcomed commercial, diplomatic, and cultural relations, first with their Latin correligionists, the crusaders, who arrived in the region toward the end of the 11th century, and later with the French, who formally proclaimed the Maronites under French protection in the year 1250 (Hitti 1967:321). This friendship pact with France was maintained through later centuries, reaching its climax when Napoleon III sent troops to help the Maronite inhabitants of the mountains in a civil war with their Druze neighbors in 1860, and again at the time of the French Mandate after World War II.

Buoyed by French protection, the Maronites began a move from their mountain villages toward the more populated coastal areas of Lebanon. There, they established a link in the silk trade between the Near East and Europe (Salibi 1965:12). They also welcomed missionary activities by French and Italian priests. These outsiders became the advisors of the Maronite patriarchs and rulers, and assisted in the supervision and administration of not only church matters, but also of all the social, educational, and economic matters affecting the community (Salibi 1965:12).

Openness to the commerce and culture of the West became two-sided when missionaries encouraged the native Maronite clergy to complete their religious education in Rome. In 1584, Pope Gregory XIII agreed to open a Maronite college (in reality a seminary) for the training of Maronite priests (Harik 1966:44). Upon return to their village or town in the mountains of Lebanon, the graduates of this college became leaders of a movement for the advancement of education in Lebanon, building schools and encouraging people to attend.

When the Turks invaded the area in 1516, the Maronite clergy championed the cause of their small community against the demands of the ruling *emirs* and their representatives, the *muqaddams*. A traditional opposition between the clergy and the feudal aristocracy developed. This opposition remained until the end of feudalism when, interestingly enough, the Maronite patriarch inherited some of the influence and power of the feudal landlords (Salibi 1965:xxi). By the beginning of the 19th century, members of the Maronite community became so influential and powerful that some prominent members of other religious groups, such as the Druze *emirs,* converted to Christianity, an act considered at that time heresy by the Ottoman Turks (Dib 1962:120). This increase in Maronite prestige, coupled with internal changes such as the gradual abolition of the semi-feudal system and the growing influence of foreign powers, were some of the direct causes of the violent conflicts that erupted between the Maronites and other Lebanese religious communities, mainly the Druze. The conflict reached its climax in 1860. Within a brief period of three months, some 12,000 people were killed, crops were destroyed, and churches, mosques, and monasteries were burned down (Suleiman 1967:12). Weakened and threatened, the Maronites sought the protection of the Europeans, who agreed to send troops to Lebanon. France alone acted. In August 1860, 7,000 troops landed on the coast of Lebanon, remaining there for a period of two years (Hitti 1967:439).

Deeply affected by the events of 1860, leaders of the Lebanese Maronite community reinforced their ties with the Western powers. They welcomed all the missionary activities of the Catholic French and helped them establish in 1875 one of Lebanon's most famous universities, St. Joseph University (Hitti 1967:453). Cooperation between the Maronite leaders and American Protestant missionaries was not a fruitful one at first, mainly because of the purely religious aspect of the early American missionaries. When these differences in belief were overlooked, many Lebanese Christians, including the Maronites, responded and helped the American missionaries establish the American University of Beirut. This university, which was built in 1863, was to become in later years one of the most prominent universities in the Middle East (Salibi 1965:134–136).

Encouraged by missionaries, some members of the Maronite community decided to leave their native country in search of better economic opportunities. Although conflicting interpretations make it difficult to be accurate, it is estimated that in the fifty year period between 1863 and 1915 the populations of Mt. Lebanon diminished by one-fourth (or 100,000) through emigration (Suleiman 1967:11–13). Prior to 1878, most emigrants traveled to Egypt. They were driven by a desire to escape the pressures of overpopulation, a worsening economic situation, and a newly established military draft (Saliba 1982:8). By 1899, however, a large number of migrants headed to the United States, Australia, and Canada, attracted by economic opportunities and religious, social, and political freedoms. Political insecurity, the lack of economic enterprise, ruinous taxation, and the threat of starvation were the primary motivating factors. In addition, French and Italian missionaries presented a rosy picture of life in a democratic country filled with promises of virgin land awaiting ambitious individuals who would cultivate and partake of its unlimited riches. The Maronites were thus motivated to flee a worsening situation of material scarcity, and were lured likewise by a material dream of plenty.

SOCIAL BACKGROUND IN LEBANON

The early Maronite migrants transplanted with them the traditional familial and social patterns they had inherited from their agrarian Middle Eastern background. Of primary concern to them was the integrity, reputation, pride, and prestige of their family, a functionally extended unit, not residentially nucleated, but nevertheless performing the same functions (Farsoun 1970:257). In Lebanon, young couples lived in separate dwellings, but referred constantly to their elderly kin, who determined religious affiliation, and marital and occupational choices (Keatings and Khayat 1960:21). Wives were taught by their parents to respect and obey their husbands, and to plan for a family immediately after marriage, as children were considered economic assets, and one's future security depended upon them as well (Touma 1965:98–100). Parent-child relationships were based on respect for both parents, especially the father, whose authority was almost always final. In all, familial emotional ties were very strong. Their strength often appeared in customs observed during the illness of a family member, marriage, pregnancy, childbirth, death, farewells, and homecomings (Keatings and Khayat 1960:97–98).

Visiting, conversations, and heated political discussions constituted the core of Lebanese Maronite social life in the early 1900s, especially for those living in villages and small coastal towns. While women would gather in houses of friends or relatives, men were more in the habit of frequenting the coffeehoues, usually to converse with friends, or more often to play backgammon or exchange political views. Special occasions like formal celebrations of family events, or observances of religious and national holidays, would bring the entire family and sometimes the whole village network together (Des Villettes 1964:109–110).

Religion was the primary form of arbitration, not only in spiritual matters, but also in such personal matters as marriage, education, travel, and occupation. The Maronite priest served as a principal source of counsel and held a prominent position in the villages or small coastal towns. He was responsible for education and was supported in his tasks by nuns operating small schools established across the country. As a result of this clerical leadership and an effective religious socialization, the Maronites remained a deeply religious people, acutely conscious of their minority status in the Ottoman empire.

EARLY MIGRATION TO AMERICA

The first Maronite to arrive in the United States was Antonious al-Bishallany, 27 years of age, who landed in Boston in 1854. He died in New York two years later, in 1856. His youth, ambition, and early death inspired eloquent accounts of his life endeavors and imaginative ornamentation on his resting place. Not only was his biography published in English and Arabic, but his tombstone was adorned with the figures of a lion, a serpent and a lamb, designed to represent his fearlessness, wisdom, and blamelessness (Hitti 1924:47).

It was not until 1876, however, that the stream of migration between Mount Lebanon and the United States became more regular. At that time, Christian tradesmen had been encouraged by the Ottoman sultan to travel and exhibit their goods at the Philadelphia International Exposition. Their successful trip, economic success, and enthusiastic reports confirmed the early missionary accounts and stimulated a widespread migratory movement all over the country (Naff 1980:130). Later expositions, such as the Chicago Fair of 1893, and the St. Louis Fair of 1906, only reinforced this pattern, attracting individuals in search of better economic opportunities and hopefully an easier life in the New World (Saliba 1982:9).

The majority of the newly arrived migrants to Detroit encountered their first experience with the United States when they disembarked at New York, Boston, or Philadelphia. These early pioneers settled in small communities, earning their livelihood as unskilled laborers filling temporary jobs. Once settled, they corresponded with relatives and/or co-villagers, sent money home, or returned to visit their village of origin, all of which encouraged the others to migrate as well. Migration was so popular that it became converted into a family affair. In such cases, members of large functionally extended families pooled their resources to finance the emigration of their most promising young adults, who pledged in return to provide for their parents, spouses, and children. The migrants committed themselves to maintain a communication link with their relatives and, when possible, to dispatch money to their villages to be used for investments in land and for the economic betterment of their kingroup (Farsoun 1970:257–271). According to Hitti (1967:475), the emigrants, particularly the early ones, undertook the double burden of supporting themselves and of contributing to the support of the "old folks" back home. Rare indeed were the migrants who destroyed all bridges behind them. Remittances to families, charitable organizations, and educational and religious institutions were numerous, so numerous that they came to be considered by the government as a major economic resource. Till this day, Lebanese citizens speak of two Lebanons: the Lebanon of "the resident," and the Lebanon of "the emigrant," literally, the resident abroad (Hitti 1967:475).

As a rule, the early immigrants wished to accumulate sufficient wealth to be able to return home and enjoy the privileges that their new financial status would grant them. Few, however, returned to their villages to live permanently. Increasing family commitments, economic failures, and dissatisfactions with the way of life in the village motivated many to settle permanently in the United States and to send for their immediate family to join them. Transportation in those days was regularly available monthly, if not weekly. In addition, emigrants were not yet burdened by such requirements as passports, visa applications, and medical examinations in Lebanon. Fare tickets were bought at the port of departure, where Lebanese immigration officials often determined the destination of the migrants. The lack of procedures at the point of departure sometimes backfired for those migrants who were heading to the United States. They were not aware that they would be asked to pass a physical examination before being allowed into the United States. If ill, they were not permitted to disembark and were sent back home in the same vessel. Tragic stories abound, such as that of a mother who, with her two young children, could not join her husband in Worcester, Massachusetts, because of the children's illness; or that of an immigrant who was denied entry because of trachoma in 1908 (Saliba 1982:10).

EARLY SETTLEMENT PATTERNS

Many Lebanese Maronites who finally settled in Detroit were originally en route to Alabama, Texas, California, or even South America. Their original destination was determined by two major factors: one, the presence of relatives and/or friends already established there, and two, the presence of a climate and a natural environment similar to that of their country. During their passage to the New World, many soon learned of the plentiful job opportunities available in the northern states. They heard stories about "streets paved with gold" and the financial success of their compatriots. Consequently, they often changed their plans and either stayed in New York, Boston, or Philadelphia or headed to Detroit, Buffalo, or Cincinnati (Ahdab-Yehia 1974:141).

With the exception of a small educated minority, the early Maronite immigrants were predominantly young, illiterate, and totally lacking in vocational and formal training. As such, they started at the bottom of the occupational ladder, working primarily as peddlers and blue collar laborers. Despite its hardships, peddling was preferred over other occupations because it offered independence from the monotony of factory work and the isolation of the farm. In addition, peddling offered a chance to master the art of salesmanship in a foreign language, and was thus a possible stepping stone to a more rewarding occupational trade.

The first Lebanese Maronite arrived in Detroit around 1890. He settled on Congress Street, an area located east of what is presently downtown Detroit. Armed with experience in peddling, and trained by several years of hardship, he managed to prosper in the grocery business. His quick success opened the door to a migratory chain; thereafter the number of Maronite immigrants to Detroit increased from 417 in 1910 to 5,520 by 1930.

Following the example of their predecessors, the Lebanese Maronites who arrived in Detroit in the early 1900s settled on Congress Street and in adjacent areas: St. Jean, Orleans, Larned, Fort, Franklin, La Belle, Sherman, Multett, and Jefferson streets. Immigrants from the same village or family tended to cluster together. Successful relatives acted as middlemen, bonding newly arrived migrants, finding them jobs in the wholesale food outlets of the Eastern Market, and renting them rooms in the few apartments they owned. As the later arrivals became more self-sufficient and managed to accumulate money, they invested in small grocery stores, restaurants, or other retail businesses. They in turn acted as sponsors to members of their immediate families, who were invited to help operate the expanding business (Ahdab-Yehia 1974:141).

In the various accounts of their early experiences, many immigrants have expressed a nostalgia for the days when the spirit of cooperation that could be found in their village of origin was also found in their new surroundings. This was a time when successful members of the newly established community were committed to the well-being of the new arrivals. Men like Nicholas Nahra, Anthony Peter, John Doueihe, and Peter Jacob are nostalgically remembered by their families and friends for all the assistance they provided many immigrants. They not only sheltered these immigrants in their homes, but they also established the necessary contacts between Detroit and the New York wholesalers in order to secure goods that could be peddled by the new arrivals in the Michigan area (Ahdab-Yehia 1970, chap. 2).

With the advent of the automobile, and the opening of the Detroit auto plants, many Lebanese Maronite immigrants prospered by catering to the needs of the large influx of factory workers. Their stores were conveniently located on the corners of busy intersections, often serving as the sole food supplier for an entire neighborhood. Once again, the village spirit and close kin networks were transplanted into the new work environment. Extended family members would often own and manage one or more stores. They would sometimes live above their stores or in close proximity to them. Social life was constantly intermixed with the world of work. One second-generation member of the community recalled his early childhood as a time filled with impromptu visits by friends and relatives, lively political discussions, backgammon games, and bargaining over the price of merchandise, all occurring at the same time. Not surprisingly, the store-house complex, just as the village, became the main focus of the immigrants' lives and their primary group network (Semaan 1979).

Later, when the Detroit auto plants began attracting a large number of migrants because of the relatively high hourly wages, most of the new Maronite arrivals went to work on the assembly line. Some stayed there until retirement, while others used this occupation as a means to save money and invest in private businesses, in the same spirit of their predecessors who had used peddling as a stepping-stone to upward mobility.

Following the example of other middle-class Detroiters, established members of the Maronite community began to leave the original settlement area for the nearby suburbs. By 1920–25, enough parcels of land had been purchased in the Grosse Pointes, St. Clair Shores, Roseville, and the east side of Detroit to facilitate a gradual move away from inner-city neighborhoods. The ability to relocate depended heavily on the individual's or family's economic success and degree of ambition, or on the intensity of their desire to flee from inner-city problems (Ahdab-Yehia 1970:54–55).

What made the Maronite immigrants so adaptable and relatively successful in their new environment can perhaps be explained by their minority status in their country of origin. Their religious distinctiveness over the centuries provided the Maronites with an openness to the Latin

West, to its commerce, culture, and occupational values. Communication with Christian institutions was not prohibited, nor was an acceptance of their philosophy or modernistic tendencies. Similarities in religious beliefs were emphasized more than dissimilarities in attitudes. Consequently, the Maronites traveled to the West with great expectations of economic gain in a land offering opportunity in return for hard labor.

RELIGIOUS IDENTIFICATION

For most Lebanese Maronites, religious affiliation and ethnicity overlap. In Lebanon, the Maronites have worked at establishing a collectivity which in the early 19th century succeeded in representing the national church of the Lebanese Christian population. The Maronites gained a reputation for their strict adherence to Catholicism and an intrinsic obedience to the Roman church. In turn, this basic deviation from their Eastern Orthodox Christian neighbors, and inherent differences from their Islamic surroundings, contributed to their increasing alienation, and enhanced group consciousness and ethnic identity.

When the first Lebanese Maronites arrived in Detroit, they joined the nearest Catholic church, Sts. Peter and Paul, located on 628 East Jefferson. Their integration in the church was facilitated by their favorable predisposition to Latin rites and by a strong desire to quickly assimilate into the mainstream of American culture. As the community grew in number, however, the need emerged for a gathering place that could preserve the community's ethnic identity as well as provide a setting in which to indulge in an episodic submergence in one's cultural, social, and religious heritage. The community decided upon establishing its own church.

Responding to a formal request submitted by the Detroit Maronite community, the Maronite patriarchate in Lebanon asked a member of its clergy to help in the planning and construction of a church. Joseph Shabaia, well known for his organizational abilities, arrived in Detroit in 1915. The Detroit church, St. Maron, was built at 1555 E. Congress, and the first mass was celebrated on the 30th of April, 1916. Elias P. Asmar was appointed the first pastor and continued in this capacity until his death in 1933. During this time, a school and a convent for nuns were built in the vicinity of the church. They operated from 1921 until 1934, when they were closed because of financial problems resulting from the Great Depression. A lack of interest on the part of the Maronite immigrants, who preferred to send their children to schools run by local Catholic churches, also contributed to the demise of the school and convent (Ahdab-Yehia 1974:143).

After Elias Asmar's death, Peter S. Sfeir directed the parish until 1937, when he was succeeded by Michael Abdoo. The latter remained pastor of the church until his death in 1971. It was under Abdoo's leadership that membership in the church reached its peak, as he encouraged all Eastern rite Catholics to attend religious events and celebrations along with the church's Western rite. Michael Abdoo also broadened the functions of the church, integrating business and social activities, thereby attracting various segments of the community to attend church activities (Ahdab-Yehia 1970, chap. 4).

As the community grew in size and influence, more members moved to the surrounding suburbs outside the sphere of influence of the church. In response, Father Abdoo undertook a campaign to raise funds for the construction of a new church which would be more centrally located. He succeeded, and a new place of worship was built on the corner of Kercheval and St. Jean streets in 1966. That year also saw the seat of the exarchate of the Maronite rite in the United States established in Detroit, adding another psychological boost for the community. The exarchate was raised to the full rank of diocese in 1972, allowing the Maronite church to govern its members in the United States according to its own discipline and without interference from the clergy of any other rite. The new diocese included at that time about 150,000 members distributed among 43 parishes. The Detroit parish numbered about 20,000 members.

After Michael Abdoo's death, many affluent church members withdrew their membership and financial support from St. Maron, which severely limited its activities. As if to nourish this decline of membership and activities, the Maronite See was moved to New York in 1978, and St. Maron reverted from a cathedral to a church. Membership steadily declined as more and more suburban church members began attending local Catholic church services out of convenience. Today, the Maronite church includes approximately 6,000 regular members and about 10,000 to 12,000 individuals who attend the church only for special religious ceremonies, such as baptisms, weddings, and funerals.

Various plans have been recently discussed by the church board regarding the possible relocation of the church to the eastern suburbs of Detroit in the hope of regaining many of the former church members who live in the area. So far the discussions have remained cautious, as there is an increasing realization that the second- and third-generation Lebanese Maronites are much more difficult to reach. Most are already established members of local churches and, despite a general notion of pride in a religious and cultural past, are effectively integrated into the American society.

ASSIMILATION CHARACTERISTICS

The Lebanese Maronite community is described as one of the most successfully assimilated Middle Eastern immigrant groups in the United States. This process began with their integration into the Roman Catholic religious institutions and spread gradually into every aspect of their social life. Most families are socially very mobile. While the first generation of migrants was largely self-employed, the second and third generations are moving rapidly into professional and managerial occupations.

Arabic surnames are rare, as Maronites have always preferred European, especially French, surnames, even in their country of origin. It is interesting to note that even in the very early days of migration, many newly arrived immigrants changed their Arabic-sounding names to American ones, either by changing the spelling or by translating them. Thus, Najib became James; Boutros became Peter; Suleiman, Solomon. Conflicting reasons are given to explain this behavior. Some immigrants attribute it to a need to become immediately integrated into American society through the loss of visible reminders of one's foreign origin. Others claim that the early immigrants, the majority of whom were illiterate, were compelled to change their names by immigration officials who could neither pronounce nor spell them (Ahdab-Yehia 1970:74–76).

As for their native language, Arabic, its usage varies with each generation. The first generation still uses Arabic with family members, relatives, and friends, and listens frequently to the local Lebanese radio program broadcast in Arabic. Most, however, revert to English with their children and grandchildren, a pattern which is characteristic of most immigrant groups. Second-generation members understand Arabic, but rarely use it in everyday conversation, except perhaps to refer to food names and kinship terms. Third-generation members rarely understand the Arabic language. Lebanese ethnic cuisine appears to have remained intact and may be the only visible link between third-generation members and their ethnic heritage. However, here too, many have stated that although they enjoyed the food, they tended to reserve its preparation for weekends, religious holidays, or certain celebrations (Ahdab-Yehia 1970:74–76).

Although it is easy to pinpoint the visible signs of acculturation exhibited by the Lebanese Maronite community, it is difficult to single out those elements of attitudinal modernity that relate to their primary relationships with their family. The family structure of the Maronites still revolves around a highly endogamous marital pattern, and divorces are very rare. Even members of the second generation return to their native village in Lebanon searching for brides among their distant relatives. When cross-ethnic intermarriages occur, they are, interestingly enough, primarily with Italian, Irish, and Polish Catholics, rather than with Chaldeans, Melkites, or other Eastern Catholic groups. On the other hand, partners of exogamous marriages are expected to convert to the Maronite rite, and are easily accepted as new members of the religious community (Ahdab-Yehia 1970:91–93).

Another characteristic of assimilation is the loosening of extended family ties in the community. The extended family where parents, children, grandchildren, and their offspring live together is practically nonexistent among the Maronite community in Detroit. The dominant form of family system in this community varies from a nuclear pattern where the household unit consists of the father, the mother, and the children, to the expanded pattern where a widowed mother or father, and maybe an unmarried brother, sister, or niece are added to the nuclear family. This latter structure is also more apparent among first-generation groupings than second and third generations (Ahdab-Yehia 1970:86).

Attitudes of community members toward the independence of their children is still characterized by ambivalence. Individualism and independence for young adults are emphasized as valuable traits to be learned in a modern industrialized society, especially as they apply to the occupational world. Expectations for social dependence, however, are still high. Children and grandchildren are expected to visit regularly, and especially during holidays and special occasions. They are expected to exhibit strong affectional bonds and gratitude toward their parents and to provide them with financial security, if needed, in their old age. Children are also expected to care for their parents, if they become disabled or infirm. Nursing homes are frowned upon, and to many indicate a loss of family cohesiveness and identity. While close family ties are still valued, some of the problems facing the American family are beginning to appear among Maronites, including a lack of communication and generational conflicts between the older members and the younger, who are starting to rebel against parental authority and control.

Social activities are still essential to all three generations of Maronites. Home visits are very frequent among first-generation members who prefer to visit individuals from their family and native village. Second- and third-generation members tend to visit among friends. Interaction with Americans varies, as expected, by generation, with more third-generation members claiming friendships with non-Maronites. Similarly, membership in Maronite formal organizations, such as societies attracting members from the same village, charitable organizations, occupational groups, and social groups, is slowly diminishing. There are many possible reasons for this trend, including interethnic feuding, inability to attract younger persons, political squabbles, lack of communication with outsiders, and competing commitments arising from occupational interests (Ahdab-Yehia 1970:98–99).

FUTURE TRENDS

As a result of these assimilation patterns, the Maronite community seems to be following the trend of religious group communalism described by Lenski (1963:43–44). According to Lenski, the American population was—until a generation ago—divided into a multitude of small ethnic groups, each trying to preserve its organizational integrity. Economic pressures and the occurrence of intermarriages have reversed this tendency, however, creating a new successor to the ethnic subcommunity: the socioreligious community. Consequently, American ethnic communities have slowly drifted toward compartmentalization, thus identifying themselves progressively with the three main socioreligious groups rather than with their own ethnic background.

The gradual integration of the Maronites into the Catholic religious community is a prime example of the process to which Lenski refers. A lack of "institutional completeness" has acted to facilitate the group's assimilation. As Hitti stated years ago, the early immigrants were individuals without strong nationalistic sentiments (1924:26). Their allegiance was reserved for members of their kin, village, or religion. There was little group cohesiveness or cooperation within the larger community, and therefore the ability to develop viable political and social institutions was seriously hampered. That has been the general tendency among Lebanese Maronites in Detroit over the past two generations.

And yet, in spite of this gradual affiliation with the Roman Catholic socioreligious grouping, the Lebanese Maronite community is a typical example of a grouping which has also jealously guarded some selected distinctive aspects of their cultural heritage. Although the most visible signs of the community distinctiveness, such as the use of the Arabic language, or affiliation to the Maronite rite, are weakening from generation to generation, other more traditional cultural traits are deeply rooted into their ways of life. Strong affectional bonds and family ties still regulate social interactions. Marriages are highly endogamous, even among second- and third-generation members. In turn, indentification with the Maronite community's ethnic background is still highly advocated, mainly through a common pride in ethnic food and music.

The persistence of selective cultural traits among members of the Lebanese Maronite community has been recently reinforced by a renewed consciousness of their national origin and familial roots. This resurgence in interest is due to various factors, among them the present turmoil in Lebanon and the Middle East, and the recent wave of migrant-refugees who are still coming to join their families and relatives in the United States. A growing number of refugees are settling in the Detroit area. As a result, members of the Maronite community, especially second- and third-generation individuals, are organizing searches into their history and culture, as well as fund-raising activities for special projects to be developed in Lebanon. In turn, some are also joining such organizations as the American Lebanese Association, the Arab-American University Graduates, and the American-Arab Anti-Discrimination Committee, three organizations which attempt to improve the status and image of Arab-Americans.

Whether or not the events in Lebanon will be able to reshape the Lebanese Maronites is difficult to say. What is clear at this point is the fact that the community is now subject to conflicting cross-pressures between continued assimilation, on the one hand, and a renewed sense of ethnic identity, on the other. The newly arrived immigrant-refugees will pose new questions concerning the assimilation process and search for a way to preserve their ethnic and religious identity, an identity which is broader in many respects than that of their already established countrymen. The mix of new immigrants with old will rekindle earlier issues which may have been glossed over in the race to assimilate. Regardless of the direction taken, some Lebanese Maronites will continue to view themselves as religiously distinctive even while others work to broaden their relationships with the larger Lebanese and Arab-American communities.

REFERENCES

Ahdab-Yehia, May
1970   Some General Characteristics of the Lebanese Maronite Community Residing in Detroit: A Sociological Investigation. M.A. thesis, Wayne State University, Detroit, Mich.

1974   The Detroit Maronite Community. In *Arabic Speaking Communities in American Cities.* Barbara Aswad, ed. Staten Island: Center for Migration Studies and AAUG.

Al-Qazzaz, Ayad
1981   The Changing Characteristics of the Arab American Community in the U.S. *Arab Perspectives* 2:4–8.

Des Villettes, Jacqueline
1964   *La Vie des Femmes dans un Village Maronite Libanais: Ain el Kharoube.* Tunis: Publications des Belles Lettres Arabes.

Dib, Pierre
1962   *Histoire de l'Eglise Maronite.* Archevêqué Maronite de Beyrouth: Editions "La Sagesse."

Farsoun, Samih K.
1970   Family Structure and Society in Modern Lebanon. In *Peoples and Cultures of the Middle East.* Louise Sweet, ed. New York: Natural History Press.

Harik, Iliya
1966   The Maronite Church and Political Change. In *Politics in Lebanon.* Leonard Binder, ed. New York: Wiley.

Hitti, Phillip K.
1924   *Syrians in America.* New York: Doran Co.

1967   *Lebanon in History.* London: Macmillan; New York: St. Martin Press.

Keatings, Margaret, and Marie Khayat
1960   *Lebanon, the Land of the Cedars.* Beirut: Khayats.

Lenski, Gerhard
1963   *The Religious Factor.* New York: Doubleday and Co.

Maloof, Louis J.
1962   *Intact and Immaculate.* Atlanta, Ga.: St. Joseph Maronite Church Press.

Naff, Alixa
   1980   Arabs. In *Harvard Encyclopedia of American Ethnic Groups*. Stephan Thernstrom, ed. Cambridge, Mass.: Harvard University Press.

Saliba, Najib E.
   1982   Emigration from Syria. *The World* 26:7–12.

Salibi, K. S.
   1965   *The Modern History of Lebanon*. London: Weidenfeld and Nicolson.

Semaan, Anthony
   1979   The Patterns and Processes of Settlement of Detroit's East Side Lebanese-Maronite Community. Unpublished paper. Wayne State University.

Suleiman, Michael W.
   1967   *Political Parties in Lebanon*. New York: Cornell University Press.

Touma, Toufic
   1965   *Un Village de Montagne au Liban, Hadeth el Jobbe*. Paris: Mouton and Co.

ABSTRACT

Located in a distant corner of Dearborn, Michigan is the oldest and most highly concentrated community of Arab Muslims in North America. The "Southend" as it is popularly referred to serves as an immigrant reception area to the growing number of new Arab immigrants arriving in Dearborn and Detroit. The area is home to three nationality groups including Lebanese, Palestinian, and Yemeni residents, all of whom share a common language, religion, and cultural heritage. The community's solid working-class status clearly distinguishes it from the rest of Dearborn and the surrounding Detroit area Arab-American communities. Two culturally distinctive institutions, the Islamic mosque and Arabic coffeehouse, play a vital role in the life of the community and give the neighborhood its unique ethnic character. Since the early 1950s the Southend has also been the center of demonstrations, meetings, and other political organizing activities which reflect the strength of Arab nationalism among the area's residents. The importance of the Southend in this regard is underscored by its special status in the eyes of other Arab-Americans, who consider it to be the "heart" of Detroit's Arab-American community.

The Southend:
An Arab Muslim
Working-Class Community

by Sameer Y. Abraham, Nabeel Abraham, and Barbara Aswad

Over the years, Dearborn, Detroit's nearby suburban neighbor, has become known as a very "nice" place to live because of the low property taxes[1] and the reputation of the city for being "lily white."[2] Few people are aware that in a distant corner in the city's industrial hub is a working-class community of Arab immigrants. That community is home to the oldest and most highly concentrated population of Arab Muslims in North America.[3] The purpose of this paper is to present a profile of that community, its function as an "immigrant reception area," and the working-class status of its residents. The mosque and the coffeehouse, two key social institutions, will be examined because of their distinctive cultural origins. Finally, Arab nationalism, which plays a central role in the life of the community, will also be analyzed.

---

[1] Until recently, the Ford Motor Company and its subsidiaries paid almost half the local property taxes in Dearborn. A state re-equalization in 1981 had the effect of redistributing more of the tax burden to home owners. Many homes which had been under-assessed have had their property taxes increased by an average of 50%.

[2] In 1970, the U.S. Census identified only .4% of the Dearborn population as "non-white"; by 1980, the non-white population had increased to 1.6%. It is suspected that some of these individuals were actually Arabs who had been "misclassified" by census enumerators.

To a certain extent, it is unfair to single out Dearborn for its segregationist policies and practices, as most other suburbs in the Detroit area pursued similar housing policies with similar results. Dearborn appears more visible, perhaps, due to the dominant role played by its former mayor, Orville Hubbard, who after almost thirty years in office was closely and vocally associated with the shape of these activities in the community.

[3] In 1980, Dearborn's population totaled some 90,660; approximately 5,000 (or 5.5%) of the city's inhabitants are located in this area. Arab-Americans also reside in other parts of Dearborn, especially in the northeast area where their numbers are on the increase (cf. Katarsky 1980).

The Dearborn Arab community is popularly referred to as the "Southend" because of its ghetto-like geographical concentration in the southeast corner of the city along the Detroit-Dearborn boundary. In an earlier study, Wigle described the physical isolation of this area in the following terms:

> Upon entry into the Southend, an observer is immediately struck by its geographical isolation from the rest of Dearborn and Detroit. It is surrounded on three sides by large factories, and on a fourth side, it is enclosed by a park [and cemetery]. (1974:155)

While adequate, this description does not provide the observer with a sufficiently graphic picture of the foreboding physical appearance of the area. To the west of the community stands the towering Ford Rouge Plant, perhaps the world's largest integrated manufacturing complex. Its mile-long presence appears like an industrial wall which casts an awesome shadow over the community. The smokestacks are forever spewing clouds of smoke into the atmosphere, as if to remind the inhabitants of the area of the auto industry's former preeminence. Dix Avenue, the major highway which bisects the community and divides it into north and south, plays an important role as the industrial corridor for trucks moving back and forth between plants in Detroit and Dearborn and the downriver industries. Rarely is there a moment of quiet along this major thoroughfare where a majority of the area's commercial establishments are located. The immediate sight, sound, and smell of industry are always present.[4] To the outsider, the physical setting of the community makes it a very depressing place.

THE ARAB CHARACTER OF THE COMMUNITY

Over the course of this century, a number of ethnic communities have developed alongside the automotive industries of Detroit. When the Ford Motor Company decided in the 1920s to expand its original facilities in Highland Park (a city within the heart of Detroit), it relocated them in Dearborn, a suburb on the immediate western boundary of Detroit. The Southend has served as the home for a number of immigrant groups from Central and Eastern Europe as well as Americans from the rural south

---

[4]In a recent survey of the community, Bowker found that while the vast majority (85%) of her respondents were generally satisfied with life in the community, the most frequent complaints (83%) had to do with noise, air pollution, dirt, and dust (1979:38).

In 1981, the Wayne County Air Pollution Control agency measured atmospheric pollutants at the annual geometric mean of 116 per cubic meter of air. The Federal Related Standard is established at 75 micrograms (Nieson 1982). The level was much higher before Ford moved its foundry several years ago and increased its regulation of pollution.

and other parts of Michigan.[5] During the first half of this century, the Southend was home to a group largely composed of Italian, Romanian, and Polish immigrants. The Arabic-speaking population was relatively small during this time but steadily grew in number. Arab immigration appears to have peaked in two periods: the years 1927–1933 and 1946–1953, according to Elkholy (1966:19). Another wave of immigration to the area began in 1967 and has continued to intensify ever since.

While remnants of these earlier groups continue to reside in the Southend, the aggregate Arab population appears to have become the majority sometime in the 1960s. In a recent survey of the area, Aswad (1973) found that over half the population (52%) were Arab immigrants or descendants of Arab immigrants. Less than a decade later, Bowker (1979:13) found that this simple majority had grown into an overwhelming majority: three-quarters (73%) of the population identified their ethnicity as Arab.[6] The Arab population is in turn divided into three main nationality groups. When place of birth is used to classify the population, the Lebanese constitute the majority (44%), Yemenis the second-largest group (12%), while the Palestinians constitute the smallest group (8%) (Bowker 1979:23). Where once the non-Arab residents resisted identifying the Southend as an Arab community, most now have resigned themselves to this fact.

Well before the Arabs constituted the majority of the Southend's population, the community revealed its Arab character in the many small business establishments which are interspersed along Dix Avenue and scattered throughout some of the residential side streets. An earlier researcher described the Arab character of the area in these terms:

> The Arab community is not only a physical but also a cultural niche. Many traditional Middle Eastern customs are maintained …the Arabic atmosphere is marked. Numerous coffeehouses are interspersed with Arabic restaurants and grocery stores which import much of their food from the "old country." Females are rarely seen on Dix; it is a congregating place for males. Advertisements are written in Arabic and Arabic is the main language spoken on the streets. (Wigle 1974:155–156)

Men and women can often be seen in their dresses of national origin as if they were still in their villages. Groups of men stroll along Dix Avenue and congregate at street corners near the coffeehouses, restaurants, billiard halls, and the nearby mosque. The regular calls of the *muezzin* (the prayer caller) at the mosque are now carried across a public address system which can be heard throughout the area, reminding the Muslim residents of their

---

[5]When birthplace is used as an indicator, the current non-Arab population falls into three groups: 18% from other parts of Michigan; 6% from other states; and 6% of European birth (Bowker 1979:23).

[6]Today it is reasonable to assume that approximately 80% or more of the Southend's inhabitants are Arab immigrants or of Arab ancestry. Hereinafter, we shall refer to the Southend as a purely Arab-American community and treat it as such in our discussion unless otherwise indicated.

obligations. As one passes along the commercial district (the *souq* or marketplace as it is sometimes referred to) one engages many of the sights and sounds familiar to the bazaars so common in the countries from which these immigrants came. So pervasive is the Arabic atmosphere that to many non-Arabs who work and live in the area, the most frequent expression heard is the feeling of being in a "foreign country" in one's own neighborhood.

AN IMMIGRANT RECEPTION AREA

Another distinguishing feature of the Southend is that it is considered a *primary* community because of its function as an "immigrant reception area." Many newly arrived Arab Muslim immigrants tend to locate in the Southend because kinsmen and/or co-villagers have already established themselves in the area. The extent to which this activity continues can be partially gleaned from a recent study of northeast Dearborn in which one investigator found that over half of his Lebanese respondents had originally settled in the Southend before moving to the newly emerging northeast community (Katarsky 1980:24). A pattern of "family chain migration" has been responsible for one family member sponsoring another in an ever-widening circle. Another indicator of the primacy of the community is revealed in the fact that over *two-thirds* of the Arab respondents in Bowker's study were born in the Arab world and emigrated to the United States *after* 1974 (1979:23–24). In other words, a significant portion of the Southend's population is composed of recent immigrants, a pattern which is likely to become more accentuated in the future. The prevalence of new immigrants in recent years has so radically altered the face of the community that Elkholy's study which was conducted in 1959 (1966) and the study by Wasfi (1964) refer to a community which for all intents and purposes no longer exists in the Southend. It is not as though one group had settled in the area many years ago and passed through the phases of community growth, development, and change over a generation or two. Rather, the Southend is constantly being infused with such a large number of new immigrants in a short span of time that it is undergoing the process of formation and re-formation every ten years or so. It is for that reason that the many early residents and their children who left the Southend in the last twenty years tend to lament the fact that the "Southend is not what it was during my childhood...it's not the same community," as one former resident nostalgically stated.

As some immigrants become economically mobile, there is a tendency for them to relocate in areas outside the Southend. Some have settled in northeast Dearborn in a newly emerging Lebanese community; others have found nearby neighborhoods in southwest Detroit more to their liking; and still others have preferred the downriver suburbs of Allen Park, Lincoln Park, Wyandotte, and Ecorse or have moved to other states. In a sense, the Southend acts like a hub through which immigrants are first drawn and eventually channeled to satellite neighborhoods usually in the surrounding area. As these "secondary" settlements grow in size, many new immigrant arrivals will be able to bypass the Southend community and locate directly in these areas much as many immigrants are doing in northeast Dearborn today. In fact, the day may not be too far off when the "Northend" (i.e., northeast Dearborn) becomes the "middle-class" counterpart of the working-class Southend (cf. Katarsky 1980).

THE SOUTHEND AS A WORKING-CLASS COMMUNITY

One of the characteristics which clearly sets the Southend apart from the rest of Dearborn and other Arab communities in the Detroit area is the fact that the Southend is a working class community *par excellence.*[7] According to any definition of social class, the Arab immigrants are firmly situated in the working class. A number of empirical indicators can be used to establish the community's socioeconomic status. When home ownership, for example, is used as an indicator, Elkholy in 1959 found that a full three-quarters of the Arab residents were home owners (1966:41). A little over a decade later, Aswad in her survey (1971) found that home ownership for all Southenders, Arab and non-Arab alike, had fallen to less than half (46%) (1974:67). By the end of the decade, Arab home ownership had fallen once again, reducing the percentage to only one-third (Bowker 1979:9). The fact that two-thirds of the Arab residents are today renters is only partially due to the decreasing earning power of the working-class. Other factors also enter into the picture.[8] The city of Dearborn has been responsible for tearing down many single and multistory houses in an "urban renewal" effort over the past thirty years which has reduced the size of the local housing market[9] (cf. Aswad 1974:53–84). But even with these qualifications, other indicators like occupation, income, and education point to solid working-class status.

Bowker in her study found that almost the entire Arab population surveyed were either white-collar or blue-collar wage earners (96%), whereas only 4% of the population were self-employed (1979:49). Of those employed, a full 80% were semiskilled or unskilled laborers. This finding is very much in keeping with Elkholy's earlier survey in which he found that a majority (60%) of his first-generation respondents were manual laborers (1966:57). (Of the balance, almost a fifth (17%) were self-employed owners of small retail establishments.) A noticeable change is clearly discernible in the twenty-year period between surveys: the percentage of manual laborers has significantly increased while the percentage of self-employed proprietors has substantially decreased. In other words, the Arab population

---

[7]Unless otherwise indicated, all comparisons between the Southend and Dearborn are based on U.S. Census data. The various sources used are cited in the references.

[8]Yemenis are particularly noted for their preference to remain renters rather than become home owners owing to their desire not to settle permanently in the United States (see the article by N. Abraham in this volume).

[9]The Southend's home ownership rate compares rather poorly with the rest of Dearborn. In 1970, the rate was 80% and remained stable in 1980 at 78%.

is becoming more *proletarianized* with each succeeding generation.[10]

Like occupation, income is usually, but not always, directly related to social class. In 1980, the median income for a Southend family was $13,981, which contrasts rather sharply with the $26,935 for Dearborn as a whole. Put in different terms, Dearbornites had a median income which was almost *twice* as large as that of the Southend residents. Over a twenty-year period, the gap appears to have widened considerably. While the difference in 1960 was only $3,401 and was reduced in 1970 to $3,001, the income gap in 1980 had increased *fourfold* to $12,954. It is unlikely that such an enormous difference between groups will be quickly or easily reduced in the near future. Given the recent downturn in the automotive and related industries, upon which this community is so heavily dependent, it is likely that the income gap will widen even further.

The fluctuations in the automobile industry have left a deep economic scar on the Southend community. Because so many residents are employed in the automobile plants, unemployment and poverty are on the increase. In 1980, nearly one-third (31%) of the Southend population was unemployed,[11] as compared to less than a tenth (8%) of the remaining Dearbornites who suffered a similar fate. Put differently, the unemployment rate in the Southend is *four times* greater than that of the rest of Dearborn. In the past, the gap between groups was not as large. In 1960, for example, the unemployment rate was 11% for Southenders and a mere 5% for the remaining Dearbornites. By 1970, the rate for both groups had decreased slightly, 10% for the Southend and 4% for Dearborn, but the difference between groups remained unchanged. Unlike the previous two decades where the difference was only twice as large, today the gap is four times as great.

A similar picture emerges when poverty rates are considered.[12] Whereas one-quarter (27%) of the Southend population fell below the poverty line in 1980, only 5% of the remaining Dearborn population was impoverished.

---

[10]The Southend community contrasts sharply with other Arab populations in the Detroit area. For example, Sengstock in her study of the Iraqi Chaldeans found that less than one-third (29%) of her respondents were semiskilled or unskilled workers, whereas over half (54%) were self-employed proprietors of middle-class standing (1967:113). Similarly, Ahdab-Yehia in her study of Detroit's Lebanese Maronites found that only a tenth of the population surveyed fell into unskilled or semiskilled occupations, while over two-thirds (72%) were either self-employed or professionals and managers, i.e., middle class (1970:73).

[11]Persons are classified as unemployed if, at the time of the census, "they were civilians 16 years old and over and (a) were neither 'at work' nor 'with a job but not at work' during the reference week, (b) were looking for work during the last 4 weeks, and (c) were available to accept a job. Also included as unemployed are persons who did not work at all during the reference week and were waiting to be called to a job from which they had been laid off" (U.S. Census 1980:B-5).

[12]The poverty level is defined according to income for a non-farm family of four. In 1970 it was $3,721 and in 1980 reached $7,412 (U.S. Census 1970:App-30; U.S. Census 1980:B-6, respectively).

The gap between groups was just as substantial in 1970 when one-fifth (20%) of the Southenders were below the poverty line as opposed to 5% of the remaining population. While the poverty rate has remained stable for most Dearbornites, the number of impoverished Southenders increased by 7% over the course of a decade. The gloomy economic forecasts of the early 1980s indicate that poverty may become a permanent feature of the community as the current recession worsens.

Education is a third variable which is usually highly correlated with social class. Generally speaking, the latest immigrant arrivals appear to have attained a higher educational level than earlier immigrants. Whereas only 16% of the pre-1974 arrivals had completed high school, almost twice as many (29%) of the post-1974 immigrants had received their diplomas (Bowker 1979:26). Overall, however, the Arab community contrasts poorly with the other inhabitants of Dearborn. In 1980, over twice as many Dearbornites (70%) had received a high school diploma as compared to their Southend counterparts (31%). As was the case with other measures, the education gap between groups appears to have widened over the course of two decades. In 1960, one-quarter (25%) of all Southenders had received a high school degree as opposed to one-half (51%) of the remaining Dearborn population. A decade later, the gap between groups had increased from 25% to 32%, that is, 27% for Southenders as opposed to 59% for the balance of Dearborn in 1970. Today, the difference between groups is 39%. While both groups have increased the percentage of high school graduates over the course of two decades, the Southend increases have been extremely meager as opposed to the gains of the remainder of Dearborn's population. It is unlikely that such a major gap can be closed in the very near future, especially as the number of new immigrants to the area increases.

To a great extent the low educational attainment of the Southend is in turn responsible for the predominance of the Arabic language in the community. In 1959, Elkholy found that almost all of the respondents in his survey did not know English before emigrating to the United States (1966:84). Two decades later, Bowker found that facility in the English language greatly varied, from one-third who knew "no" English at all to the remaining two-thirds who had some "limited" conversational, reading, and/or writing abilities (1979:27). While Arabic remains the dominant language in the area, especially among first-generation members, some 40% of the Arab respondents in Bowker's study had attended English language classes (1979:29). Even so, the community strongly identifies with the Arabic language, so much so that 80% of Bowker's respondents wanted their children to learn Arabic (1979:30). The continuing infusion of new immigrants into the area, coupled with their production-type work which limits communication on the job, virtually insure that Arabic will remain the area's dominant language. Many children who have entered Dearborn's public schools have encountered difficulties because of their limited facility in English. As a partial remedy, the Dearborn Public Schools introduced an Arabic bilingual/bicultural program in 1976 which currently involves eight schools in which there is a growing Arab student population.[13]

Clearly, then, the Southend was and remains a working-class community. Over the course of two decades, the inhabitants of the area have become more proletarianized. Their recent immigrant status and rural backgrounds tend to insure that they will be relegated to manual occupations with the greatest instability and have little opportunity for advancement. The increasing unemployment and poverty among Southend residents also points to a community with a sizable and growing "underclass." Given the downsizing of the automobile firms, it is likely that a significant portion of the Southend's residents will be reduced to this impoverished status permanently. In every respect, however, the Southend remains a thriving and vibrant community in the fullest sense of the term. Not only do the residents of the area share the same physical niche, but they also strongly identify as a community. Of the various organizations and institutions which make up the life of the community, two institutions in particular stand out: the mosque and the Arabic coffeehouse.

THE MOSQUE IN AN ARAB MUSLIM COMMUNITY

Religion is another distinguishing feature which sets the Southend community apart not only from the wider society, but from the majority of Detroit's Arab-Americans as well. In 1959, Elkholy surmised that approximately ten percent of Arab-Americans located in the Detroit metropolitan area were Muslims (1966:27). Today, Arab Muslims comprise anywhere from 30% to 40% of the 200,000 Arab-Americans in the Detroit area and their numbers are steadily on the increase (see the article by S. Abraham in this volume). In her survey of the Southend, Bowker found that almost 73% of the inhabitants were Arab and of that number only 3% were non-Muslims (1979:8). Because of its Muslim identity, the Southend community is unique among Detroit's Arab-American communities. In effect, the Southend Arab Muslims constitute a *minority within a minority.* The two major "factions"[14] in Islam, Sunni and Shia (and among Yemenis,

---

[13] Arabic-speaking students represent the single largest group of bilingual students in the Dearborn Public Schools. In 1976–1977 their number totaled 238, whereas in 1981–1982 they had increased to 1,481, a *six-fold increase* in less than five years. In a home language survey conducted in October, 1982 the school district determined that approximately 2,100 of Dearborn's 12,300 enrolled students were of Arab ancestry. In other words, almost two out of every ten students (or 17%) in Dearborn is an Arab-American. It is more than likely that the home survey may have actually underestimated the total Arab-American student population since many second- and third-generation families do not speak Arabic at home.

[14] There are two main divisions in Islam: Sunni, who follow the *Sunna*, the traditional practice of Muhammad as set forth in the *Hadith* ("Traditions"), and Shia. The Shia is a "faction" that held that only the descendants of the Prophet Muhammad and his son-in-law Ali should legitimately head the Islamic community. The Shafeis represent one of the four major schools which constitute the Sunni branch, whereas the Zeidis form a Shia following in Yemen.

Shafei and Zeidi), are present in the community and have played a role in the choice of religious leadership and the building of three mosques over the years (cf. Elkholy 1966:73–78).

As a visitor enters the Southend, he is immediately struck by the architecture of the Dearborn Mosque with its large gold dome topped by a crescent moon symbolic of the Islamic faith. Even in its simple brick facade, the mosque tends to leave a lasting impression among the otherwise largely soot-grey, nondescript commercial buildings, duplex homes, and rundown tenements that comprise the neighborhood. Located at the major crossroads of Dix Avenue and Vernor Highway—the latter a major street leading into Detroit—the "Moslem Mosque," as it is officially named, stands conspicuously at the eastern entrance of the community, serving as a constant reminder of the Southend's unique ethnic and religious character. In recent years the Islamic call to prayer, ritually announced from the upper floors or minarets of the mosques before each of the five daily prayers, have been broadcast over a large loudspeaker perched atop the upper floor of the building.[15] This innovation came about as a result of the influx of more traditionally oriented Muslims into the congregation, mostly unaccompanied males who are recent arrivals to the community. Their increasing influence led to a "takeover" of the mosque culminating in the ouster of the presiding American-born imam and his replacement by a more traditionally-minded imam from the Arab world.[16] The change in religious leadership brought to an abrupt close a long chapter in the history of the "Moslem Mosque" and of the larger Southend Arab community as well. As the mosque's original congregation was becoming more "Americanized," the mosque began to function more like an "ethnic church." Given recent events, that process has been totally reversed.

Until recently, there were two mosques in the Southend, both of which were established by an earlier generation of immigrants. One of them, the "Hashmite Club" was established in 1933 by a group of Lebanese immigrants organized under the Hashmite Renaissance Society, a Shia association. The society established the Hashmite Club in a former bank building which was bought and remodelled in 1936 (Wasfi 1964:133). Located on the corner of Dix Avenue and Salina Street in the heart of the Southend

---

[15]The prayer caller's use of a loudspeaker has not been without its share of difficulties. On the basis of twenty-five complaints of residents living near the mosque, Dearborn's city attorney filed a formal complaint in 1979 in the Dearborn district court charging three mosque officials with violation of the city's noise ordinance. Ultimately the charges were dismissed on the basis of the Muslims' first amendment rights, and consequently the call continues to be broadcast five times a day. Officials of the mosque point out that the chimes of the Christian churches, the harsh cacophony of trains coupling in a nearby railroad yard, and the blare of rock concerts in a neighborhood park also continue even, at times, into the wee hours of the morning without a formal "noise" complaint.

[16]The "takeover" of mosques by more fundamentalist-oriented Muslims appears to be a widespread phenomenon (see the article by Haddad in this volume).

business district, the Hashmite Club consisted of a meeting hall on the ground floor and a large prayer room adjoining several smaller classrooms and a business office on the upper floor. An accidental fire destroyed the building in early 1977, and it was subsequently razed in 1980. The mosque had long since ceased functioning as a place of worship by the mid-1960s after a rival group of Lebanese Shia led by another imam built the Islamic Center of Detroit. Although this new mosque was located several miles north of the Southend, it succeeded in attracting a large number of Southend Shia and former Southend residents and their offspring. Because many second- and third-generation Lebanese Shia frowned upon the old Southend neighborhood and were reluctant to attend the mosque there, the Islamic Center appears to have filled the vacuum (cf. Wasfi 1964; Elkholy 1966).

Not to be outdone by their compatriots, rival Lebanese Sunni in 1939 began construction of the Dearborn "Moslem Mosque" several blocks away. Working under the auspices of the *Manaret al-Hoda*, the Sunni were only able to finish the ground floor of the mosque, while the main upper floor with its distinctive dome had to await completion in 1952. The upper floor includes a large prayer room, an adjacent room for the performance of ritual ablution, an office for the imam, and a classroom. The unpartitioned ground floor with its accompanying small stage and kitchen was used as a multipurpose hall for weddings, funerals, social occasions, and religious and Arabic-language instruction. Adjacent to the mosque was a large empty field belonging to the sponsoring association, which was renamed the "American Islamic Association" in 1952. The lot seems to have been purchased with the intention of future expansion of the mosque facility. For as long as anyone can remember, however, a large advertising billboard has stood in the middle of the empty field, where it is readily visible to passing motorists on Vernor Highway.

The mosque's religious importance to the community extends beyond the neighborhood. Elkholy described the role of the mosque in these terms: "The mosque institution plays a vital role in the life of the entire community, for religion's vital psychological functions integrate the individual personality with that of the surrounding society" (1966:134). Although the mosques in the Southend primarily served the local community, their congregations, at least in the case of the Moslem Mosque, included Muslims from the surrounding communities. Thus, the two Southend mosques and later the Islamic Center of Detroit, have been a constant source of pride for Arab Muslims throughout the Detroit area.

As a place of worship the mosque is used for the weekly Friday-noon communal prayer, although Islamic theology permits a Muslim to pray on any clean spot on earth, which in a practical sense means praying at home. Because of the difficulties encountered in leaving work to worship on Fridays, the weekly communal prayer has traditionally been observed only by the elderly and retired men of the Southend. Although women are not barred from the Friday services, and in fact do attend services at the larger urban mosques in the Muslim world, they rarely attend the communal service beyond the two major Islamic holidays of *Eid al-Fitar* and *Eid al-Adha.*[17] The Friday communal prayers, rarely attended by more than a handful of pious men, almost disappeared as the custom of Sunday worship became the preferred norm (Elkholy 1966; Wasfi 1964). In recent years, a group of men of varying ages, numbering up to one hundred at times, can be found attending the Friday communal prayer. In contrast to the past, this attendance represents a virtual revival of the Friday prayer, a revival which appears after almost two decades of decline and near extinction of the custom. To a great extent, the revival of the mosque is a direct result of the influx of a large number of new immigrants to the Southend. The recent arrivals have brought with them a "fundamentalist" Islamic consciousness which has recently spread throughout many of the Arab and Muslim countries.

While the religious functions of the mosques have been vital, the mosques have also played an important social and educational role. In fact, the Southend mosques were primarily established with the equal purpose of servicing the immigrant community's social needs as much as their religious needs. Funerals, weddings, holidays, and celebrations were constantly attended in the mosque, so much so that the ground floor, the "social domain" of the mosque, saw greater use over the years than the upper floor or the "sanctuary." The educational role of the mosques was just as important, although not as pervasive. Throughout the 1960s, both Southend mosques organized Arabic-language and religious instruction classes intermittently. The classes, however, were never completely institutionalized. At best they averaged two to four years in duration. An unspoken competition appears to have emerged between the Sunni mosque and the Shia Hashmite Hall in the offering of classes, whereby the termination of one group's classes would prompt the rival to start similar classes (cf. Elkholy 1966; Wasfi 1964). The importance of these classes, especially religious instruction, was underscored by Elkholy, who, in studying the degree of religiosity in the Southend and the Toledo (Ohio) Muslim communities, wrote: "The great majority of those second-generation members in both communities who are religious were found to have learned about their religion from the mosque rather than from their parents" (1966:148).

In the decades of the 1960s and 1970s both mosques often served as the site of numerous political meetings, rallies, and demonstrations. When these accommodations proved too confining owing to their limited size and facilities, many Southend members turned to the more spacious Islamic Center of Detroit. Many Southend Sunni, however, still appear reluctant to use the tightly managed Center facilities for their religious observances. In recent years, the community has had to turn to non-Arab-owned private social halls outside the community to host many of their social and political events. This alternative will probably become the norm as the funda-

---

[17]*Eid al-Fitar* or "Lesser Bairam" marks the end of the month-long fast of *Ramadan*. *Eid al-Adha* or "Greater Bairam" falls seventy days after *Eid al-Fitar* and commemorates the redemption of Abraham's son, Ishmael. It coincides with the end of the Islamic pilgrimage to Mecca.

mentalist-oriented group led by a traditionally minded imam has led to a "ban" on social and political activities taking place in the Moslem Mosque. The continuation of this policy will lead to an increase in tension between groups and may act as a stimulus in the establishment of yet another mosque.

THE ARABIC COFFEEHOUSE

Of all the many commercial establishments which exist in the Southend, one institution in particular stands out as a foreign transplant, the Arabic coffeehouse. The coffeehouse is a traditional Middle Eastern social institution wherein a primary level of social interaction is maintained among men and usually age peers. It is a segregated institution *par excellence*, for it is within the physical setting of the coffeehouse that men socially and politically interact. In fact, the coffeehouse resembles a closed club more than a commercial enterprise. Should an unsuspecting outsider enter one of the many coffeehouses scattered throughout the Southend to purchase a cup of tea or thick Turkish coffee, he may find himself in a rather awkward situation, as all those who frequent such establishments usually know one another intimately.

The coffeehouses cater to men of all ages, but are usually frequented by men over the age of eighteen, though there is no rigid regulation which prohibits younger males from entering. As a traditional preserve of the Arab male, the coffeehouse provides a unique social environment in which leisure time and recreational activities are pursued. After a day's work at the nearby factory, and a short trip home for dinner, the men turn to the coffeehouses to spend their evenings with relatives and friends. The same group of men can be observed in their daily routine of card playing and backgammon, the two most popular forms of entertainment. In some cases, a traditional village hierarchy is maintained within the coffeehouses. Certain tables which are known to be frequented by the elderly village heads are avoided by the younger men as a gesture of deference to their status and importance.

The coffeehouse also functions as a center where community problems are discussed, where news from the home village is exchanged, and where disputes emerge, end, and reemerge. Family feuds have a habit of finding their way into the coffeehouse. Because the proprietor may be related to one of the families, the contending family may find it expedient to "boycott" his establishment in retaliation. By the time a boycott is underway, family alliances have been formed and the villagers have been divided into major factions. The coffeehouse is many times defined as the battlefield. Most issues, however, are usually not so volatile.

Coffeehouses also serve as an important center for political communication and discussion. Events in the Middle East are openly discussed and debated among the patrons. When events are particularly critical, the owner or clients will bring their shortwave radios and televisions to the coffeehouse to follow the news. Most coffeehouse owners openly display their nationalist affiliations and the coffeehouse clientele in turn tend to identify coffeehouse proprietors according to their political loyalties. During the heady days of pan-Arab nationalism, one coffeehouse owner named his establishment "Nasser's" after the president of Egypt (Wasfi 1964:126). Today one can find the "Palestine" coffeehouse which reflects the growth of Palestinian nationalism and the identity of the owner. Pictures of political personalities like Gamal Abdel-Nasser and Yasser Arafat freely adorn the walls of most of these establishments (Wigle and Abraham 1974:293). As if to signal their concrete commitment to the "cause," some establishments display the official receipts of contributions sent by their clientele to Palestinian charitable organizations. Local activists find the walls of the coffeehouse provide a ready space on which to publicize cultural and political events. The coffeehouse also provides access to a pool of residents who can be easily mobilized for the demonstrations which occur with growing frequency in the community. The strategic location of these establishments and the daily visitations by community residents insure the immediate transmission of information.

New coffeehouses in the Southend are constantly being opened while others, faltering financially, are closing their doors. In the early 1960s, Wasfi located five coffeehouses, three of which were owned by Italian-Americans, but whose clientele was predominantly Arab (1964:86–87). By 1975, their number had increased to ten and all were owned by Arabs. Some were located on Dix Avenue and others were scattered along the residential side streets. Among these coffeehouses, two were Lebanese, three Palestinian, and five Yemeni.[18] The coffeehouses are distinguished not only on the basis of nationality, but also according to the village their proprietors represent. Of the three Palestinian coffeehouses, for example, one is owned by a member of El Bireh and the other two by natives of Beit Hanina, two West Bank villages. A similar pattern of representation characterizes the Yemeni and Lebanese establishments. Each of the enterprising proprietors caters to a specific clientele, usually the compatriots of his village, many of whom are related to the owner. The changing character of the community's residents has been responsible for the perpetual opening and closing of numerous coffeehouses over the years.

The existence and perpetuation of the coffeehouse institution in the Southend appears to be directly linked to three factors: 1) the social need created by the continuing influx of new immigrants; 2) the working-class and rural background of the residents; and 3) the ecological concentration of the community. In the surrounding Arab communities[19] where middle-class status has been attained and residential dispersion is the pattern, first-

---

[18]The fact that most Yemenis have emigrated without their families may explain the larger number of coffeehouses among this group.

[19]Two exceptions stand out: coffeehouses have been established among the working-class immigrants of Detroit's Iraqi Chaldean community, although they are not found among their middle-class suburban counterparts. Another exception is the growing Lebanese community located in northeast Dearborn where one coffeehouse has recently opened (Katarsky 1980:28). Although it is argued that this is a

generation members have redirected their leisure time and social activities into the establishment of more westernized clubs, church associations, and home visitations (cf. Saba 1971; Ahdab-Yehia 1970). This tendency is not limited to Detroit area residents. In the Chicago Arab community, Haddad noted the early disappearance of the coffeehouses there as a consequence of the residents' economic mobility and residential scattering (1969:96). Once a higher socioeconomic status is attained, social circumstances and a changed class outlook tend to lead to a dissolution of this age-old institution.

A CENTER OF ARAB NATIONALISM

Since the early 1950s, the Southend has been the site of repeated political demonstrations, meetings, and organizing activities centering almost exclusively on issues stemming from the Middle East. In the aftermath of the Palestine War (1948) which led to the creation of the state of Israel and the forced exodus of nearly a million Palestinians from their homeland, the Arab world has been locked in a bitter and often bloody struggle with Israel into the present. During the interim period, the Arab world itself has witnessed successive periods of political turmoil and instability, as contending political personalities, ideologies, and movements have vied with one another for power and influence. The events of the past three decades have reverberated throughout the Arab world and beyond, influencing events in the Southend community as well. In the period leading up to the June War (1967), the dominant themes in Arab politics centered on the charismatic personality of the late Egyptian leader, Gamal Abdel-Nasser. Millions of Arabs identified with Nasser's leadership of the entire Arab nation, his quest for independence, unity, and the restitution of Palestinian national rights.

While Nasser came to power in a 1952 military coup which overthrew the corrupt rule of the Egyptian monarch, King Farouk, it was not until the Suez War (1956) in which Egypt defended itself against a combined attack by Britain, France, and Israel that his popularity spread throughout the Arab countries. The Egyptian leader's popularity also extended to the Southend community. Evidence of this is revealed in the remarks of a prominent community member, who on the eve of King Hussein of Jordan's visit to Detroit in 1959 stated:

> Whenever a party is opened in the name of the Prophet, no one is particularly moved. If it is opened in the name of God, no one cares either. But the name of Gamal Abdel-Nasser electrifies the hall. (Quoted in Elkholy 1966:48)

"middle-class" community, it is suspected that the definition of social class has been too loosely defined, as the bulk of Katarsky's respondents were employees, most of whom were semiskilled or unskilled laborers (1980:32–33).

Nasser's defiance of Israel and the Western European powers and his subsequent rise to world prominence reawakened a sense of nationalism among the Southend Arabs. For them, Nasser represented the quintessence of the Arab nation and continuity with the Arabs' "glorious" past. Community members acknowledged identification with Nasser by adorning the walls of their homes with his picture (Elkholy 1966:48). Through Nasser, many Arab-Americans were able to forge a new sense of pride and self-esteem. Whereas during an earlier period, many first-generation parents would attempt to hide their ethnic origins, some to the extent of changing their names, many now freely and openly acknowledged their Arab identity (Wasfi 1964:113). The former feelings of "inferiority" as an unknown minority group, which agonized many, tended to fade in the wake of the Suez War (Wasfi 1964:173).

The Arab-Israeli war of June 1967 was a major turning point for the Arab world and for the Arab nationalist movement. The humiliating defeat inflicted on the Arab armies by Israel paved the way for the emergence of the Palestinian resistance movement. Arab students at a nearby university took the lead in introducing this new, more militant nationalism to the Southend (N. Abraham 1978:124). Like Arabs elsewhere, the Southend community placed their renewed hopes and national aspirations on the Palestinian *fedayeen* ("guerillas"). Wigle and S. Abraham summed up the prevailing mood of the Southend in the post-1967 period when the Palestinian resistance had risen to prominence:

> Though the Palestinian sector of the community felt closest to the Resistance, every Arab identified himself with the struggle to liberate Palestine. In place of Nasser's photo, posters of the *fedayeen* were pinned up in homes, stores, restaurants and many coffeehouses. (A pro-Nasserite sentiment lingered on, however, as many merely added a poster next to Nasser's photo.) Talk turned from Nasser and the affairs of Arab states to the activities of the *fedayeen*. (1974:295)

The decade of the 1970s was an extremely turbulent one for the Middle East. A seemingly endless cycle of bloody events shook the region: the Arab-Israeli war of October 1973; the Lebanese civil war (1975–1977); the Israeli invasion of southern Lebanon (March 1978). Each of these events precipitated a reaction on the part of the Southend residents, who organized political demonstrations, meetings, and lectures and collected financial contributions to aid the wounded and homeless. These events were usually preceded by the mass distribution of political leaflets and announcements written for the most part in Arabic. Nationalist activity appears to have peaked during the October War (1973), when the Southend was the scene of a mass demonstration in front of the offices of the United Automobile Workers (UAW) Local 600, which are located in the heart of the Southend. Nearly 2,000 persons took part in the demonstration, making it one of the largest in the community's history (cf. Georgakas 1975:15; Ahmed 1975:19). The demonstration began as a rally at the nearby Moslem Mosque and then made its way to the UAW local where the demand was raised that the UAW dispose of the Israeli government bonds in its possession.

Nearly six weeks later, on November 28, 1973, Southend activists called for another demonstration to coincide with a B'nai B'rith fund-raising dinner at which then-UAW President Leonard Woodcock was scheduled to receive the organization's "Humanitarian Award of the Year." Unlike the previous demonstration which took place in the Southend, the November 28th demonstration was held in front of Cobo Hall in downtown Detroit, some ten miles from the Southend. Although Arab-Americans throughout Detroit were mobilized, the Southend residents constituted the backbone of the demonstration. The Southend neighborhood functioned as the nerve center of the organizing effort. Ismael Ahmed, a Southend activist and one of the demonstration's organizers, described the frenzied atmosphere in the days leading up to the event:

> The organizing for the demonstration went on within the [auto] plants and in the community. This was the first time that the plight of the Arab people had been taken to the workers in any mass way. Nearly 70,000 leaflets calling people in Arabic and English to join the demonstration were distributed. Arab radio stations and newspapers joined in. Local religious leaders declared a day of mourning and wrote absence excuses for workers. On the day of the demonstration Arab high school students went to the plants to turn back workers who had not gotten the news. (1975:19–20)

Well over 2,000 persons participated in the demonstration, making it the largest in the history of the Detroit Arab-American community.

In an earlier study of the political activities in the Southend, Wigle and S. Abraham argued that the community's responses were "situational," that is, they were contingent upon events taking place in the Middle East (1974:283). A distinct pattern was discerned whereby the community reacts in a burst of activity to major crises occurring in the Middle East. These activities were characterized as the "overt manifestations of Arab nationalism." After the crisis subsides "latent nationalism replaces overt nationalism, activities dwindle, organizations fold, and the community reverts to its traditional mode of behavior until the next crisis comes around" (Wigle and S. Abraham 1974:283). The situational character of the community's responses precluded the emergence of pan-community formal organizations that would extend beyond the short-lived, crisis-oriented ad hoc committees. Aside from two locally oriented organizations, the Arab Community Center for Economic and Social Services (ACCESS) and the Southeast Dearborn Community Council (SEDCC),[20]

---

[20]SEDCC was established in 1953 in response to the city of Dearborn's plans to rezone the Southend for heavy industrial use. In 1971, a class action suit was filed

both of which are social service organizations, no major community-wide organizations have been sustained in the Southend for any appreciable period. The lack of such organizations has not prevented the community's activists from *institutionalizing* certain events, however. The "Palestine Day Parade," which has been held on a continuous basis since 1974, has gained wide support and recognition throughout the Southend and Detroit areas. The Parade routinely involves over 1,000 individuals and proceeds through the main shopping district of Dearborn, ending at the doorstep of City Hall. Annual fund-raising dinners are also organized to collect funds in support of Palestinian charitable institutions. These and other activities constitute a growing part of the life of the community.

Given its history and current activities, the Southend can be viewed as a major center of Arab nationalism. The importance of the Southend is underscored by the fact that Arab-American organizations and activists recruit members and conduct many of their activities in the community. Because of its unique function as a primary community, the Southend has earned a special status among Arab-Americans as the "heart" of Detroit's Arab-American community. The Southend's status is reinforced as new immigrants make their way to the area from such politically turbulent areas as the West Bank (Palestine), southern Lebanon, and the border regions of North and South Yemen. In addition to their cultural baggage, the new arrivals bring with them their nationalist sentiments and political consciousness. So long as a large number of immigrants continue to make their way to the Southend, and the political turmoil in the Middle East continues, the Southend will remain a vibrant center for Arab nationalist activities.

CONCLUSION

The Southend is the oldest and most highly concentrated community of Arab Muslims in North America. As home to an earlier group of central

---

in Federal District court by the community council to block the city's controversial urban renewal plans. Buoyed by a victory in the courts, SEDCC has continued to lead the struggle for improved housing and the introduction of federally subsidized low-income housing for the Southend. The community organization, which represents Arab as well as non-Arab members, recently initiated a drive for the establishment of an ethnic heritage museum along with a local labor history archive in the neighborhood.

ACCESS was established in October 1972 by a group of Arab-American professionals and Southend residents. In the period since its founding, the social service organization has come to play an increasingly vital role in the life of the community, especially in the area of assisting new immigrants. "ACCESS has functioned to provide legal aid, employment counseling, instruction in English, and advice in dealing with government bureaucracies" (Wigle and Abraham 1974:300). Although mostly Arab-American in membership, its services are available to all Southend residents.

and eastern European immigrants, the community has functioned and continues to function as an important "reception area" for new Arab immigrants arriving in Dearborn and Detroit. The Southend today consists of three distinct nationality groups, including Lebanese, Palestinians, and Yemenis, who are bound together by a common language, religion, cultural heritage, and socioeconomic status. The ghetto-like enclave in which the community is located and the working-class status of its residents radically set the community apart from the white, middle-class residents of the rest of Dearborn and the surrounding Arab-American communities in the metropolitan area. Over the course of two decades the community has undergone a process of almost complete proletarianization and is currently confronted with the prospect of developing a permanent and impoverished "underclass" among a portion of the residents.

Against a world of economic uncertainty, Islam has served as a unifying force in the life of the three Arab nationality groups which inhabit the Southend. The multifaceted role played by the mosque institution stands as a constant reminder of the Southend's unique ethno-religious character. Perhaps because of its centrality, the mosque has also served as a catalyst in stimulating internal divisions with each passing generation. The Arabic coffeehouse is another key institution, one of the hallmarks of the community, which serves a social as well as political function for its clientele. Through these two institutions, the Southend has been able to transplant and perpetuate part of the "old country" and a distinct way of life. The continuing influx of new immigrants to the Southend also insures that the community will preserve its rich ethnic identity while simultaneously slowing the forces of acculturation and assimilation. The prevalence of the Arabic language and the increasing number of Arab nationalist activities are clear indications that the immigrants have not forsaken their native lands. In fact, the contrary appears to be the case, for once outside their countries, the immigrants manifest a political consciousness which remains current with the changing character of political events in the Arab world. Thus, even with their feet firmly planted in a Western home, thousands of miles distant, the Arab Muslims of the Southend remain firmly transfixed eastward.

REFERENCES

Abraham, Nabeel
1978　National and Local Politics: A Study of Political Conflict in the Yemeni Immigrant Community of Detroit, Michigan. Ph.D. dissertation, University of Michigan, Ann Arbor.

Abraham, Sameer Y.
1975　Arabic Speaking Communities of Southeastern Dearborn: A General Overview. Mimeo. Madison: University of Wisconsin.

Ahdab-Yehia, May
1970　Some General Characteristics of the Lebanese Maronite Community in Detroit. M.A. thesis, Wayne State University, Detroit.

Ahmed, Ismael
1975　Organizing an Arab Workers Caucus. *MERIP Reports* 34:17-22.

Aswad, Barbara
1973　Results of Study on Southeast Dearborn. First Series Revised. Mimeo. Detroit: Wayne State University.

1974　The Southeast Dearborn Arab Community Struggles for Survival Against Urban 'Renewal.' In *Arabic Speaking Communities in American Cities*. B. C. Aswad, ed. New York: Center for Migration Studies and Association of Arab-American University Graduates.

Bowker, Joan P.
1979　Health and Social Service Needs Assessment Survey. Mimeo. Dearborn: University of Michigan.

Elkholy, Abdo A.
1966　*The Arab Moslems in the United States: Religion and Assimilation.* New Haven: College and University Press.

Georgakas, Dan
1975　Arab Workers in Detroit. *MERIP Reports* 34:13-17.

Haddad, Safia H.
1969　The Woman's Role in Socialization of Syrian-Americans. In *The Arab-Americans: Studies in Assimilation.* E. C. Hagopian and A. Paden, eds. Wilmette, Ill.: Medina University Press International.

Hussaini, Hatem
1974　The Impact of the Arab-Israeli Conflict on Arab Communities

182

in the United States. In *Settler Regimes in Africa and the Arab World*. Ibrahim Abu-Lughod and Baha Abu-Laban, eds. Wilmette, Ill.: Medina University Press International.

Katarsky, Anthony P.
  1980 Family Ties and the Growth of an Arabic Community in Northeast Dearborn, Michigan. M.A. thesis, Wayne State University, Detroit.

Nieson, M. J.
  1982 A Brief Comparison of Two Working Class Communities in Metropolitan Detroit. Unpublished paper, Department of Anthropology, Wayne State University, Detroit.

Saba, Leila
  1971 The Social Assimilation of the Ramallah Community Residing in Detroit. M.A. thesis, Wayne State University, Detroit.

Sengstock, Mary C.
  1967 Maintenance of Social Interaction Patterns in an Ethnic Group. Ph.D. dissertation, Washington University, St. Louis.

U.S. Bureau of the Census
  1960 *U.S. Censuses of Population and Housing*. Census Tracts. Final Report PHC(1)-40 (Detroit, Michigan SMSA).

  1970 *Census of Population: 1970. General Social and Economic Characteristics*. Final Report PC(1)-C24 (Michigan).

  1970 *Census of Population and Housing*. Census Tracts. Final Report PHC(1)58 (Detroit, Michigan SMSA).

  1980 *Census of Population and Housing: 1980*. Census Tracts. Final Report PHC80-2 (Detroit, Michigan SMSA).

  1980 *Census of Population and Housing 1980: Summary Tape File 3A*.

Wasfi, Atif A.
  1964 Dearborn Arab-Moslem Community: A Study of Acculturation. Ph.D. dissertation, Michigan State University, East Lansing.

Wigle, Laurel
  1974 An Arab Muslim Community in Michigan. In *Arabic Speaking Communities in American Cities*. B. C. Aswad, ed. New York: Center for Migration Studies and Association of Arab-

American University Graduates.

Wigle, Laurel, and Sameer Y. Abraham
   1974   Arab Nationalism in America: The Dearborn Arab Commu-
           nity. In *Immigrants and Migrants: The Detroit Ethnic Ex-
           perience.* David W. Hartman, ed. Detroit: New University
           Thought Publishing.

Part Three

Select Bibliography
on Arab-Americans

ABSTRACT

A bibliographic guide to the subject of Arab immigration and settlement in the United States is presented. This select bibliography is the result of 1) a review of existing bibliographies; 2) an examination of published books and articles, as well as unpublished dissertations and theses; and 3) personal letters and telephone calls of inquiry to appropriate scholars. Primary and secondary sources are included. These works are intended to provide the reader with a reliable guide for further reading and research.

A Select Bibliography on Arab-American Immigration and Settlement

by Mohammed Sawaie

Any peruser of the literature on immigration to the United States cannot fail to notice the dearth of bibliographic materials on immigrants from Arabic-speaking lands as compared with the materials available about many other ethnic groups. To the best of my knowledge, there is not a single completed compilation of materials relevant to Arab immigration to America. This fact is readily apparent to anyone involved in a search of the literature. In order to remedy the situation, this writer currently is engaged in compiling an annotated bibliography on the subject.

In compiling this select bibliography on Arab migration and settlement, a number of standard bibliographies were first consulted. These included the bibliography compiled by Philip Kayal (1974) at the end of *Arabic Speaking Communities in American Cities,* edited by Barbara C. Aswad; the chapter "Arab Americans: A Guide to the Arab-American Experience" in *A Comprehensive Bibliography for the Study of American Minorities,* vol. I, pp. 263–276 (1976) by Wayne Charles Miller, et al.; and the article by Barbara C. Aswad (1974) titled "Arab-American Studies" in *The Middle East Studies Association Bulletin* 8 (3):13–26.

Published books and periodical articles, as well as unpublished university dissertations and theses were examined next. The bibliographies and lists of references in these works provided a wealth of material. Some of these items are included in this bibliography.

Finally, correspondence, telephone calls, and personal visits to various researchers were helpful in filling the remaining gaps. At times these efforts proved fruitful; at other times, the rewards were only partial. This bibliography represents a search process which extended over a year's time.

The writer encountered two general problems in preparing this survey. Many of the primary materials about early Arab immigration have not been preserved, or if they have, their location has not been documented for reference purposes. The early Arab immigrants published newspapers, magazines, business directories, etc. Many of these items have not been deposited in archival centers for future generations to study. Consequently, many of these valuable early sources of information may be permanently lost. An additional problem that has been pointed out by others in the articles of this book and elsewhere is that the early immigrants were not classified as "Arabs" by the U.S. Immigration authorities. Rather, they were often registered as Ottomans, Syrians, Turks, Armenians, or some other nationality group. The task of the researcher has been complicated enormously as a result of this confusion.

Despite these difficulties, it is significant to note that as early as the turn of this century there was some interest in the documentation and study of Arab immigrants and their adjustment to the new environment. This was initiated either by the immigrants themselves, as in the case of Salloum Mokarzel (1928), or by early "social scientists," such as Lucius Hopkins Miller (1904) and Louise Seymour Houghton (1911). Some theses and dissertations were also written about the early immigrants, such as those by Edith Stein (1922) and Morris Zelditch (1936). In order to learn more about the world of the early Arabic-speaking immigrants, the researcher must delve deeply and tirelessly into the archives and collections of public and private libraries spread across the United States. The location of these materials is widely dispersed due to the fact that while the early immigrants tended to settle in and around the industrial centers and major urban centers, their settlements extended from as far as the Dakotas to the Deep South (see Afif Tannous, 1943; and the article by Alixa Naff in this volume).

Since the early 1950s and 1960s there has been a growing interest in the study of Arabic-speaking immigrants and their communities, assimilation, and acculturation patterns. A growing number of university theses and dissertations have addressed these and other issues. Included among these are the works of Younis (1961), Al-Tahir (1952), Elkholy (1960), and Othman (1970). Some of these dissertations have now been published in book form and are available to a wider readership. These include Elkholy (1966) and Othman (1974), to cite two examples. The Association of Arab-American University Graduates, Inc. (AAUG) has also published two important volumes which focus on Arabs in America. The first was edited by Elaine C. Hagopian and Ann Paden (1969) and the second by Barbara C. Aswad (1974), which was jointly published with the Center for Migration Studies in New York. In these works the reader will find reference to other materials helpful for further research. The Immigration History Research Center at the University of Minnesota also possesses a growing archive of primary materials on Arab immigration and history.

In the selections cited in this bibliography, an attempt was made to provide the reader with a broad compilation of principal works on Arab immigration and settlement. The criteria used for selecting materials were based on either their historical significance in documenting the presence of Arabs in America or their breadth of treatment of this topic.

There was an attempt to provide sufficient representation of the Arabic-speaking groups that are the focus of this book. Additionally, early works were included to highlight the fact that the phenomenon of Arab migration was of interest not only to the immigrants themselves but also to some of the people with whom they came into contact. Finally, the materials were selected to reflect the various facets of immigrant life: literature and language, adjustment to new environments, conflict, religion, and so forth.

These selections are divided into two major categories, published and unpublished materials. Under each category are citations of books, journal or newspaper articles, documents, theses and dissertations, and so on. A word of warning is in order. Some of these works are, undoubtedly, already outdated, and they should be used judiciously as a guide for further investigation.

PUBLISHED MATERIALS

Books and Monographs:

Abraham, Sameer Y., and Nabeel Abraham, eds.
   1981   *The Arab World and Arab-Americans: Understanding a Neglected Minority*. Detroit, Mich.: Wayne State University, Center for Urban Studies.

Abu-Laban, Baha
   1980   *An Olive Branch on the Family Tree: The Arabs in Canada*. Toronto, Canada: McClelland and Stewart Ltd. in association with the Multiculturalism Directorate.

Al-Qazzaz, Ayad
   1979   *Transnational Links Between the Arab Community in the U.S. and the Arab World*. Sacramento: Cal. Central Press.

Aswad, Barbara C., ed.
   1974   *Arabic Speaking Communities in American Cities*. New York: Center for Migration Studies and the Association of Arab-American University Graduates, Inc.

Chandras, Kananur V.
   1977   *Arab, Armenian, Syrian, Lebanese, East Indian, Pakistani and Bangla Deshi Americans: A Study Guide and Source Book*. San Francisco: R and E Research Associates, Inc.

Elkholy, Abdo A.
   1966   *The Arab Moslems in the United States: Religion and Assimilation*. New Haven, Conn.: College and University Press.

Hagopian, Elaine C., and Ann Paden, eds.
   1969   *The Arab Americans: Studies in Assimilation*. Wilmette, Ill.: The Medina University Press International.

Haiek, Joseph R., ed.
   1975   *The American Arabic-Speaking Community 1975 Almanac*. Los Angeles: The News Circle.

Hitti, Philip K.
   1924   *The Syrians in America*. New York: George H. Doran.

Katibah, Ibrahim Habib, and Farhat Ziadeh
   1946   *Arab-Speaking Americans*. New York: The Institute of Arab American Affairs, Inc.

Kayal, Philip M., and Joseph M. Kayal
1975 *The Syrian-Lebanese in America: A Study in Religion and Assimilation.* Boston: Twayne Publishers.

Macron, Mary Haddad
1979 *Arab Americans and Their Communities of Cleveland.* Cleveland, Ohio: Cleveland Ethnic Heritage Studies, Cleveland State University.

Mehdi, Beverlee Turner, ed. and comp.
1978 *The Arabs in America, 1492–1977: A Chronology and Fact Book.* Dobbs Ferry, New York: Oceana Publications, Inc.

Miller, Lucius Hopkins
1904 *Our Syrian Population: A Study of the Syrian Population of Greater New York.* N.p. (Columbia University, New York University, and Harvard University libraries).

Othman, Ibrahim
1974 *Arabs in the United States: A Study of an Arab-American Community.* Amman, Jordan: Shashaa and the University of Jordan.

Sengstock, Mary C.
1982 *Chaldean-Americans: Changing Conceptions of Ethnic Identity.* Staten Island, New York: Center for Migration Studies.

Wakin, Edward
1974 *The Lebanese and Syrians in America.* Chicago: Claretian Publishers.

Wasfi, Atif A.
1971 *An Islamic-Lebanese Community in the U.S.A.: A Study in Cultural Anthropology.* Beirut, Lebanon: Beirut Arab University.

Articles:

Abraham, Nabeel
1977 Detroit's Yemeni Workers. *MERIP Reports* 57:3–9.

Ahmed, Ismael
1975 Organizing an Arab Workers Caucus. *MERIP Reports* 34:17–22.

Aruri, Naseer
    1969   The Arab American Community of Springfield, Massachu-
           setts. In *The Arab Americans: Studies in Assimilation.* Elaine
           C. Hagopian and Ann Paden, eds. pp. 50–66. Wilmette, Ill.:
           The Medina University Press International.

Barclay, Harold B.
    1968   An Arab Community in the Canadian Northwest: A Pre-
           liminary Discussion of the Lebanese Community in Lac La-
           Biche, Alberta. *Anthropologica* 10:143–156.

Benyon, E. D.
    1944   The Near East in Flint, Michigan: Assyrians and Druze and
           their Antecedents. *Geographic Review* 24:234–274.

Berger, Morroe
    1958   America's Syrian Community. *Commentary* 25(4):
           314–323.

    1959   Americans from the Arab World. In *The World of Islam.*
           James Kritzeck and R. Bayly Winder, eds. pp. 351–372. New
           York: St. Martin's Press.

Bisharat, Mary
    1957   Yemeni Farmworkers in California. *MERIP Reports*
           34:22–26.

Bousquet, G. H.
    1935   Moslem Religious Influences in the United States. *The Mus-
           lim World* 25:40–44.

Georgakas, Dan
    1975   Arab Workers in Detroit. *MERIP Reports* 34:13–17.

Germanns, A. K. J.
    1966   Arabic Literature in America. *Islamic Literature* 12(2):
           17–26.

Haddad, Safia
    1969   The Woman's Role in Socialization of Syrian-Americans in
           Chicago. In *The Arab Americans: Studies in Assimilation.*
           Elaine C. Hagopian and Ann Paden, eds. pp. 84–101. Wil-
           mette, Ill.: The Medina University Press International.

Houghton, Louise Seymour
    1911   The Syrians in the United States. *Survey* 26(1–4):480–495;
           647–665; 786–802; 957–968.

Hussaini, Hatem I.
1974 The Impact of the Arab-Israeli Conflict on Arab Communities in the United States. In *Settler Regimes in Africa and the Arab World.* Ibrahim Abu-Lughod and Baha Abu Laban, eds. pp. 201–222. Wilmette, Ill.: The Medina University Press International.

Ismael, Jacqueline S., and Tareq Ismael
1976 The Arab Americans and the Middle East. *Middle East Journal* 30(3):390–405.

Jaafari, Lafi Ibrahim
1973 The Brain Drain to the United States: The Migration of Jordanian and Palestinian Professionals and Students. *Journal of Palestine Studies* 3(1):119–131.

Kassees, Assad S.
1972 Cross Cultural Comparative Familism of a Christian Arab People. *Journal of Marriage and the Family* 34(3):539–544.

Kayal, Philip M.
1973 Religion and Assimilation: Catholic "Syrians" in America. *International Migration Review* 7(4):409–426.

1974 Problems in Classification: Estimating the Arab American Population. *Migration Today* 2(5):3.

Khuri, Fuad I.
1967 A Comparative Study of Migration Patterns in Two Lebanese Villages. *Human Organization* 26:206–213.

Lovell, Emily
1973 A Survey of the Arab-Muslims in the United States and Canada. *Muslim World* 43(2):139–154.

Makdisi, Nadim
1959 The Moslems in America. *The Christian Century,* pp. 969–971.

1962 The Maronites in the Americas and in Atlanta. *Golden Jubilee Book.* Atlanta: Atlanta Maronite Community.

Mokarzel, Salloum
1928 Arabic Newspapers in America. *Syrian World,* p. 36.

Naff, Alixa
1980 Arabs. In *Harvard Encyclopedia of American Ethnic Groups.*

Stephan Thernstrom et al., eds. pp. 128–136. Cambridge, Mass.: The Belknap Press of Harvard University Press.

Saliba, Najib E.
1981   Emigration from Syria. *Arab Studies Quarterly* 3(1):56–67.

Sanderson, Iris
1975   Who Are the Detroit Arabs? *The Detroiter* (September), pp. 28–32.

Semaan, Khalil I. H.
1968   The Crisis of Arabic in the U.S.A. *The Muslim World* 58:334–344.

Sengstock, Mary C.
1970   Telkaif, Baghdad, Detroit—Chaldeans Blend Three Cultures. *Michigan History* 54:293–310.

1974   Traditional and National Identity in a Christian Arab Community. *Sociological Analysis* 35(3):201–210.

1977   Social Change in the Country of Origin as a Factor in Immigrant Conceptions of Nationality. *Ethnicity* 4:54–70.

Simsar, Mehmed A.
1955   Muslims in the United States. In *Twentieth Century Encyclopedia of Religious Knowledge,* Vol. 2. Lefferts A. Loetscher, ed. p. 768. Grand Rapids, Mich.: Baker Book House.

Smith, Marlene K.
1981   The Arabic-Speaking Communities in Rhode Island: A Survey of the Syrian and Lebanese Communities. In *Hidden Minorities: The Persistence of Ethnicity in American Life.* Joan H. Rollins, ed. pp. 141–176. Washington, D.C.: University Press of America.

Sprengling, Martin
1932   Michael Naimy and the Syrian Americans in Modern Arabic Literature. *Open Court* 46:551–563. (Reprinted in *The New Orient* 1 (1933):313–324.)

Swan, Charles, and Leila Saba
1974   The Migration of a Minority. In *Arabic Speaking Communities in American Cities.* Barbara C. Aswad, ed. pp. 85–110. New York: Center for Migration Studies and the Association of Arab-American University Graduates, Inc.

Tannous, Afif
1942 Emigration, a Force of Social Change in an Arab Village. *Rural Sociology* 7(1):62–74.

1943 Acculturation of an Arab-Syrian Community in the Deep South. *American Sociological Review* 8(3):264–271.

Tuma, Elias H.
1981 The Palestinians in America. *The Link* 14(3):1–14.

Wigle, Laurel D., and Sameer Y. Abraham
1974 Arab Nationalism in America: The Dearborn Arab Community. In *Immigrants and Migrants: The Detroit Ethnic Experience*. David W. Hartman, ed. pp. 279–302. Detroit, Mich.: New University Thought Publishing.

Wilson, Howard Barrett
1903 Notes on Syrian Folklore Collected in Boston. *Journal of American Folklore* 16:133–147.

Wolf, C. Umhau
1960 Muslims in the American Mid-West. *The Muslim World* 50(1):39–48.

Yazbek, Joseph
1923 The Syrians. In *Catholic Builders of the Nation*. C. E. McGuire, ed. Boston: Continental Press, Inc.

UNPUBLISHED MATERIALS

Doctoral Dissertations, Master's Theses, and Mimeographs:

Abraham, Nabeel
1978 National and Local Politics: A Study of Political Conflict in the Yemeni Immigrant Community of Detroit, Michigan. Ph.D. dissertation, University of Michigan, Ann Arbor.

Abraham, Sameer Y.
1975 Arabic Speaking Communities of Southeastern Dearborn: A General Overview. Mimeograph. University of Wisconsin, Madison.

Ahdab-Yehia, May
1970 Some General Characteristics of the Lebanese Maronite Community in Detroit: A Sociological Investigation. M.A. thesis, Wayne State University, Detroit, Mich.

Allhoff, John
   1969   Analysis of the Role of St. Raymond's Maronite Church as an Agent in the Assimilation of Lebanese Families in St. Louis. M.A. thesis, University of Mississippi.

Al-Nouri, Qais Naiman
   1964   Conflict and Persistence in the Iraqi-Chaldean Acculturation. Ph.D. dissertation, University of Washington, Seattle.

Al-Tahir, Ali Abdul Jalil
   1952   The Arab Community in the Chicago Area: A Comparative Study of the Christian-Syrians and the Muslim-Palestinians. Ph.D. dissertation, University of Chicago.

Ansara, James M.
   1931   The Immigration and Settlement of the Syrians. A.B. thesis, Harvard University.

Azat, Issa Yacoub
   1974   The Nonreturning Arab Student: A Study in the Loss of Human Resources. Ph.D. dissertation, University of Southern California, Los Angeles.

Campbell, Milo Kay
   1972   An Analysis of the Relationships between Self Concept and Sociological Receptiveness of Lebanese Ethnic Children in the Detroit Metropolitan Area. Ph.D. dissertation, Wayne State University, Detroit, Mich.

David, J. K.
   1954   The Near East Settlers of Jacksonville and Duval County. Paper presented at the May 12, 1954 meeting of the Jacksonville Historical Society, Jacksonville, Florida.

Dlin, Norman
   1961   Some Cultural and Geographic Aspects of the Christian Lebanese in Metropolitan Los Angeles. M.A. thesis, University of California, Los Angeles.

Doctoroff, A. M.
   1978   The Chaldeans: A New Ethnic Group in Detroit's Suburban High Schools. Ph.D. dissertation, University of Michigan, Ann Arbor.

Dweik, Bader Saed
   1980   Factors Determining Language Maintenance and Language Shift in Arabic-American Communities. Ph.D. dissertation,

State University of New York, Buffalo.

Elkholy, Abdo A.
1960   Religion and Assimilation in Two Muslim Communities in America. Ph.D. dissertation, Princeton University.

Gezi, Khalil Ismail
1959   The Acculturation of Middle Eastern Arab Students in Selected American Colleges and Universities. Ph.D. dissertation, Stanford University.

Hanna, Suhail
1973   An Arab Expatriate in America: Khalil Gibran in His American Setting. Ph.D. dissertation, Indiana University, Bloomington.

Jaafari, Lafi Ibrahim
1971   Migration of Palestinian Arab and Jordanian Students and Professionals to the United States. Ph.D. dissertation, Iowa State University of Science and Technology, Ames, Iowa.

Kassees, Assad S.
1970   The People of Ramallah: A People of Christian Arab Heritage. Ph.D. dissertation, Florida State University, Tallahassee.

Katarsky, Anthony P.
1980   Family Ties and the Growth of an Arabic Community in Northeast Dearborn, Michigan. M.A. thesis, Wayne State University, Detroit, Mich.

Kayal, Philip M.
1970   The Churches of the Catholic Syrians and Their Role in the Assimilation Process. Ph.D. dissertation, Fordham University, New York.

Khattab, Abdelmoneim M.
1969   The Assimilation of Arab Muslims in Alberta. M.A. thesis, Department of Sociology, University of Alberta, Edmonton.

Kleem, Ferris A.
1982   The Maronite Lebanese in the Cleveland Metropolitan Area and Education. Ph.D. dissertation, Wayne State University, Detroit, Mich.

Lewis, Ralph Kepler
1967   Hadchite: A Study of Emigration in a Lebanese Village. Ph.D. dissertation, Columbia University, New York.

McHenry, Stewart Gaylord
 1973   The Syrians of Upstate New York: A Social Geography.
        Ph.D. dissertation, Syracuse University, New York.

Melki, Henry H.
 1972   Arab-American Journalism and Its Relation to Arab
        American Literature. Ph.D. dissertation, Georgetown Uni-
        versity, Washington, D.C.

Oschinsky, Lawrence
 1947   Islam in Chicago: A Study of the Acculturation of a Muslim-
        Palestinian Community in that City. M.A. thesis, Depart-
        ment of Anthropology, University of Chicago.

Othman, Ibrahim Issa
 1970   An Arab Community in the United States: A Study of the
        Arab-American Community in Springfield, Massachusetts.
        Ph.D. dissertation, University of Massachusetts.

Pannbacker, R.
 1982   The Levantine Community of Pittsburgh. Ph.D. dissertation,
        University of Michigan, Ann Arbor.

Rouchdy, Aleya
 1972   Bilingualism Among Detroit Arabs. Paper presented at
        AAUG, Inc. Fifth Annual Convention, Berkeley, California.

Saba, Leila B.
 1971   The Social Assimilation of the Ramallah Community
        Residing in Detroit. M.A. thesis, Wayne State University,
        Detroit, Mich.

Semaan, Anthony
 1979   The Patterns and Processes of Settlement of Detroit's East
        Side Lebanese-Maronite Community, 1896–1979. Mimeograph.
        Wayne State University, Detroit, Mich.

Sengstock, Mary C.
 1967   Maintenance of Social Interaction Patterns in an Ethnic
        Group. Ph.D. dissertation, Washington University, St. Louis.

Sesi, Georgette
 1973   The Middle Eastern Children in Detroit Public Schools.
        M.Ed. thesis, Wayne State University, Detroit.

Stein, Edith
 1922   Some Near Eastern Immigrant Groups in Chicago. M.A.

thesis, University of Chicago.

Swanson, Jon C.
1970 Mate Selection and Intermarriage in an American Arab Moslem Community. M.A. thesis, University of Iowa, Iowa City.

United Community Services
1975 Arabic Speaking Peoples of Metropolitan Detroit: A Community Profile. Mimeograph. Detroit: Research Department, United Community Services of Metropolitan Detroit.

Wasfi, Atif A.
1964 Dearborn Arab-Moslem Community: A Study of Acculturation. Ph.D. dissertation, Michigan State University, East Lansing.

Wassef, Nadia Hanna
1977 The Egyptians in Montreal: A New Colour in the Canadian Ethnic Mosaic. M.A. thesis, Department of Geography, McGill University, Montreal, Canada.

Younis, Adele Linda
1961 The Coming of the Arabic-speaking People to the U.S.A. Ph.D. dissertation, Graduate School of History, Boston University.

Yousef, Fathi Salaama
1972 Cross-Cultural Social Communicative Behavior: Egyptians in the U.S. Ph.D. dissertation, University of Minnesota, Minneapolis.

Zaghel, Ali Shteiwi
1973 Arab American Communities and Voluntary Organizations in the Chicago Area. Manuscript.

1977 Changing Patterns of Indentification Among Arab Americans: The Palestine Ramallites and the Christian Syrian-Lebanese. Ph.D. dissertation, Northwestern University, Evanston, Ill.

Zelditch, Morris
1936 The Syrians in Pittsburgh. M.A. thesis, University of Pittsburgh.

Appendix

National Arab-American Organizations, Publications, and Elected Officials[1]

MAJOR ARAB-AMERICAN ORGANIZATIONS[2]

American-Arab Anti-Discrimination Committee (Washington, D.C.)
Association of Arab-American University Graduates, Inc. (Belmont, Massachusetts)
National Association of Arab-Americans (Washington, D.C.)

CHARITABLE ORGANIZATIONS

Middle East Philanthropic Fund (Boston, Massachusetts)
Palestine Aid Society (Detroit, Michigan)
Palestine Arab Fund (San Francisco, California)
Save Lebanon, Inc. (Washington, D.C.)
United Holy Land Fund (Chicago, Illinois)

FOUNDATIONS

American Palestine Educational Foundation (Washington, D.C.)
Arab American Cultural Foundation (Washington, D.C.)
Attiyeh Foundation (Washington, D.C.)

RESEARCH ORGANIZATIONS

American-Arab Anti-Discrimination Research Institute (Washington, D.C.)
Institute of Arab Studies (Belmont, Massachusetts)
Middle East Research Group, Inc. (Fresno, California)

---

[1] This compilation is not meant to be exhaustive but simply illustrative.

[2] Other national organizations are identifiable but are not listed above because of their restrictive memberships. These include: American Federation of Ramallah, Palestine; Federation of Syrian-American Clubs; General Union of Palestine Students; Islamic Federation of America; Muslim Student Association; Organization of Arab Students; Palestine Congress of North America.

MAGAZINES AND JOURNALS

American-Arab Affairs (Washington, D.C.)
Arab Perspectives (Washington, D.C.)
Arab Studies Quarterly (Belmont, Massachusetts)
Journal of Arab Affairs (Fresno, California)
The Search: Journal of Arab and Muslim Studies (Burlington, Vermont)

ELECTED OFFICIALS (1982)

James Abdnor, Senator (Republican, South Dakota)
George Mitchell, Senator (Democrat, Maine)
Abraham Kazen, Jr., Congressman (Democrat, Texas)
Mary Rose Oakar, Congresswoman (Democrat, Ohio)
Nick Joe Rahall II, Congressman (Democrat, West Virginia)
Victor Atiyeh, Governor (Republican, Oregon)
John Sununu, Governor (Republican, New Hampshire)

Index

Abd al-Hamid, Sultan, 37
Abdoo, Michael, 156–57
Abourezk, James, 27, 60
Acculturation, 3, 49, 66, 158
Adenis, 117, 118, 125, 126
Age of early immigrants, 15
Agriculture, 33–34; impact of emigration
  on, 40
Ahmed, Ismael, 179
Al-Amal (magazine), 71
al-Bishallany, Antonious, 152
al Faruqi, Ismail, 75
Ali, Muhammad Kurd, 37
American-Arab Anti-Discrimination
  Committee (ADC), 1, 26, 60, 102, 160
American Islamic Association, 173
Americanization: new immigrants and,
  74–75; religious integration and, 52
American Lebanese Association, 160
Arab Banner Society, 68
Arab-Chaldean Social Services Council
  (ACSSC), 102
Arab Christians. See Christians
Arab Community Center for Social
  Services (ACCESS), 89, 102, 179–80
Arab-Israeli wars, 24, 25, 55, 57, 177,
  178; Palestinian emigration and, 92–93
Arbili family, 38
Asmar, Elias P., 156
Assimilation, 3, 66; Christian Arabs
  and, 53; lessening of trend toward, 60;
  Maronites and, 157–60; religious
  identity and, 49–50; Yemeni immigrants
  and, 126
Association of Arab-American University
  Graduates (AAUG), 4, 26, 59, 76, 160
Auto plants: Maronite workers in, 155;
  Southend (Dearborn) and, 164 n.1,
  165, 169; Yemeni workers in, 111,
  113, 115

Blatty, William, 20
Boston, 17, 21, 39
Bourjaily, Vance, 20

"Brain drain" from Arab lands, 24, 67

Canada, 35
Catholicism: Eastern Christianity and,
  46; ethnic heritage and, 51; Maronites
  and, 156–57, 159–60; Syrian-Lebanese
  integration into American, 52
Catholics: in Arab world, 12; Chaldean,
  137; ethnicity and, 54; Irish, 49, 50;
  Syrian (in U.S.), 49–50
Chaldeans: in Detroit, 86, 88, 89 Table 2;
  differences from Arabs and, 140–43;
  discrimination against (in Iraq), 141;
  future prospects of, 143–44; historical
  background on, 136–37; identified with
  Arabs, 144; language and, 136–37, 138,
  140–41, 143, 144; migration patterns
  and, 138; national identity and, 100;
  reasons for emigration of, 94; regional
  origin of, 141; religion of, 87 Table 1,
  136–37, 140; residential patterns of,
  95, 96 (map), 97–98; socioeconomic
  status of, 139–40
Chicago Fair of 1893, 36, 153
Christian rites: Coptic, 58; Eastern
  Christianity and, 45; Maronite, 149, 157
Christians: in Arab world, 12, 45;
  Chaldean, 87 Table 1, 136–37, 140;
  contemporary Syrian-Lebanese
  American consciousness and, 55–59;
  Coptic, 12, 13, 24, 58; in Detroit area,
  86–87, 90, 91; Eastern Christianity
  and, 46–48; ethnic dilemma of Christian
  Arab-Americans and, 53–55; ethnic
  loyalty and, 27; ethnopolitical
  community evolution and, 59–61;
  industrial labor and, 17; Lebanese
  national identity and, 100; Ottoman
  oppression and, 47; overview of Arab,
  45–48; percent of Arab (U.S.), 9–10;
  postwar (WW II) immigration of, 24;
  residential patterns and, 95, 97, 98,
  101; Syrian (in U.S.), 48–53; Syrian
  emigration and, 37, 38. See also

Christians (cont.)
Catholicism; Catholics; Clergy;
Christian rites; Churches; Maronite
religious tradition; Melkite religious
tradition; Orthodox Christians
Churches: Americanization of, 54;
Chaldean, 139–40; Christian Syrian, 18;
in Detroit, 90; ethnicity and, 54, 55;
Maronite, 156–57; parishioners of, 58;
religious instruction in, 25, 174
Class. *See* Social class
Clergy: Christian Syrian, 18; Maronite, 150
Coffeehouses, 152; in Southend (Dear-
born) 175–77; in Yemeni immigrant
community, 129
Cole, William, 56
Conscription: emigration and, 48; in
WW I, 34
Coptic Christians, 12, 13, 24, 58
Corey, George, 58–59
Cotton, 33, 34
Council of Masajid, 70
Culture: attempts to maintain Arab, 22;
cleavages in Arab, 12; Maronites and,
160; Syrian-Lebanese and Arab, 56;
Syrian, in U.S., 20

Davis, Joe, 124
Dearborn. *See* Southend (Dearborn)
Detroit: changing Arab identity in,
98–100; factors of fusion and diversity
in Arab communities in, 101–103;
immigrant population estimates for,
88–89; Maronite settlements in, 154–56;
nationality of immigrants in, 86–87;
occupations of immigrants in, 111,
114, 115, 122, 139, 140, 153, 154, 155,
157, 168–69; patterns and reasons for
immigration to, 90–94, 119–23, 137–38;
152–54, 167–68; reasons for emigration
to ("push-pull" factors), 91–94;
religious identity of immigrants in,
86–87; residential patterns of immigrants in, 94–98, 112 (map), 113, 115,
118–19, 154; study focus and, 5, 6;
Syrian settlements in, 17; Yemeni
community in, 86, 88, 89 Table 2, 115,
118–19. *See also* Southend (Dearborn)
Dietary laws (Muslim), 76–77
Discrimination: against Chaldeans (in
Iraq), 141; against Muslims (in U.S.), 78
Dixon, Paul Rand, 59
Druze, 48, 150, 151

Eastern Christianity, 46–48. *See also*
Christians
The Eastern Federation of American

The Eastern Federation (cont.)
Syrian-Lebanese Clubs, 25
Economic factors: Arab immigration
and, 15–17, 92; Chaldean immigration
and, 139–40; Syrian economy (WW I)
and, 33–34; Syrian emigration and, 36;
Yemeni immigration and, 121
Education: Arab (between WW I and
WW II), 23; Chaldean emigrants and,
140; of Muslims in U.S., 67, 170;
role of mosque in, 174; in Syria
(1878–1920), 36–37; Syrian emigrants
and, 39. *See also* Schools
Egypt: "brain drain" from, 24; Coptic
Christians in, 13; emigration of Copts
from, 24, 58; Syrian immigration and,
34, 35, 38; U.S. foreign policy (1950s)
and, 26
Eisenhower, Dwight David, 69
Emigration: reasons for early, 13–15;
Syrian (1878–1920), 31–40. *See also*
Immigration
England, 13, 14
Ethnicity: Arab-Americans and loyalty
toward, 27; Arabs as "hidden minority"
and, 1; Christian Arab-Americans and,
53–55, 59–61; increase of interest in, 25;
neighborhoods and, 3; organizations
and, 20–21; religion and Maronite,
156; Syrian-Lebanese identification
with Arabs and, 55–59
Ethnic organizations. *See* Organizational
activities

Family: "chain migration" and, 92, 137,
167; Chaldean, 140, 142–43; early
emigrants and, 39; group maintenance
and, 21–23; Maronite, 151–52, 153,
158–59, 160; Muslim, 21, 73–74;
religious identity and, 47–48; values
of Arab, 15–17; Yemeni immigrant,
121–22, 123–24, 126, 127
Famine in Syria, 32–33, 151
The Federation of Islamic Associations
(FIA), 68–69
Food: Islamic dietary laws and, 76–77;
Maronites and Lebanese, 158
Ford Sociological Department archives,
nationality analysis and, 90
Foreign policy, 45; Arab influence and
U.S., 25–26
France: 14, 40; Christian religious groups
and, 13, 20, 47, 52, 150, 151

Geographical distribution: of Arabs in
Detroit, 94–98; of Chaldeans in U.S.,
137, 139; map of, 2; of Muslims in

Geographical distribution (cont.)
U.S., 67, 77; population estimates and, 1; religious and national identity and, 101; of Yemenis in U.S., 119
Gibran, Gibran Khalil, 20
Gregory XIII, Pope, 150
Grocery stores, 17, 139, 140, 154, 155

Hashmite Club (Southend, Dearborn), 172–73
Herberg, Will, 54
Hitti, Philip K., 4, 13, 48, 92, 153, 160
Howar, J., 68
Hussein, King, 177

Illiteracy: of early immigrants, 15, 39; Yemeni (in English), 128
Imams: family unit and, 74; reform and, 74; religious leadership and, 172; role of, 73–74
Immigration: analysis of early, 13–15; of Arab Muslims, 13–14, 65–68, 167–68; countries of origin and, 9–10, 12; examination on entry and, 39, 153–54; geographic settlement patterns and, 103; Maronite, 152–54; new Lebanese, 74; patterns of and reasons for, 90–94, 119–23; 137–38, 152–54, 167–68; periods ("new" and late) of, 1–3; postwar (WW II), 23–27, 92; records of, 10; Syrian, 31–40, 48–49; transiency versus permanency and, 123–26, 131. *See also* Emigration
The Immigration and History Research Center (University of Minnesota), 4
Immigration papers, 39, 120, 153
Industry (Syrian), 34
Ingram, Abdulla, 68, 69
Intellectuals: "brain drain" and, 67; in Syria (1878–1920), 36–37; Syrian immigrant, 19–20
Iranian Muslim Student Association, 71
Iraq, 86, 94, 100, 137, 141. *See also* Chaldeans
Iraqi-Chaldeans. *See* Chaldeans
Islam: analysis of, 10–11; reform movement and "true," 76; U.S. growth of, 72
Islamic Center of Detroit, 114, 173, 174
Islamic Center of Washington, D.C., 68
Islamic Conference of North America (1977), 69–70
Israel, 78, 177; emigration of Palestinians and, 92–93; Syrian-Lebanese identification as Arabs and, 55, 56, 57–58

Jerusalem, 57–58

Jessup, Henry H., 37
Jews, 14, 15. *See also* Israel
Jordan, 86

Kurds, 94, 137

Language: Chaldean immigrants and, 136–37, 138, 139, 140–41, 143, 144; English-speaking church-goers and, 58; Maronites and, 158; Muslims in Southend and, 170, 174, 181; renaissance in Arabic (1880s), 37; used in Arabic newspapers in U.S., 19; Yemeni immigrants and, 128–29, 131
Lebanese: as Arab-Americans, 101; citizenship in Lebanon and, 40; in Dearborn, 113–14; in Detroit, 86, 88, 89 Table 2; early emigration of, 34–39; Israel and Arab identification of, 56, 57, 58; Muslim immigration and, 65; Palestinian rights controversy and, 56; patterns of emigration of, 90, 91; reasons for emigration of, 93; religion of Detroit's, 87; religious identity and, 48–49; residential patterns of, 95, 96 (map), 97. *See also* Lebanon; Syrian-Lebanese Christians
Lebanese Maronites. *See* Maronite religious tradition
Lebanese Melkites. *See* Melkite religious tradition
Lebanon: ethnic organizations in U.S. and, 20; immigrants from, 9–10; Maronites and, 54–55, 61, 148–49, 151–52, 160; massacres of 1860 in, 37–38; Palestinian guerillas in, 93. *See also* Lebanese; Mount Lebanon
Lenski, Gerhard, 159
Literature, 20

Maloof, Fr. Alan, 50
Maria, Frank, 58
Maronite religious tradition, 12, 90; assimilation characteristics and, 157–59; Catholic community and, 156–57, 159–60; cultural accommodation and, 50–52; defined, 148; early emigration of, 152–54; early settlement patterns of, 154–56; Eastern Christianity and, 46–48; ethnic organizations and, 20; first churches of, 18; the French and, 13, 20, 47, 52, 150, 151; future trends and, 159–60; historical background and, 148–51; integration of ethnic and religious concepts and, 53, 54–55; Israel's forays into Lebanon and, 57; Latinization and, 50, 51, 52; national

Maronite religious tradition (cont.)
identity and, 100; present-day views
on, 61; religious identification of, 149,
150, 152, 156–57; social background in
Lebanon and, 151–52; study overview
and, 148
Marriage, 66; Arab students in U.S. and,
67; Chaldean immigrants and, 142; in
early Syrian settlements in U.S., 21–22;
endogamous, 142, 158, 160; Maronite
immigrants and, 158, 160; Muslims in
U.S. and, 22, 74; Syrian-Lebanese
Christians and, 53, 61; Yemeni
immigrants and, 123, 125, 126
Melkite religious tradition, 12; assimilation
and, 60; cultural accommodation and,
50–52; Eastern Christianity and,
46–47; emigrants' destinations and,
38; first churches of, 18; the French
and, 13; integration of ethnic and
religious concepts and, 54; Israel's
forays into Lebanon and, 57;
Latinization and, 50, 51, 52
Men: coffeehouses and, 175–77; early
immigration and single, 14, 39; as
single emigrants, 92; social latitude of,
22; WW I conscription (Syria) and, 34;
in Yemeni immigrant community, 129
Mosques: cooperation between, 70; in
Dearborn, 114, 166, 171–75, 181; in
Detroit, 90–91; first built in Ross
(N.D., 1920s), 19; functions of, 72–73;
increase in number of U.S., 25
Mount Lebanon: Detroit immigrants
from, 86; Druze population of, 48;
early emigration from, 13; impact of
emigration on, 40; Maronites and, 151,
152; Protestant schools in, 13; as
religious refuge area, 12; role in
emigration, 31–33, 34–35, 36, 38, 39.
See also Lebanon
Mufassir, S. S., 75
Muhammad, 10–12
Muhammad, Wallace, 75
Muslim Arab Youth Association, 71
Muslims: adapting Islamic practices in
U.S. and, 72–74; American lifestyles
and, 77; converts and, 78–79; in
Dearborn, 113, 114, 164–81; in
Detroit, 86–87, 90, 91; early immigration
and, 13–14; ethnic loyalty and, 27;
family unit and, 21, 73–74; Federation
of Islamic Associations and, 68–69;
history of, 10–13; immigration of,
65–68; industrial labor and, 17; Islamic
institutions and, 68; Islam in U.S. and,
76–78; Lebanese national identity and,

Muslims (cont.)
100; marriage and, 22, 74; Muslim
Student Association and, 70–72;
Muslim World League and, 69–70;
non-Muslim society in U.S. and, 18–19;
Ottoman oppression and, 47; percent
of (in U.S.), 9–10; postwar (WW II)
immigration of, 24, 25; reform movement and, 74–76; refusal to become
Christians and, 51; residential patterns
and, 95, 97, 98, 101; sense of mission
and, 75; Syrian emigration and, 37, 38.
See also Imams; Islam; Mosques
The Muslim Star (magazine), 69
Muslim Student Association (MSA),
70–72, 73, 75, 79
Muslim World League (MWL), 69–70,
73, 74

Nader, Ralph, 59
Names (changes in), 158
Nasser, Gamal Abdel-, 26, 99, 176,
177–78
The National Association of Arab
Americans, 26, 59–60
National Association of Federations, 25
Nationalism: Palestinian, 99; in Southend
(Dearborn), 177–80
Nationality: of immigrants in Detroit,
85–86; in Southend (Dearborn), 181;
of Syrians, 98–99. See also Chaldeans;
Lebanese; Palestinians; Syrian-Lebanese
Christians; Syrians; Yemenis
Newspapers, 19; decline of Arabic, 25
New York, 17, 18, 39

Occupations: Arab-Americans in professional, 26–27; of Chaldean immigrants,
139, 140, 169 n.10; of early immigrants,
14, 15–17; of Maronites, 153, 154, 155,
157; of Muslims in Southend, 168–69;
of postwar (WW II) immigrants, 24; of
Yemeni immigrants, 111, 114, 115, 122
Omar, Muhammad, 68
Organizational activities, 3; emergence of
Arab-American, 100, 101–102, 103;
ethnic, 20–21; formation of new
immigrant associations and, 25–26; of
Maronites, 159, 160; of Muslims in
U.S., 68–72; Yemeni immigrant, 129–30
Organization of Arab Students (OAS), 70
Orthodox Christians, 12, 156; assimilation
and, 49–50, 52–53; Eastern Christianity
and, 46; emigration destinations and,
38; first churches of, 18; integration
of ethnic and religious concepts and, 54
Ottoman Empire, 12–13; early emigration

Ottoman Empire (cont.)
and, 13–14; Maronites and, 150; religious oppression and, 47; Syria and, 32–33, 98

Palestine Day Parade (Southend), 180
Palestine, influx of Jews into, 14
Palestinians: as Arab-Americans, 101; in Detroit, 86, 88, 89 Table 2; early immigration and, 14; immigration designations for, 10; in Lebanon, 93; pan-Arabism and, 99; patterns of emigration of, 90, 91; postwar (WW II) immigration and, 24; reasons for emigration of, 92–93; religion of Detroit's, 87; residential patterns of, 95, 96 (map), 98; rights of, 55, 56, 57; in Southend (Dearborn), 113, 177, 178
Pan-Arabism movement, 99, 176
Pan-Islamic movement, 99–100
Pasha, Jamal
Pasha, Midhat, 37
Paternal authority, 21, 152; generational conflicts and, 159. *See also* Family
Peddling, 15–17, 154, 155
People's Democratic Republic of Yemen, 115, 124. *See also* Yemenis
Political activity, 49, 60, 174–75
Politics: Arab-Americans and, 26, 27; Arab nationalism and, 177–80; coffeehouses and, 175–76; Syrian emigration and, 36; tension between Muslims and, 78; in Yemen, 121; Yemeni immigrants and, 128
Population estimates: Arab-American, 1, 9, 10; of Arab students in U.S., 71; Chaldean immigrant, 137; of early immigrants, 14, 35; of immigrants in Detroit, 88–89; Maronite immigrant (1910–1930), 154; Muslim immigrant, 67–68; of Southend Muslims, 166; Syrian immigrant, 48–49; of Yemen, 118; Yemeni immigrant, 110–11, 113, 114, 115
Poverty rate (Southend), 169–70
Prayer: Muslim communal, 72, 76; in Southend (Muslim), 166, 172, 173–74
Public security (Syria, WW I), 33

Rand, Ayn, 78
Religion: analysis of Muslim, 10–13, 72–73; destination of emigrants and, 38; ethnopolitical consciousness and, 61; of immigrants in Detroit, 85–86, 87, 136–37, 140, 149, 150, 152; Ottoman oppression and, 47; persecution in Syria (1860s) and, 37–38, 47; role of

Religion (cont.)
mosque in, 171–75, 181; Syrian immigration and, 18–19. *See also* Christians; Muslims
Religious holidays (Muslim), 76
Religious instruction, 25, 174
Remittances: during WW I (Syria), 40; early immigrants and, 14; Maronite immigrants and, 153; Yemeni immigrants and, 122–23, 126
Research (Arab-American), 3–5
Residential patterns: of Chaldean immigrants, 138; of Detroit's immigrants, 94–98; of Maronite immigrants, 154; of Yemeni immigrants, 112 (map), 113–14, 115, 118–19
Ross, North Dakota, 19, 68

St. Louis Fair of 1906, 153
St. Maron, 149
Schools: American University of Beirut, 37, 151; Protestant, 13; student population of Detroit's, 88–89; in Syria (1878–1920), 36–37. *See also* Education
Seafarers (Yemeni), 111, 129
Sfeir, Peter S., 156
Shabaia, Joseph, 156
Silk, 34, 66, 150
Social class: American Catholicism and, 52; education and upper and middle, 23; of Lebanese immigrants to Detroit, 91; Muslim immigrant, 65; Southend (Dearborn) and, 168–71, 181; of Syrian immigrants, 39; of Yemeni immigrants, 117
Southeast Dearborn Community Council (SEDCC), 180
Southend (Dearborn), 1–3; Arab character of, 165–67; Arab nationalism in, 177–80; coffeehouses in, 175–77; as migrant reception area, 167–68, 181; mosque in, 114, 166, 171–75, 181; as Muslim community, 24–25, 164–81; nationality groups in, 181; occupations of residents in, 168–69; residential patterns in, 98; as single nationality-religious community, 95; study overview of, 164–65; as working-class community, 168–71, 181; Yemenis in, 113–14, 126–30. *See also* Detroit
Stereotypes of Arabs, 45; imposed Arabic identity and, 100; prejudice in U.S. and, 78
Suez Canal, 65; nationalization of, 26; opening of, 34
Surnames (changing of), 158
Syria: during WW I, 31–34; emigrants

Syria (cont.)
from (1878-1920), 34-39; immigrants
in U.S. from, 9-10, 12; impact of
emigration from, 40; number of early
immigrants from, 14; as Ottoman
province, 32-33, 98. *See also* Syrians
Syrian-Lebanese Christians: analysis of,
48-53; contemporary American
consciousness and, 55-59; Eastern
Christianity and, 46-48; ethnicity
and, 53-55; ethnopolitical community
development and, 59-61. *See also*
Christians
Syrians: ages and illiteracy rate of immigrant (1889-1915), 15; characteristics
of immigrant, 14; Christian (in U.S.),
48-53; identification of nationalities
of, 98-99; intellectual aspects of
immigrant, 19-21; occupations of
immigrant, 15-17; patterns of
emigration of, 90; politics and
naturalized, 27; settlements of (in
U.S., 1910-1930), 17-18

Taxes (Southend), 164
Telkaif (Chaldean village), 136, 137,
138, 141
Textile industry (Syria), 34, 40
Transportation for emigrants, 39, 153
Truman, Harry S., 27

Unemployment in Southend, 169
Unions: demonstration in Southend and,
178-79; Yemeni immigrants and, 128;
Yemenis and Joe Davis's statement
concerning, 124
United Nations, the Muslim World

League and, 69

Wakeel al-mughtaribeen (emigrant
agent), 120
Women: early immigration and, 15;
equality question and Muslim, 78;
family unit and, 21-22; interfaith marriages and, 74; in mosques, 72, 173-74;
postwar (WW II) immigration of, 24;
Yemeni, married to Americans, 125
Woodcock, Leonard, 179
World War I, Syria and, 31-34
World War II, immigration after,
23-27, 92

Yemen Arab Republic, 115-19, 124
Yemenis: background of (in Yemen),
115-19; chief characteristics of, 130-31;
community life and organization and,
129-30; Dearborn community and,
113-14, 126-30; in Detroit, 86, 88, 89
Table 2, 115, 118-19; emigration
patterns of, 119-20; formation of
community (U.S.) of, 24; occupations
of, 111, 114, 115, 122; population
estimates of, 110-11, 114, 115; reasons
for emigration of, 93, 120-23; religion
of Detroit's, 87; residential patterns
of, 112 (map), 113, 115, 118-19;
study overview and, 110; ties to home
country and, 121-23; transiency versus
permanency and, 123-26, 131; young
people (in U.S.) of, 127. *See also* Adenis
Yorty, Samuel, 58
Young Men's Muslim Association, 68

Zogby, James, 60

Contributors

Nabeel Abraham is an anthropologist and Research Associate at the Center for Urban Studies, Wayne State University, Detroit, Michigan.

Sameer Y. Abraham is a sociologist and Research Associate at the Center for Urban Studies, Wayne State University, Detroit, Michigan.

May Ahdab-Yehia is a sociologist and President of Health Information Systems, Inc. of Grosse Pointe Shores, Michigan.

Barbara Aswad is Professor of Anthropology at Wayne State University, Detroit, Michigan.

Yvonne Haddad is Associate Professor of Islamic Studies at the Hartford Seminary, Hartford, Connecticut.

Philip M. Kayal is Associate Professor of Sociology at Seton Hall University, South Orange, New Jersey.

Alixa Naff is former Director of the Arab-American Project, National Center for Urban Ethnic Affairs, Washington, D.C.

Najib E. Saliba is Professor of History at Worcester State College, Worcester, Massachusetts.

Mohammed Sawaie is Assistant Professor of Arabic at the University of Virginia, Charlottesville, Virginia.

Mary C. Sengstock is Professor of Sociology at Wayne State University, Detroit, Michigan.